THE
SEA DOGS

THE
SEA DOGS

Privateers, Plunder and Piracy
 in the Elizabethan Age ✦

Neville Williams

Weidenfeld and Nicolson
London

For my nephew John Churchill

Designed by Sandra Shafee for
George Weidenfeld and Nicolson Limited,
11 St John's Hill, London SW11

Filmset by Keyspools Limited, Golborne, Lancashire

Printed and bound in Great Britain by
Morrison & Gibb Ltd, London and Edinburgh

CONTENTS

INTRODUCTION

EVER SINCE THE DAYS OF RICHARD HAKLUYT THE YOUNGER, who was putting the finishing touches to his first collection of the narratives of the voyages of English seamen as the Spanish Armada entered the Channel, the exploits of the sea dogs have been of absorbing interest, for it was their daring and enterprise that were transforming England into the foremost maritime power. Subsequent writers relating the achievements of Tudor mariners in the realms of discovery and maritime adventure have emphasized their effects on the establishment of sea power and in the founding of the first British Empire. In more recent years a great body of detailed research has added to our knowledge of the Elizabethan seamen and their immediate precursors. In the first place there has been the notable series of well-edited narratives of voyages and expeditions issued by the Hakluyt Society, which proudly carries on the work begun by the Elizabethan Hakluyts, and the corresponding collections of letters and papers published by the Navy Records Society. Secondly there has been the discovery of much fresh material through diligent searches among the records of the High Court of Admiralty in London and among Spanish archives, notably by Professor D.B.Quinn and Dr K.R.Andrews. Taken together these two branches of historical research have added a further dimension to scholarship and, as a result, a new account for the general reader, similar to that given by James Anthony Froude in 1895, is long overdue. The author hopes that the pages which follow will not only meet a real need but even stimulate further studies on one of the grandest of themes.

This book owes much to the staffs of Weidenfeld and Nicolson, London, and Macmillan Publishing Co., Inc., New York. In particular the author wishes to pay tribute to the kindly interest of Christopher Falkus and John Curtis. In the later stages he has leant heavily on Hilary Lloyd Jones. The choice of illustrations has been largely the work of Judith Aspinall. Once again he is indebted to Annabel Clover for her careful typing of a difficult manuscript. His wife and family, as always, have followed the progress of the work with encouragement and understanding.

N.W.
Shrove Tuesday 1975

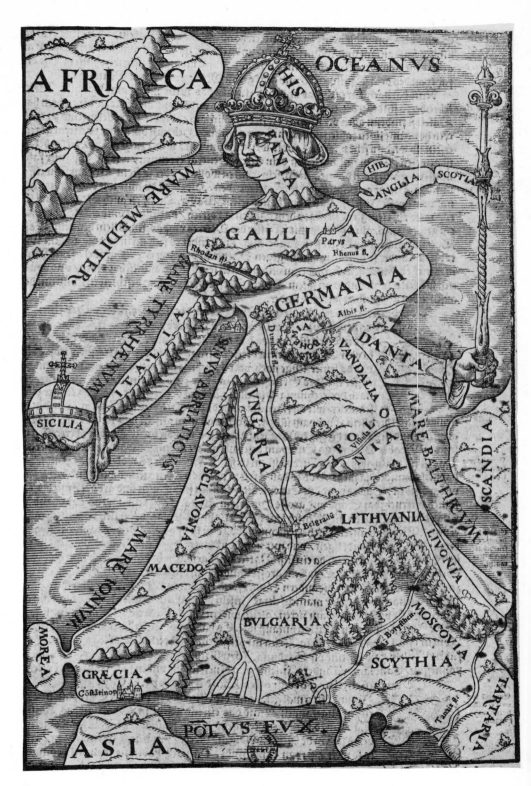

AFRICA OCEANVS

HIS

ANIA

MARE MEDITER.

HIB. ANGLIA SCOTIA

GALLIA

Parys

Rhodan fl. Rhenus fl.

GERMANIA

Albis fl.

MARE TYRRHENVM

ITALIA

BOHE

DANIA

VANDALIA

SAXONIA

VNGARIA

POLONIA

Vistula

MARE BALTHICVM

SICILIA

SINVS ADRIATICVS

SCLAVONIA

Belgradu

LITHVANIA

Vistula

LIVONIA

SCANDIA

MARE IONIVM

MACEDO

Danubius fl.

Borysthen.

MOSCOVIA

MOREA

BVLGARIA

GRÆCIA

Constinop

POTVS EVX.

SCYTHIA

Tanais fl.

TARTARIA

ASIA

8

1 NEW PERSPECTIVES

W HEN NEWS OF THE SEMINAL PORTUGUESE and Spanish discoveries in east and west reached England as the fifteenth century drew to a close, those few seamen interested in pioneering were amazed at the great strides that had been made towards reaching Marco Polo's Cathay, enlarging man's horizons and opening up seemingly endless possibilities in trade and colonization. The world was expanding and the old charts were being redrawn; it was a time for hope, for testing novel ideas about the nature of oceans and for expecting that renewed endeavour would bring great rewards. Yet with the exception of the Genoese John Cabot in the service of King Henry VII, and his enterprising friends in Bristol, English mariners were content to be spectators. The initiative remained with the Spanish and Portuguese and where opposition to their monopolies arose it came not from Englishmen but from the French. Despite the cautious support of Henry Tudor to maritime enterprise, England was to remain largely indifferent to oceanic development for over a generation. A small country, on the fringe of Christendom, it was content to concentrate its trade with northern Europe where its sovereign sought recognition from neighbouring rulers. There was no suspicion that the voyages of Columbus would affect international trade so that the centre of gravity of Europe would shift from Mediterranean lands to the north west.

Almost a century after Christopher Columbus had made his landfall at San Salvador, the geographer Richard Hakluyt traced the tremendous achievements of the English sea dogs in his lifetime, but he could not but remark on the negative attitude of their predecessors in the era of the prime discoveries: 'But alas our English nation were either altogether destitute of such clear lights and inducements, or if they had any inkling at all, it was as misty as they found the Northern Seas, and so obscure and ambiguous that it was meet rather to deter them than to give them encouragement.' To be blunt, during the thirty-four packed years between Bartholomew Diaz rounding the Cape of Good Hope and Ferdinand Magellan, with Sebastian del Cano, circumnavigating the globe, English mariners appeared to have missed the boat completely. Early promise of extensive discoveries stemming from John Cabot's voyage had not been fulfilled. By 1517, when Henry VIII was bent on outshining his rivals in Europe, the chance had slipped through Englishmen's hands. John Rastell, the brother-in-law of Sir Thomas More, lamented the gulf between what had happened and what might have been:

OPPOSITE Spain's dominance in sixteenth-century Europe is illustrated in this contemporary map.

9

O what a thing had been then,
If that they that be Englishmen
Might have been the first of all;
That these should have taken possession,
And made first building and habitation,
A memory perpetual.
And also what an honourable thing
Both to the realm and to the King,
To have had his dominions extending
There into so far a ground,
Which the noble King of late memory,
The most wise Prince, the seventh Harry,
Caused first to be found.

The laments were to become more embittered with the years when it became
clear how rich the Spanish empire really was.

   Deterrence assuredly existed in the Spanish and Portuguese monopolies
of the new oceanic trades, the one westward, the other largely in the east, for

10

these were established by governmental regulation and protected by armed fleets. As English sea dogs came to see it, Spain had unwarrantably reserved to herself an entire continent, with its numerous off-shore islands, and prohibited merchants of other nationalities from even a modest share in the trade. Before long 'all were reputed pirates that were found in those waters'. In 1493, two months after Columbus had returned to Seville from his first voyage to the West Indies, Pope Alexander VI, who was himself a Spaniard, published a bull granting to Ferdinand of Castile all lands already discovered and those to be explored in future years in the region that the Italian in his service had stumbled upon. The wily Ferdinand was anxious to guard against possible counter-claims by the King of Portugal to territories in what would be known as 'the Americas', and thus the next year he persuaded the Pope to issue further bulls. The third document, *Inter Caetera*, assigned to Spain all lands west and south of an imaginary line, drawn north to south a hundred leagues west of the Azores and the Cape Verde Islands. Not only the land but even the seas beyond the line were deemed to be in Spain's sphere of influence. A further papal edict was more far-reaching still: Ferdinand and his successors were to have sovereignty over 'all islands and mainlands whatsoever . . . in sailing or travelling towards the west and south, whether they be in regions occidental or meridional and oriental and of

Portuguese treasure carracks; an early sixteenth-century Flemish painting.

India'. King Manuel of Portugal was dismayed at this mention of India and when the Pope would not retract he negotiated with Ferdinand I and succeeded in forcing him to sign the Treaty of Tordesillas, which secured Portuguese rights not only to India and the Far East but also, as it happened, to the as yet unknown Brazil. Ferdinand reckoned he had been outwitted, for the New World produced none of the spices that now came flooding to Lisbon from the east, and it was this that led his successor, Charles v, to employ Magellan. Columbus had been dismayed at the apparent paucity of mineral wealth in the west. 'Gold is the most precious of all commodities', he wrote. 'Gold constitutes treasure and he who possesses it has all he needs in this world, as also the means of purchasing souls from purgatory and restoring them to the enjoyment of paradise.' It was forty years before Pizarro sacked Cuzco to plunder the hereditary wealth of Atahualpa, fifty years before the Potosi silver mines were discovered. Thereafter the treasure of the New World was regularly shipped to Spain to undermine the economies of Europe and envy of the Spaniard's luck became intense.

During the last quarter of the fifteenth century English deep-sea fishermen, who had largely been ousted from Icelandic waters by the Hanseatic seamen from the German ports, had been pressing further into the Atlantic in search of cod and ling, for fish played an increasingly important part in people's diet. In July 1480 two vessels, the *George* and the *Trinity* left Bristol 'not for the purpose of trading, but to seek and discover a certain island called the Isle of Brasil' – a land which, according to Master Lloyd, reckoned the most experienced mariner in England, lay in the western part of Ireland. Indeed, the isle of Brasil had been imaginatively sited by the cartographers as lying in the great western ocean as a stage on the route to Cathay, and the Portuguese discoveries of the Canaries and the Azores had seemed to point to the likelihood of another, greater island or group of islands. The voyage of the *George* and *Trinity* was twelve years before Christopher Columbus sailed across the Atlantic, though the little ships were driven by storms into an Irish harbour. Next year the same men made a further attempt at oceanic adventure which was equally fruitless. Yet Bristol merchants and fishermen did not easily give up, for the misty lore about 'Greenland' and other lands beyond, known to the cartographers, was an integral part of the vernacular traditions of Bristol. The Italian Columbus, who had sailed to Iceland in Bristol vessels for fish, was well aware of local gossip about the continent that lay to the far west, many days' sailing beyond the last sight of Ireland. He, like everyone else, took it for granted that this new continent must be Asia. The indications are that Bristol fishermen had certainly reached Dogger Bank and Nova Scotia by the year 1490, convinced that the land on which they dried their nets was 'Brasil'.

It is one of the ironies of history that while Christopher Columbus was patiently awaiting an answer to his proposal that Ferdinand and Isabella should sponsor his westward expedition to discover Cathay, his brother

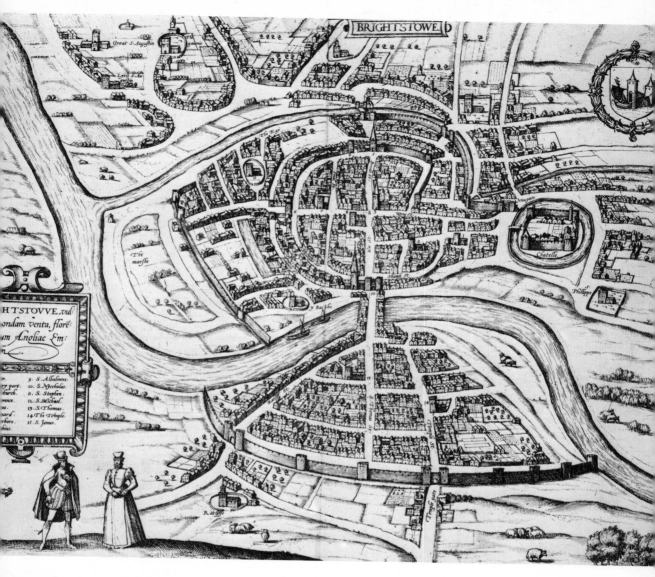

Bartholomew should take passage to England to try and attract the rival support of Henry Tudor for the scheme. Unfortunately Bartholomew had the ill luck to fall into the hands of pirates on leaving Spain so that it was not until the winter of 1488 to 1489 that he reached London. At that juncture Henry VII had his hands full and his revenue fully committed, for he was about to be involved in a war with France. With scant ceremony he declined the invitation to subscribe funds to become patron of the proposed adventure to Asia, the land of rich spices, fine silks and even gold. Accordingly Columbus sailed west in 1492 under the Spanish flag.

The Genoese John Cabot, who later became a citizen of Venice, had resided in Bristol in the mid-1480s and was well aware of the endeavours of

At the beginning of the sixteenth century Bristol was the centre of England's maritime interests.

13

Bristol mariners to find 'Brasil' that was thought to lie to the west of Ireland. Cabot was also in Seville when Columbus returned from 'the Indies' in 1493 and he at once appreciated that for all the latter's success in discovering new territories, he had failed in his objective to reach Cathay. It seemed to Cabot that the 'Brasil' of the men of Bristol could be the north-east cape of Asia and he became convinced that it was his mission to find this country. He returned from Seville to England to interest merchants in this venture and in 1496 obtained an audience with the King. Henry VII granted him a comprehensive patent for sailing to all parts of 'the eastern, western and northern sea' for discovering 'whatsoever islands, countries, etc.' that existed there and 'are unknown to Christians'. Such lands were to be occupied in the King's name and one-fifth of the net profit of the voyage was to go to the crown. The wording of Cabot's letters patent implies that no one believed that Columbus had reached Asia and that his 'Indies' was but a stage on the long route. Cabot's attempt in 1496 was unsuccessful, for gales forced him back to Bristol, yet he left with the *Matthew* a second time on 20 May 1497 and five weeks later sighted 'The New Found Land' – probably the shore of Nova Scotia. Here he went ashore to place a cross together with personal banners of Henry VII, the Pope and St Mark of Venice. The *Matthew* was back in Bristol by 6 August, thanks to favourable winds, when the crew reported to local fishermen that 'they would bring thence so many fish that they would have no further need of Iceland'.

Cabot rode confidently to London for further discussions with the King, who listened to his claims to have discovered Asia and his dreams of developing a new route for the spice trade. Henry offered the adventurer a modest reward: 'To him that found the new isle £10', runs the entry in his household accounts. That winter John Day, an Englishman living in Andalusia, wrote to Columbus, giving him information he had gleaned about Cabot's voyage and in his letter noted 'it is considered certain that the cape of the said land was discovered in the past by men from Bristol'. Cabot set out again in May 1498 and one of the five ships in his expedition belonged to the King. He sailed past Newfoundland and Nova Scotia and followed the coast to the south, but he died on the voyage; his son Sebastian would in time continue this pioneering, but the next expedition was made under royal licence by three Bristol merchants, headed by Richard Warde, joined by partners from the Azores, to trade in 'the arctic and the northern seas' and found a colony there. They returned with presents for the King of 'a brasil bow and two red arrows' and brought to court three natives wearing their homely furs, but there were no spices and not a glint of gold. About the same time the brothers Gaspar and Miguel Corte-Real visited Greenland, crossed Davis Strait to Labrador, sailed on to Newfoundland and probably penetrated the Gulf of St Lawrence. Believing these territories to fall within Portugal's sphere of colonization, they claimed the entire coast for King Manuel, yet Portugal was by now primarily concerned with exploiting the discoveries of Vasco da Gama.

Within the portrait:

EFFIGIES·SEBASTIANI·CABOTI
ANGL·[F]IL·I[I] IOHANIS·CABOTI·VEN
TI·MILITIS·AVRATI·PRIMI INVE[N]T
ORIS·TERRÆ·NOVÆ·SVB·HERICO·VII ANGL
IA·REGE

SPES·MEA·IN·DEO·EST·

Sebastian Cabot carried
on his father's search for
the north-west passage;
a watercolour copy of an
anonymous contemporary
portrait, since destroyed.

Bristol fishermen now regularly sailed to the Dogger Bank for 'Newland' fish, but discovery was shelved. Sebastian Cabot, who had accompanied his father on his first voyage, remained in Bristol after the latter's death, busying himself as a merchant, yet he was determined to lead an expedition to the north west himself and find the fabled passage to China. In 1508, just thirty, he sailed with Henry's blessing. The details of the voyage that have come down to us are tantalizingly brief; he met with a barrier of ice and his crew became faint-hearted, yet he was sure that the expanse of water he had entered in that unknown region *was* the north-west passage. He returned

15

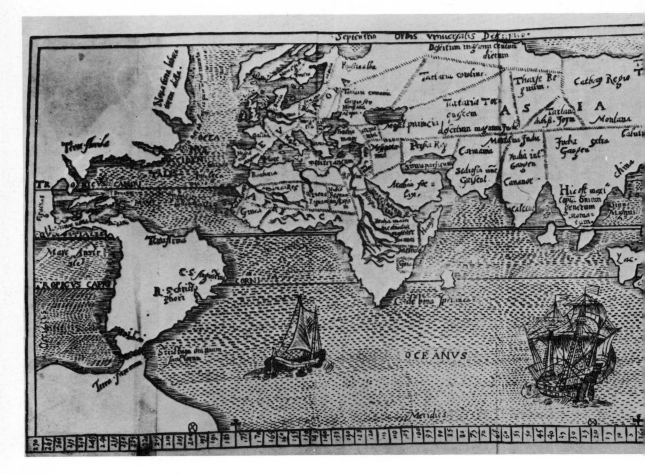

A map of the world in 1527 drawn by Robert Thorne, a friend of the Cabots, who urged Henry VIII to promote voyages of discovery.

to Bristol 'without affecting what he had intended, but with a resolve to return to that project at a time when the sea should not be frozen'. He found King Henry VII, his patron, dead and soon discovered that 'his son cared little for such an enterprise'. Despairing of royal backing, in the third year of the new reign he received permission to enter the service of Ferdinand I and was to live in Spain for thirty-six years serving as 'Pilot Major'.

The year after Sebastian Cabot had gone to Spain, Robert Thorne of Bristol, whose father had been a pioneer in the Newfoundland fishery, endeavoured to interest Henry VIII in discovery. He wrote of the wealth that would be acquired in the Indies, like ripe apples dropping from an overladen tree, in those 'richest lands and islands of the world of gold, precious stones, balms, spices and other things that are here esteemed most' and underlined that the King would win 'perpetual glory' if he backed this fresh enterprise to find the northerly passage to Cathay. Indeed, it was the plain duty of monarchs 'to extend and enlarge their dominions' and the sovereign who hesitated to act would be thought to lack courage. Not even this imputation

16

A sixteenth-century cosmographer at work in his study surrounded by contemporary instruments of navigation; an engraving by Stradanus.

on Henry's honour – a point on which he was most sensitive – had the slightest effect. Sebastian Cabot could not forget about the short route to the Indies and at one stage corresponded with Cardinal Wolsey about a fresh English venture being mounted. When England again rejected his proposals he turned to Venice, hoping the merchants whose traditional traffic was being threatened by the Turkish advance would finance him. He would, he wrote, show Venice 'a passage whereby she would obtain great profit, which is the truth, for I have discovered it'. Once more he was disappointed. But at last, after Henry VIII's death, Cabot returned to England to find himself regarded as the grand old man of English maritime enterprise.

The regular trade to Antwerp was so profitable that English merchants were not prepared, any more than their sovereign, to look further afield, particularly when such investments would be at risk. The traditional traffic with the Low Countries, hallowed by the first Tudor's treaties, made sound commercial sense, for English cloths commanded a good price. Only in 1521, a year of unexpected recession, was there any serious suggestion for giving the route to Asia a fresh hearing and before any decisions could be

17

taken, trade again improved. The only fresh enterprises to more distant parts were those of John Rut in 1527 and of the 'lawyers' excursion' in 1536. Rut sailed the *Mary Guildford* to Newfoundland and then moved south to the Caribbean, the first known venture of an English seaman into those forbidden waters. His experience did not encourage others to follow his lead, for he was driven from Santo Domingo by gunfire; the Spaniards feared that if they winked at a single English craft trading there the next year there would be a fleet of twenty vessels from London. The 1536 adventure was led by a rank amateur, Master Horne, who was accompanied by a group of young lawyers from the Inns of Court 'and divers others of good worship, desirous to see the strange things of this world'. Their laudable ambition was not matched by professional competence. It was in fact remarkable that the two ships succeeded in reaching Cape Breton and the Newfoundland coast, though they found no opportunities for trade and slender hope of provisions. Some, we are told, took to cannibalism and the rest only saved themselves

By 1536, the year of the 'lawyers' excursion', the north-east coast of America had been charted in some detail; from the world map of P. Descaliers

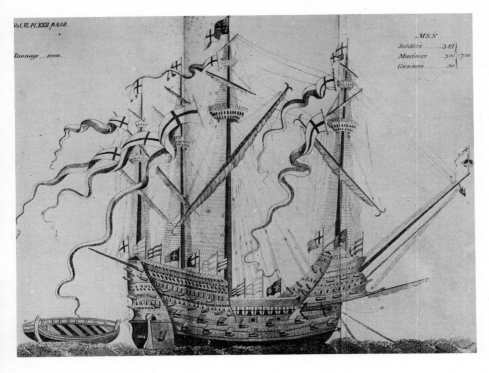

Vol. VI. Pl. XXII. p.208.

Tannage... 1000.

MEN
Soldiers........349
Mariners.......301 ⎫700
Gunners.........50 ⎭

The *Harry Grace à Dieu*, launched in 1514, was the largest vessel in Henry VIII's navy; a detail from the Anthony Roll.

through taking a French fishing vessel that was well-stocked with supplies. The survivors returned home utterly shaken, cured of their lust for adventure and one of them (Master Butts) was so broken by his experiences on the ill-planned voyage that even his parents failed to recognize him.

Despite his lack of enterprise in oceanic voyages, Henry VIII took an intense personal interest in his navy. He had been born at Greenwich where there was salt in the air and a smell of pitch, and he saw the creation of a strong force at sea as essential if England were to command the Channel and be able to pursue an anti-French policy. The *Harry Grace à Dieu* of 1000 tons was launched in 1514 and the Corporation of Trinity House for pilots was founded. New dockyards were opened to provide a fleet of seaworthy fighting ships that was the envy of rival sovereigns and these men-of-war were supported by a notable reserve of armed merchant vessels. Without such sustained developments the sea dogs of the next generation could not have come to prominence.

In the last ten years of his reign Henry listened carefully to the advice on naval affairs which William Hawkins of Plymouth offered him. Hawkins had been a pioneer of the trade with Upper Guinea (Liberia) and ventured to the Portuguese colony in Brazil. In European ports he had picked up much information about the products of those countries and the prevailing winds of the Atlantic. In 1530 he fitted out the 250-ton *Paul* of Plymouth for a triangular voyage and most probably engaged pilots who knew the hazards of the coasts. In the estuary of the Sestos River in Upper Guinea he traded for

Elizabethan shipwrights at work; an illustration from *Fragments of Ancint Shipwrighting* by Matthew Baker.

pepper and ivory without encountering Portuguese hostility and then crossed the Atlantic to Brazil, anchoring near Bahia, where he loaded his ship with brazilwood, the dye much in demand by English clothiers. Hawkins had a knack of getting on with the natives of the region and made so profitable a voyage that he returned next year, again calling at Guinea. A local chief from Bahia was persuaded to sail back to Plymouth with Hawkins, and Martin Cockerham stayed behind for a season as a hostage for the native's well-being in English hands until he should be safely returned. Hawkins took the chief to court to present him to Henry VIII. Here he was made much of for 'all his apparell, behaviour and gesture were very strange to the beholders' and Englishmen were amazed at the jewel set in his lower lip and the holes in his cheeks, in which were planted thin bones 'which in his own country were reputed for a great bravery'. Hawkins obviously wanted to arouse the King of England's interest in his new commercial ventures and sought recognition in case he should be accused of interloping on the Portuguese monopoly. In 1532 he made his third voyage and though the native chief died on the high seas 'by change of air and alteration of diet', his subjects accepted that his death was not through any fault of his English hosts, so Cockerham was restored to his compatriots. While awaiting the *Paul*'s return he had busied himself laying in stores of brazilwood.

This was the last voyage which Hawkins himself made, but there are signs that the trade between Plymouth and Brazil continued until 1540. Hawkins told Thomas Cromwell of his hopes for extending his ventures if the King would invest £2000 to be used principally for arming his ships, no doubt against the French privateers off Brazil who had destroyed the Portuguese fort at Pernambuco and were becoming a serious menace to all vessels.

20

Hawkins promised his sovereign 'to do such feats of merchandise that it shall be to the King's great advantage in his Grace's custom'. The customs ledgers of Plymouth show the *Paul* bringing back ninety-two tons of brazilwood in October 1540 together with ivory from Guinea ('elephant's teeth') worth a total of £615 and paying £30 15s in duty. Cromwell took the hint and himself invested in the voyages of the *Saviour of Bristol* which Nicholas Thorne made to Brazil and other parts. Southampton merchants, too, were making the Atlantic crossing, including Robert Reneger (whom we shall meet later), and John Pudsey who in 1542 built a fort near Bahia to protect British interests.

Trade to the Caribbean was reckoned far too risky in view of England's alliance with Spain for most of the period down to 1558. A pioneer here was John Phillips who sailed the *Barbara* of London to Hispaniola, without touching at Guinea. Here he captured a Spanish vessel with hides and sugar aboard and, as his own ship was leaking, he put the Spaniards ashore, transferred his crew to the prize, which he renamed the *Barbara*, and sank his own vessel. On his return to Dartmouth he was arrested for piracy on the complaint of the Spanish ambassador and was in dire trouble. Robert Reneger, who was to operate on a much larger scale, far from being prosecuted, was to earn the King's special protection.

There was a renewal of privateering on an unprecedented scale in the Narrow Seas when in June 1543 Henry VIII declared war on France, assured of the support of the Emperor Charles V. Yet after fifteen months of campaigning, the Emperor signed a separate peace with Francis I at Crépy,

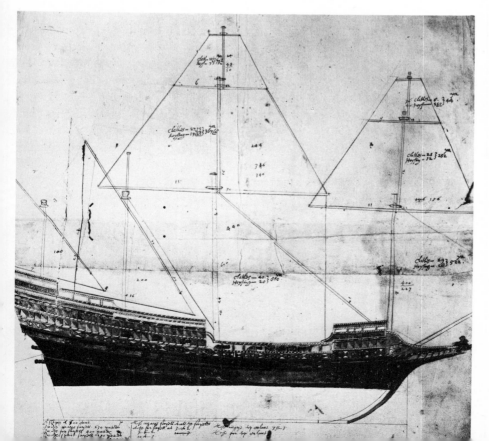

The design and sail plan of an Elizabethan galleon drawn by Matthew Baker.

leaving England isolated. In the summer of 1545 the French fleet under Admiral d'Annebault displayed its command of the English Channel by entering the Solent unopposed; it was beaten off, but the *Mary Rose*, the pride of Henry's navy, heeled over and sank in Portsmouth harbour; in the following year the French tried to force the English to give battle off Shoreham. Although the King's ships were backward in the defence of the English shores, the privateers that war with France always unleashed were in the forefront, attacking French merchant shipping with impunity. There had never before been so many prizes taken in the Channel and the quantities of goods landed became an embarrassment to merchants. Prices fell dramatically for a whole range of wares and in every port the buildings of former religious houses became converted to temporary warehouses for plunder; in London it was said that the Grey Friars was full of wine, the Austin Friars stinking with fish and the Black Friars black with prunes. With the signing of the Peace of Crépy, however, vessels from Spain, the Netherlands and German ports became neutral and quite naturally began carrying French goods, claiming these were covered by the flag of neutrality. No less naturally English privateers reckoned that French goods were a lawful prize, regardless of the nationality of the ships carrying them. There were as a result of sundry attacks forceful diplomatic representations from Brussels and Madrid resulting in a crop of law suits. William Hawkins was in trouble for taking a Spanish vessel and he had compounded his offence by disposing of the cargo before judgement was given in the Admiralty Court. When he lost his case he was committed to prison until he should make restitution to the owner, Juan Quintana Dueñas, though long afterwards it was shown that this Juan was no longer a Spanish subject but had taken French nationality before the attack by Hawkins' ship.

In 1545 the French fleet entered the Solent and attacked the English fleet in Portsmouth harbour. Henry's flagship, the *Mary Rose*, top-heavy and cumbersome, turned turtle while manoeuvring; the spot where she sank is marked by a few floating bodies in this painting executed the same year.

A brass culverin recovered from the wreck of the *Mary Rose*.

That same year an even more remarkable case occurred when an English captain astounded the courts of Europe by despoiling a Spanish treasure ship on its way home from the Indies. Robert Reneger of Southampton had found it increasingly difficult to continue peaceful trading with the Peninsula. Trade was being hampered by all kinds of restrictions and after the breach with Rome, English merchants in San Sebastian and other ports were being brought before the Inquisition; harsh fines were being imposed on some of them and a Londoner had even been burnt at the stake for heresy. Reneger had captured a French ship and brought her into a Spanish port,

where his seizure was investigated, and he agreed to surrender a part of the lading that was Spanish property. A further claim by a Spaniard was too much for Reneger to concede and when it was clear that the whole of his prize would be seized by the intransigent authorities he left port bent on revenge.

Reneger lay in wait for the *San Salvador* returning from Hispaniola with a fabulous cargo. Ten leagues off Cape St Vincent, with the help of four small English ships, he bore down on his prey and robbed her of a great quantity of gold, 124 chests of sugar and 140 hides, worth no less than 7,243,075 *maravedis*. Though under the cloak of legality, Reneger's action was sheer piracy. He apparently told the captain of the treasure ship that he would take no more than the value of the confiscated prize and offered him a certificate of restitution. But the Spanish captain begged him to keep quiet about the gold as it was being shipped illegally; it was not on the royal account, but a private venture for smuggling into Spain.

Robert Reneger knew the importance of his *coup*. As soon as he landed in England he reported the incident to the Privy Council, which ordered the bullion to be lodged in the Tower. King Henry was supposed to have been 'greatly annoyed' at Reneger's insolence and promised Spain that he would recall all privateers forthwith. Yet far from being punished 'in exemplary fashion as a pirate', the Southampton captain became a hero overnight. The Spanish ambassador in London told him to his face that it would be 'far better for everyone if he took up another profession', yet Reneger was given a wonderful reception at court 'for his fine piece of work ... and swaggers

The principal means of navigation in the sixteenth century was by taking observations of the sun with a sextant; an engraving by Stradanus.

about everywhere', as the ambassador reported, almost in tears. King Henry promptly appointed Reneger to a command in his fleet.

The event set in motion a typical series of reprisals. English goods in Spain were confiscated and in turn Spanish ships in English ports were held. Much ink was to be spilled before the vicious circle of embargoes was ended; haggling was to go on for many months over the restitution of the sugar and hides and for much longer over the bullion. The gold in the Tower was not returned to Spain for another eight years, and then it was no more than a third of the sum originally claimed. When all was finally settled Reneger was left with a vast sum. A little later the man who had shown that open piracy paid such handsome dividends petitioned the Lord Admiral about the 'great damages and losses' (to the tune of a mere £135) he had suffered through French pirates, 'to his utter subversion and undoing'. The millionaire retired from the fray and ended his days peaceably as Controller of the Customs in his native port of Southampton.

The attack on the treasure ship opened a new phase of piracy. Lesser mortals, inspired by Reneger's adventure, plundered every Spaniard that entered the English Channel. The galleons that left Spain in the summer of 1545 were attacked off the Cornish coast and soon every harbour in the Peninsula had a long list of casualties. Men like Robert Collins of Dartmouth were despoiling Spanish and Portuguese vessels in their home ports and getting away with it. Baltimore in Ireland became overnight a recognized mart for the disposal of great quantities of sugar, elephants' tusks and olive oil. For forty years of uneasy truce there was an unbroken series of incidents on the high seas in which the maritime power of Spain was seriously challenged; and when Drake, as the most natural thing in the world, plundered Philip II's plate fleet, it was to the Reneger incident that both Spanish and English courts turned for precedents. Robert Reneger was in truth the first of the sea dogs.

In 1551 Thomas Wyndham brought the *Lion* of London to Morocco (near the modern Agadir) and this pioneering voyage laid the foundation of a regular Barbary trade, principally for sugar and dates. Through the intermediary of Jewish traders newly settled in the port there was found to be a good market for English cloth in return. Wyndham was a Norfolk man, whose service as a naval officer had brought him to the attention of William Hawkins, who secured backing from the city of London and in 1553 Wyndham extended his interests to the Gold Coast and Benin. Wyndham had discovered two Portuguese pilots, at odds with their government, who were prepared to take his ships beyond Cape Palmes to the unknown territory of Lower Guinea. The commander and nearly two-thirds of his men succumbed to fever, but the survivors returned to England with gold, pepper and ivory. Thereafter there were to be annual sailings from London to Lower Guinea which soon provoked strong diplomatic representations from Lisbon so that the English crown officially prohibited the traffic, yet took no active steps to prevent it.

Sir Hugh Willoughby; an anonymous contemporary portrait.

Robert Thorne had urged his King in 1527 to promote searches for a north-east passage, on the grounds that 'of the four parts of the world, it seemeth three parts are discovered by other princes. For out of Spain they have discovered all the Indies and seas occidental, and out of Portugal all the Indies and seas oriental ... so that now next to be discovered [are] the North parts, the which it seemeth to me is only your charge and duty; because the situation of this your realm is thereunto nearest and aptest of all other.' It was a shrewd argument and more relevant than the attempts to find a north-west passage. Henry VIII was, however, in no position to finance undertakings of this kind nor, with England's special relationship with the

26

Netherlands still prospering, was there a compelling reason to search for new markets. The project was taken up again in the early fifties when the slump in the clothing markets on the continent had begun to bite. A group of London merchants, headed by the Greshams and with the investors including Lord Treasurer Winchester and Secretary Cecil, subscribed £6000 to fit out three ships for the 'discovery of the northern parts of the world'.

The arms of the Russia Company incorporated under letters patent of Queen Mary in 1555.

The expedition was led by Sir Hugh Willoughby with Richard Chancellor as his second-in-command. They sailed from the Thames in May 1553, as Edward VI lay mortally ill, but as they passed Greenwich on their great adventure to Cathay via the Arctic seas, 'the courtiers came running out and the common people flocked together, standing very thick upon the shore'. Willoughby's vessel was to be caught in the ice off the coast of Lapland and all hands perished; a second ship met the like fate, so that only Chancellor managed to cross the White Sea to reach the mouth of the River Dvina, where he learnt that the land was Muscovy, not China. From here he made his way to Moscow, where the Tsar received him and granted him and his countrymen freedom to trade. On his safe return to England a company was formally incorporated under Queen Mary's letters patent as 'the Merchants Adventurers of England for the discovery of lands unknown'. Old Sebastian Cabot was appointed governor. There was great hope, if not of finding a sea route to Cathay, of extending their trading activities to India and there were dreams of spices being brought by caravans through Persia to Muscovy and the English outpost. Anthony Jenkinson left on a three-year expedition in 1557 and on reaching Moscow sailed down the Volga to Astrakhan, crossed the Caspian Sea and then trekked by camel to Bokhara, intent on inaugurating direct trade with China.

Jenkinson had the ebullience of a pioneer: 'We set up the red cross of St George in our flags which I suppose was never seen in the Caspian Sea before.' He, Reneger, Wyndham and Hawkins were the precursors of the sea dogs of the Elizabethan age, who were to meet the triple challenge of the perils of the seas, the hazards of the unknown and the guns of the Spanish fleet.

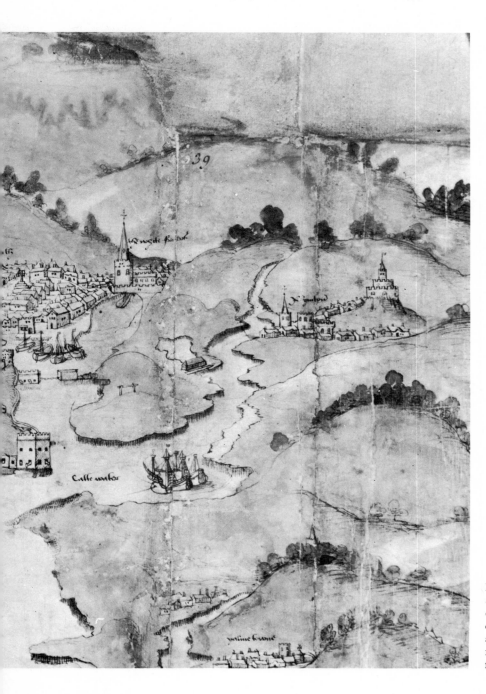

Plymouth; a detail from
an anonymous sixteenth-
century map of the south
coast of England
annotated with
navigational instructions
for mariners.

THANKS TO THE ACTIVITIES AND PERSONALITY of old William Hawkins, who had died at the beginning of 1554, Plymouth was becoming the pioneering port of oceanic trading, the base of a new generation of maritime adventurers seeking by their endeavours to acquire for England a regular share of the wealth of the New World. By the accession of Elizabeth I Plymouth was already synonymous with the re-orientation of maritime enterprise, much as Bristol had been in the heyday of John Cabot sixty years back. Throughout her reign the West Country port was to a very large extent to dominate England's efforts at becoming an oceanic nation, for it was the home port of the sea dogs John Hawkins, his cousin Francis Drake and the Devonian Walter Raleigh, and the key base of the Queen's navy in its role of challenger to Spanish supremacy.

The elder of the sons of William Hawkins, another William, was the fore-most ship-owner in Plymouth and was to serve on three occasions as mayor of the borough, though even when not in office he remained the chief lynch-pin of the government in overseeing the maritime affairs of the West Country. He had accompanied his father on the voyages to Brazil, perhaps even on the earliest, when no more than eleven years old, but now he for-sook active service afloat, keeping to the wharves and counting-house. His brother John, a dozen years his junior, was by contrast an adventurer who was never so happy as when at sea. He was destined in 1578 to become Treasurer of the Navy, which enabled him to have a decisive voice in develop-ing a naval construction programme. From the outset of the reign John saw the importance of cementing relations with the City of London to provide finance for his voyage on a scale which Plymouth could never hope to match. He bought a house in the capital in 1551 and the same year married Katherine Gonson, the daughter of the Treasurer of the Navy, and intro-duced himself at court. This set the stage for the next thirty years, for John Hawkins' ventures required support from city financiers and courtiers as well as the active encouragement of the Queen herself and were to be inti-mately bound up with the development of the navy. Hawkins was to a large extent an oceanic adventurer trying to struggle free from the character of a public servant.

John Hawkins was to be closely supported by his brother William, though their formal partnership in the Plymouth syndicate founded by their father was wound up in 1560, when John's share of the proceeds was £10,000. Each brother, however, continued to invest in the particular ventures of the other for many years to come. John was very hopeful of acquiring privileges in the Spanish trade to the West Indies, because he had made himself known to Philip of Spain when he came to England to marry Mary Tudor and stories were told that the King had been beholden to Hawkins for his personal service; at any rate for years afterwards he referred to Philip II as 'my old master'. It is worth emphasizing the reluctance of Elizabeth to break with Spain on commercial no less than on political grounds, and it was not until 1586 that relations in Europe became so strained, after years of spasmodic

conflict beyond the line, that war was inevitable. In the early 1560s the chief threats to Spain's New World colonies came from French sailors who regularly interloped on the trading monopoly, sacked Cartagena, Santa Maria, Havana and other ports and terrorized local officials.

Hitherto Hawkins had traded peaceably with the Canaries, where the ports were open to all-comers. Because the Portuguese had not made an effective occupation of the coastal territories they had conquered in West Africa, it was accepted by the powers that trade was free to all nations, yet in the Caribbean Spain resisted all rival claims. When pressed by the Privy Council to signify those areas which Philip maintained were his own, the Spanish ambassador in London replied 'All the West India continent and islands'. By now the line of Alexander VI's papal bull of 1493 had been more clearly defined, for during the negotiations between France and Spain at Cateau-Cambrésis in 1559, the Spaniards had insisted that 'the lines of amity' were the Tropic of Cancer and the prime meridian passing through Ferro in the Canaries. Any breach of the Spanish monopoly west and south of those lines was to be disregarded so that the activities of an adventurer from Britanny in the Caribbean did not technically prejudice Franco-Spanish relations in Europe, though there would naturally be no redress for actions taken by Spanish colonial officials in defending themselves from French intruders. The position of English seamen in those waters was as yet uncertain but was soon to be put to the test by Hawkins.

West African tribesmen; a sixteenth-century engraving.

In his voyages to the Canaries Hawkins had regular dealings with Pedro de Ponte, a Genoese merchant residing in Teneriffe, who was able to give him fairly precise information about the slave trade on the African coast and the markets for wares in the West Indies. It was on the basis of such details that Hawkins was able to make plans sufficiently realistic to attract sound financial backing – the founding of a triangular trade between West Africa, the West Indies, and England. The London syndicate that put up the money for this new venture included his father-in-law, Gonson, Sir William Wynter, the Surveyor of the Queen's Ships, Sir Thomas Lodge and Sir Lionel Ducket, who were most interested in seeing the results of a preliminary voyage, for experience would surely show whether the new pattern of trade could be developed as Hawkins anticipated. He left Plymouth in October 1562 taking the *Salomon*, the *Swallow* and the *Jonas*, with Thomas Hampton as second-in-command. These little vessels were indeed launched on voyages with another dimension – the passage of uncharted waters, sailing at the mercy of Atlantic seas, winds and perils unknown for months on end. Their first port of call was Teneriffe, where Hawkins consulted with Pedro de Ponte, who introduced to him Juan Martinez, a pilot from Cadiz, well acquainted with the Caribbean. Then he sailed on to Upper Guinea, proceeding as far south as Sierra Leone to find slaves.

On the African coast he certainly obtained some of his human cargo by capture, yet it is equally clear that others were acquired through legitimate trading with the half-caste Portuguese factors in the river ports. To cover

Hawkins challenged the Portuguese monopoly of the West African trade and sailed down the coast of Guinea buying slaves and ivory. A chart of Portuguese possessions in the Southern Atlantic by Diogo Homen, 1588.

themselves from charges of dealing with interlopers these factors prepared a bill of complaints for sending to Lisbon accusing the Englishmen, for instance, of overwhelming them 'with many insults and tortures, who despoiled of their goods were cast upon the bank of the Mtombi River'. It was surprising, however, that if Hawkins' operations were entirely military, no one on either side was killed or seriously injured in the process of seizing perhaps five hundred Negroes as well as ivory, money and at least one Portuguese slave ship which was not returned to its owners. On his second voyage his raiding cost seven of his party their lives with twenty-seven wounded, but the outright piracy of which he was to be accused in Lisbon for his 1562 visit to West Africa seems rather to have been forced trading. The three Plymouth vessels and the Portuguese slaver, aided by the north-east trade winds, reached Hispaniola where Hawkins was expected by Spanish officials and planters in Santo Domingo, thanks to messages sent by Pedro de Ponte from Teneriffe. But while the colonists were eager for slaves to work in the plantations they were anxious to give the government in Madrid no cause for suspecting them of breaking the law, and so a contingent of soldiers was sent against the English. Without a shot being fired the Spanish captain and John Hawkins came to terms and the latter was given a permit to trade, though, since his West Indies customers were short of ready money, most of his deals were achieved by barter or by bills on finance houses in Seville. For the return voyage most of the lading was in hides and by April 1563 Hawkins was back in England with two of his vessels. But he had also laden two other ships for Seville – a caravel which he hired in Hispaniola and put under the command of Thomas Hampton, and the Portuguese slaver which was left under her original crew. Both these cargoes were seized in the Peninsula by the Spanish and Portuguese authorities respectively, since reports from the Guinea coast and the Spanish Main, taken at their face value, suggested that Hawkins had illegally infringed the trading monopolies in both continents. He must have known that there was a strong probability of these

In the 1550s French privateers were the greatest threat to Spanish interests in the Caribbean; an engraving by Theodore de Bry of the sacking of Cartagena by the French in 1555.

goods being impounded and perhaps he had deliberately gone out of his way to show the Spaniards and Portuguese that he had been able to exploit a chink in their armour not at this time in a spirit of bravado, but as an argument on diplomatic grounds. Meanwhile the two cargoes brought to England produced for their investors a very favourable return, showing beyond doubt that the Atlantic trade was both practicable and profitable.

Hawkins was banking on being granted a dispensation from the laws Old Spain had made to protect its monopoly of trade in the New World, for he had proved to his own satisfaction that the men of Hispaniola at heart welcomed his initiative and they had been able to buy from him at prices below the rates charged by the merchants of Seville. It was much the same state of affairs on the Guinea Coast where, despite prohibitions from Lisbon, the Portuguese factors had proved very ready for business with the interloper. While Hawkins began a formal action in the High Court of Admiralty for the

34

return of the cargo seized in Portugal, he put his case for seeking redress from Spain to the Privy Council. The Queen herself wrote to Philip II commending Hawkins and also alerted Sir Thomas Challoner, her ambassador in Madrid – a flurry of diplomatic activity which seems out of all proportion to the fate of a mere cargo of hides. Clearly Elizabeth and her ministers had been persuaded by Hawkins of the importance of being regarded as a special case. He was prepared to travel to Spain to plead in person but seems in the end to have been represented. In the event he never received restitution of his goods, nor could he secure special privileges from Philip II.

We may suspect that in these diplomatic discussions Challoner in effect offered Hawkins' services while in the Caribbean to Spain to protect her colonial settlements and shipping, which were vulnerable to the Huguenot settlers in Florida, led by Jean Ribault. For a generation there had been intermittent attacks by French sea dogs, but now they had a foothold on the continent ideally situated for plundering the plate fleets, since the Gulf Stream and the prevailing winds dictated that Spanish treasure ships bound for Spain left the Caribbean by the Florida Channel. It is hard for us, with our knowledge of later events, to grasp the situation as it appeared to John Hawkins and his Queen in 1563. Spain was still England's traditional ally and England's trade with the Peninsula, and even more so with the Spanish Netherlands, was of overriding importance to the economies of each country. Politically, Elizabeth I needed Philip's support in Europe at this stage as much as the King of Spain relied on England's help to counter French domination, and at this very time, with the grand objective of regaining Calais and the hope of overturning the Guise faction, England had intervened to aid the Huguenot party in the civil war in France. Hawkins the merchant adventurer found himself involved in high politics. The Anglo-Spanish alliance could be refurbished by granting the British syndicate limited rights to supply slaves and other desperately needed commodities to the West Indies leading perhaps to more widespread concessions; in return for these trading privileges the Queen's ships when in those waters would afford the colonists the protection against the French that Spain herself could not provide. In theory there were great attractions for both sides, yet no agreement was reached. The wave of English privateering in the Channel which came with the French war led to indiscriminate plundering of Spanish vessels and cargoes, which soured relations, and Philip II could not commit himself to employing 'heretic' seamen. He procrastinated about giving an answer, but Elizabeth chose to assume that if he were not for the present relaxing his prohibitions on trade, he was not ruling out future co-operation on these lines, and she was intent on proving to him the value of reaching such an accord.

The shareholders in Hawkins' second voyage comprised five distinct categories. As in the first voyage there was the group of Plymouth merchants, headed by William and John Hawkins, the stalwarts of the Navy Board, John's father-in-law Gonson and Admiral Wynter, and merchants

Lord Admiral Clinton, one of the group of courtiers who sponsored Hawkins' voyage of 1564; by an unknown artist.

from the City of London, such as Edward Castlyn, who had long experience of the Spanish trade. But now a group of courtiers also put money in the venture, including the favourite Lord Robert Dudley, Lord Clinton the Lord Admiral, the Earl of Pembroke, and most probably Cecil, the Secretary of State. Even more significant was the Queen's own interest in the voyage, for she supplied one of her largest warships, the *Jesus of Lubeck* and regarded the adventure as essentially a naval expedition. She summoned Hawkins to court to be briefed, commissioned him to sail under her personal standard and regarded his squadron as an integral part of her navy. Elizabeth also required him while in the West Indies to serve 'in the interests of the King of Spain'. The fleet left Plymouth Sound on 18 October 1564, with Hawkins commanding the *Jesus*, an impressive vessel of 700 tons which had, however, been inadequately maintained ever since Henry VIII had bought her from the Hanseatic League. In company sailed three Plymouth ships, the largest being the *Salomon* of 130 tons, the smallest the *Swallow* of 30. Among the officers were John Sparke, who had been on Hawkins' maiden trans-Atlantic voyage and was to write the authoritative account of the second, Anthony Parkhurst, but recently returned from Spain where he had most probably been involved with Challoner in the secret conversations, and George Fitzwilliam who was related to Jane Dormer, the English wife of the Spanish Duke of Feria, a minister close to Philip II. These Spanish connections emphasized Hawkins' unique role.

After waiting on the wind at Ferrol, Hawkins made for Teneriffe for further consultations with Pedro de Ponte, whose up-to-date information about conditions for trading in the New World was invaluable. When subsequently the Englishmen's activities became known to him, the Spanish ambassador in London commented, anent Pedro, 'were it not for these Spaniards helping them in the islands, these expeditions would never have commenced'. Thence the squadron sailed for the African coast for slaves and though Cape Verde was unprofitable, there was successful raiding and trading at Sambula and at Taggarin in the region of Sierra Leone. The Portuguese suggested Hawkins might join them in attacking a neighbouring town but the action produced more English casualties than Negroes captured. These losses dismayed Hawkins and if outwardly he remained cheerful, 'his heart inwardly was broken in pieces for it'. This was characteristic, for he looked on his crews as if they were sons or brothers, but such a setback did not deflect him from his objectives. Soon he explored the estuary of the River Caceroes with his pinnaces and in five days captured or purchased six hundred Negroes as well as seventeen Portuguese ships, ivory and a little gold. This was a notable haul. The reports sent to Lisbon of these further depredations included one witness's statement that 'he heard the English shout loudly to him that the contract belonged neither to the King of Portugal nor to the contractors, but to the realm of England and John Hawkins'. Suitably adapted to the Spanish colonial monopoly, this was to be the battle cry of the English sea dogs for the next half century.

OPPOSITE Sir John Hawkins; a portrait attributed to Hieronymo Custodis.

FOLLOWING PAGES A map of the world in 1536 by Pierre Descaliers.

ÆTATIS SVÆ LVIII
Anno Dñi 1591

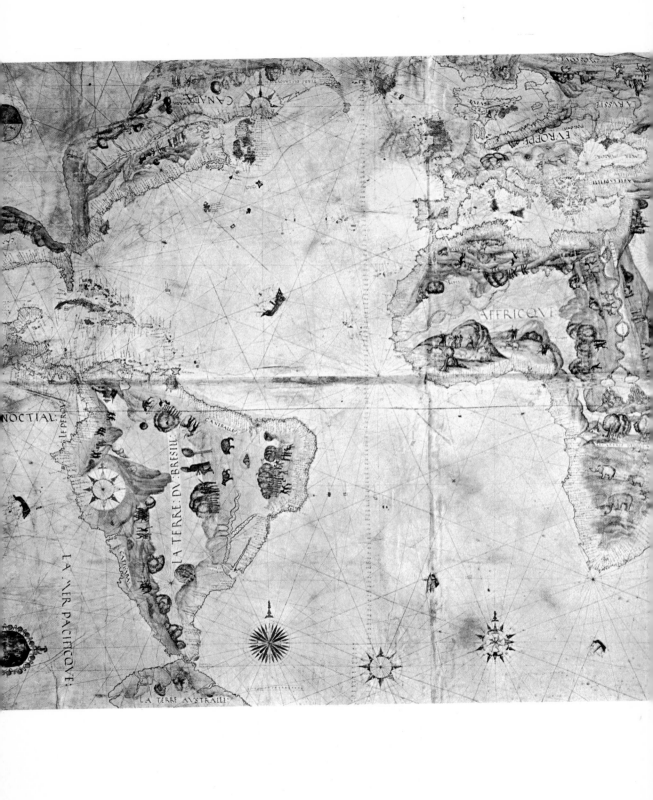

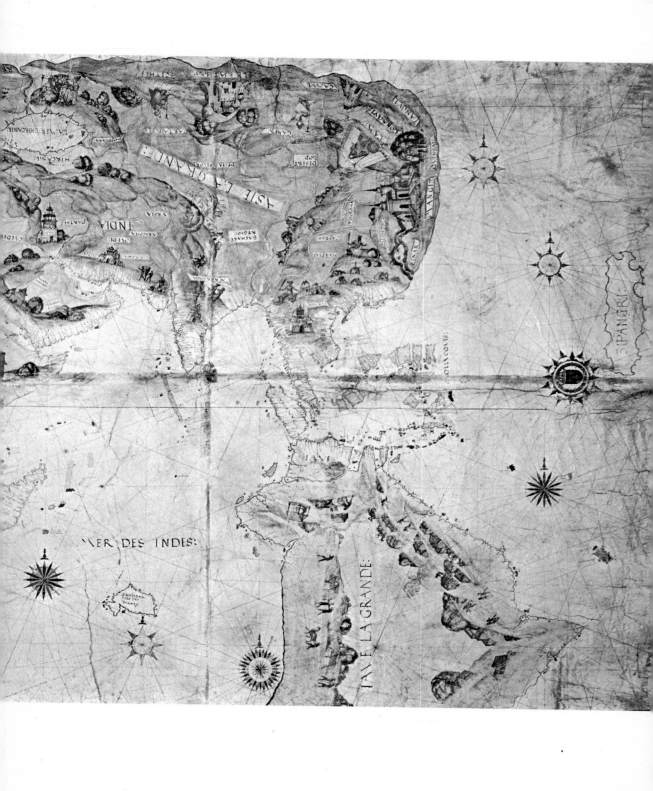

SIC PARVIS MAGNA

They reached the Spanish Main in mid-March, but found the governor of the island of Margarita hostile, for he prevented Hawkins from engaging a Spanish pilot and alerted officials in the ports to the west that the English were back and must be boycotted, though in fact such warnings were a helpful advertisement that trading was about to begin. When they came to Borburata Hawkins proffered an introduction to the governor, Alonso Bernaldez, provided by his uncle Lorenzo of Santo Domingo, but Alonso was away from his post. The men of Borburata, fearing the approaching squadron was French, had fled, but when Hawkins through an interpreter made it known that his purpose was peaceful, the deputy governor agreed to let him land some of the Negroes who were ill from the voyage and the ease with which they were sold suggested that there would be brisk business for the robust slaves when Alonso returned. 'This captain promises to please everybody', wrote the deputy. Bernaldez was careful not to grant a licence until the English had threatened the use of force; a Spanish witness helpfully recorded for transmission to Spain 'the Englishman grew violent and swore an oath that he was a great servitor of King Philip, our master, and that if the permit were not given him from here down the coast he would not leave a thing standing, that he will do all the damage he could and that we were not to think he was a corsair thief'. The man who heard Hawkins' words added his own gloss on the situation: 'God, Our Lord and his royal majesty will be better served by granting the said licence that by ruining the people of this city and . . . risking the safety of the whole province and entire coast'. The threats made by Hawkins, one suspects, were a neat exercise in collusion made to show Philip II that Governor Bernaldez had no alternative but to grant a permit, though in fact a show of force was needed to avoid the levying of excessive customs duties. There was a month of mutually profitable trading and the Spaniards paid in gold.

After obtaining hides and beef at Curacao Hawkins moved on to Rio de la Hacha where there was a further comedy. The treasurer, Miguel de Castellanos, hesitated about nodding his approval until the English should threaten to set fire to their houses 'in order that they might take various depositions of witnesses and prove that they were forced to trade with him'. Once further problems about the prices of slaves had been settled the men of Rio bought three hundred Negroes as well as cloth, linens and other wares with gold and silver. They were so delighted at Hawkins' initiative that they booked firm orders for his next voyage and the treasurer even issued him with a testimonial praising the behaviour of his men. Before leaving American waters he called at the French settlement in Florida, offering to evacuate Laudonnière and his men; had he been able to persuade them to abandon their foothold Hawkins' stock with Philip II would have been high. Since the Huguenots would not leave as they daily expected reinforcements from France, Hawkins generously let them have provisions he could ill spare, so that he had to sail to the Newfoundland Banks for cod which provided the staple diet for the homeward passage. His visit to Florida is chiefly of interest

OPPOSITE Sir Francis Drake; a portrait by an unknown artist.

41

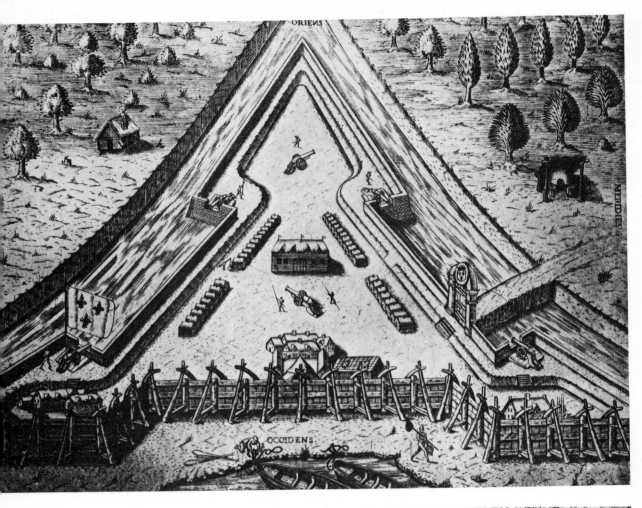

ABOVE The French
Huguenot settlement in
Florida; an engraving by
de Bry.

RIGHT The French settlers
copied the natives' habit of
tobacco smoking; an
engraving by Thevet
published in 1575.

in that it affords the earliest description in English of tobacco smoking, with an account of the natives' use of pipes that the Huguenots had copied. Hawkins returned to Padstow in north Cornwall in September 1565 after an absence of eleven months, to cheer the investors with news of a most favourable return on their money.

Hawkins wrote to the Queen that he had carried out her personal instructions 'so as I doubt not but it shall be found honourable to Your Highness, for I have always been a help to all Spaniards and Portugals that have come in my way without any harm or prejudice'. As a mark of her esteem she granted him the privilege of a coat of arms. The reports which reached Spain of events on the Main greatly alarmed Philip who regarded Hawkins' voyage as unqualified harm and prejudice to Spanish interests. Far from persuading his 'old master' of the strategic importance of allowing an English squadron to protect his New World colonies, Hawkins was seen as a freebooter, brazenly flouting commercial regulations. Alonso Bernaldez was sent home from Borburata as a prisoner and the treasurer of Rio da la Hacha reprimanded.

Even before Hawkins had reached the Main, Philip II had decided to tighten the screws against unauthorized trade and also to increase his efforts to protect his colonies. In 1565 he commissioned Pero Menéndez de Avilés, a soldier of considerable reputation, to sack the French base in Florida prior to founding a Spanish settlement at St Augustine and, as a result, Jean Ribault and most of his companions were massacred. The same year, too, the King issued much stricter rules for conducting the convoys of treasure ships between the West Indies and Spain. Menéndez himself was to be admiral of a squadron of twelve guardships, the largest of them a galleon with thirty-six guns, that were to form the Galleons of the Indian Guard. To eliminate illicit trafficking, the admiral was under orders to put all interlopers of whatever nationality to death.

Once Hawkins was back in London, the Spanish ambassador, Guzman de Silva, sought a meeting with him to try and fathom his next moves and afterwards wrote to Philip, 'it may be best to dissemble so as to capture and castigate him on the next voyage'. The two men had further meetings and when it was clear that Hawkins was bent on promoting further voyages to the Caribbean, de Silva advised his King on the importance of getting him away from England, 'so that he may not teach others, for they have good ships and are greedy folk with more liberty than is good for them'. The ambassador made the surprising suggestion to Hawkins that he should fit out a squadron to serve Philip against the Turks in the Mediterranean and the Englishman, eager for action, leapt at the idea, for he *still* believed that service to Spain in whatever quarter of the globe could ultimately lead to his being awarded trading privileges in the West Indies. The topic was explored during the spring and summer of 1566 while Hawkins fitted out four ships at Plymouth, and when still no answer had come from Spain about the Mediterranean project, he decided to send this squadron on a further triangular trading venture under John Lovell, to meet the orders for slaves made at

Borburata and Rio de la Hacha the previous year, while he himself would remain in England to be at hand when news arrived from Madrid.

De Silva heard about the preparations in Plymouth and, drawing the obvious conclusion, complained to the Privy Council. As a result Hawkins was summoned to Whitehall for cross-questioning, when he solemnly declared that neither he nor his ships were bound for the West Indies and entered into bonds for £500 that he would not violate the Spanish commercial monopoly. This undertaking satisfied the ambassador, who withdrew his request to the government to prohibit the squadron from sailing. Hawkins must have found it hard to keep a straight face, for although we do not know who besides himself and his brother were investing in Lovell's voyage, it would have been unlikely if the three privy councillors who had enjoyed such a profitable return on their outlay the previous year were not again subscribing. On this occasion, however, the Queen was not lending any of her ships and the venture was on a smaller scale. In any case £500 was a minimal sum for Hawkins to forfeit. John Lovell may possibly have been related to Hawkins

Don Diego Guzman de Silva, the Spanish ambassador to England in the 1560s; a contemporary woodcut.

and he certainly had his complete confidence. Among the others were Thomas Hampton, who had been on Hawkins' first voyage, James Ranse, who was to see much service with Francis Drake, and the young Drake himself on his first trans-Atlantic voyage, which was to prove the turning-point in his career.

Drake, destined to become the English sea dog *par excellence*, was about twenty-two when he sailed with Lovell and for his years already had considerable experience of life afloat. He had been born to the sea for his paternal grandmother was a Hawkins and his father, Edmund, had been a seaman before his marriage, when he settled down as a shearman on Lord Russell's estate at Tavistock. Tradition has it that Edmund Drake's voyages to the ports of northern Europe led to his conversion to Protestantism. He rejoiced when under Cranmer's guidance England became a Protestant state in 1547, ending the period of religious reaction which characterized the last years of Henry VIII's reign. At the time when the West Country rose in protest at the First Prayer Book of Edward VI, the Drakes and their young family decided to flee from Devonshire, making first for Plymouth, which surrendered to the rebels, and then finding a boat for London. This uprooting from Tavistock and the years of poverty that the family endured as refugees in Gillingham, where they lived on a hulk by the River Medway, had a profound effect on the young Francis. Edmund Drake obtained the post of chaplain to the naval squadron based at Gillingham Reach and though his sons had no formal schooling he brought them up as staunch Protestants; 'Make the most of the Bible' he said at his end. Francis was to become a Protestant hero in the duel England was destined to fight with Catholic Spain; while many English sea dogs justified their attacks on Spanish ships and settlements in the New World on nationalist, political grounds no less than on sound commercial commonsense, Drake was never to play down the religious issues. Though Hawkins took morning and evening prayers every day at sea, he never infected men with his religious zeal as did Francis Drake, who constantly talked about being an instrument of 'God's purpose'. On this first voyage with Lovell he converted a Welsh seaman from Roman Catholicism. He also kept up a close friendship with John Foxe, the martyrologist, writing to him after the sack of Cadiz to continue his prayers: 'Our enemies are many, but our Protector commandeth the whole world. Let us all pray continually and our Lord Jesus will hear us in good time mercifully.'

Those early years on the Medway provided a wonderful opportunity for a prentice seaman. From the age of ten Drake served in a small bark in the Thames approaches and sometimes journeyed as far as the French Channel ports and the Netherlands. He quickly found his sea legs and the old pilot was so impressed with his seamanship and his promise as a master mariner that when he died childless early in 1561 he left Francis his ship. This was tremendous good fortune. For a few further years he continued to sail her on the coasting trade and to north European ports as a maid-of-all-work, until he felt he was ready for more distant ventures. After joining a larger vessel as third officer for a voyage to Spain, he decided to sell his own bark and return to his native Devon to find employment with his Hawkins cousins. News of John Hawkins' first trans-Atlantic voyage had reached the Medway and the promise of trading to the New World fired the youngster's imagination. He was determined to play a part himself in this great adventure and, by investing his modest capital, to stake his own claim to the riches that would reward successful enterprise. Two of his young brothers and a number of friends decided to accompany him to Plymouth to seek their fortune, but by the time they arrived in port in the late autumn of 1564, John Hawkins had already left on his second expedition. While he awaited his return from the West Indies there was work enough for Drake to do in western waters as a very junior member of the Hawkins family business; and then came the chance of joining Lovell.

De Silva's complaint had meant that sailing had been postponed for at least a fortnight, so Lovell made straight for West Africa, instead of calling at Teneriffe. Perhaps, too, Hawkins thought that his own contacts with customers on the Main were so good that there was no need for further consultation with Pedro de Ponte, though had Lovell been able to consult him he would have learnt that conditions in the Indies were going to be tougher than the English had previously experienced. In the Cape Verde Islands Lovell took a number of Portuguese prizes with cargoes of Negroes, sugar, ivory and wax, one of them being a Lisbon vessel bound for Brazil. What we know of these activities suggests that there was much less trading proper with the half-caste factors and much more outright piracy than on Hawkins' voyages. The *Swallow* was sent back to Plymouth with sugar and ivory, while the other three ships sailed westwards, calling first at Margarita. When the new governor of Borburata forbade the Englishmen to trade they kidnapped two Spanish merchants who obligingly had their pockets full of money, which was taken in return for twenty-six Negroes. They were put ashore and soon business proper began – not only for slaves, but for provisions and manufactured goods as well. These transactions were completed in a hole-and-corner way to avoid the wrath of the straight-laced governor, who reported to Philip that the colonists 'buy at night and cover each other, and no measures suffice to prevent it'.

Lovell next sailed to Rio de la Hacha, where treasurer Castellanos was determined to resist any suggestion of trafficking, even by night, for he was still suspected in Madrid of being too easy-going with the English interlopers and was scared of falling foul of the new governor of Venezuela, his provincial chief. A few days before, a French vessel had come to Rio with slaves and Castellanos had mustered his forces to send it away, so when Lovell anchored on Whit Monday the treasurer was determined to see him over the horizon. For a week Lovell remonstrated with him: the slaves, he said, had been ordered by men in Rio de la Hacha, who he knew were most anxious to buy them. Eventually, when Castellanos would not shift his

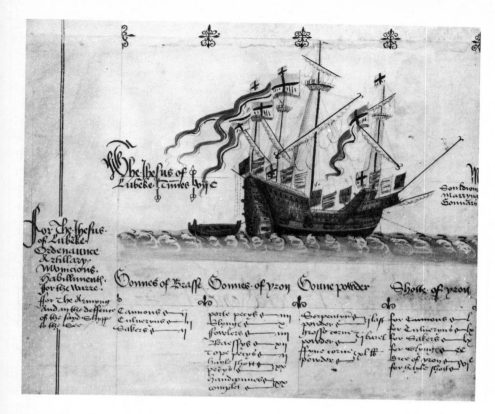

The *Jesus of Lubeck*
loaned by Elizabeth for
Hawkins' expeditions of
1564 and 1567; a
detail from the Anthony
Roll.

ground, he landed the remaining nintety-two Negroes and sailed for Hispaniola to take aboard hides before returning to Plymouth in September
1567. The official report from Rio mentioned 'the thousand calamities' endured in 'fighting off this corsair', but this purple passage can only have been
introduced to support the treasurer's request to King Philip that the inhabitants might legitimately share out amongst themselves the ninety-two slaves.
As a trading venture it was not utterly disastrous, for a valuable cargo had
already been sent home in the *Swallow* and there had been useful pickings at
Borburata, yet the days wasted at Rio had netted nothing. Hawkins lamented 'the simpleness of my deputies who knew not how to handle these
matters' and he never again employed John Lovell. Hawkins, assuredly,
would have provoked a showdown with Castellanos, as he achieved on his
following visit to Rio. Lovell's lack of audacity was a useful education for
Drake who early on practised strong-arm methods, yet he never forgot
Lovell's bad luck and misjudgement and for years afterwards he spoke very
movingly about 'the wrongs received at Rio Hacha with Captain John
Lovell'.

Long before Lovell's return, Hawkins had been planning a further voyage
on a much larger scale, for the chance of employment by Philip in the
Mediterranean had faded way. The Queen was providing two of her ships,
the *Jesus of Lubeck* and the *Minion* of 300 tons. The other four vessels were

47

Plymouth owned, including the *Swallow* and the *Judith* of 100 tons. It was a quick turn-round for Drake, James Ranse and Thomas Hampton who were all engaged for the new voyage. In the summer it had been given out as a blind that the fleet was sailing to find a new gold mine in West Africa of fabulous wealth, according to information provided by two Portuguese renegades that had offered themselves as guides. These two dubious adventurers had already approached Philip of Spain with their proposals which he had unceremoniously rejected. But soon there was news that two of the Queen's ships lying on the Thames were being laden with beans, the staple diet of Negroes crossing the Atlantic, and also fine cloths unsuitable for the West African market. Spies reported this to the Spanish ambassador who felt sure a further triangular voyage was contemplated and made vigorous representations. The Queen summoned some of the merchants to her presence and required them to swear that John Hawkins was not bound for the Indies, and de Silva seemed satisfied, so the *Jesus of Lubeck* and the *Minion* sailed round to Plymouth to join the rest of the fleet. Once again Hawkins was to sail under the Queen's commission.

A few days before Lovell's ships returned there had been a remarkable incident in Plymouth Sound. Seven Spanish warships commanded by Baron de Wacher, the Flemish admiral who was apparently cruising in the Western Channel to meet Philip, half-expected to be voyaging from Spain to his Netherlands provinces, took refuge in Plymouth in very dirty weather. Instead of finding a clear anchorage he made straight for Cattewater, the confined area where Hawkins had anchored his squadron. It seemed to the Englishmen that the Flemish admiral was deliberately set on ramming down the *Jesus of Lubeck*. Worse, he had not dipped his flags as was the recognized custom for any naval vessels entering a foreign port. Could it be that the Baron had divined the true purpose for which Hawkins' fleet had been assembled and was bent on preventing it from sailing? Much was at stake and without hesitation Hawkins ordered the guns from both the *Jesus* and the *Minion* to fire on the Flemish flagship and this produced belatedly the customary salute and an alteration of course so that the visitors came to anchor to the north of St Nicholas's Island. Their flagship had been hit on the hull, so the admiral made a vigorous protest, not at first to Hawkins, but to the mayor of Plymouth; soon he sent a messenger to the *Jesus*, who was received by Hawkins in state and told very firmly that 'the haven which he entered was the Queen's, the ships that ride therein hers also, that any stranger ought to be obedient in such case to this prince and not seem to enter after such manner'. A truce was sealed with a gift of poultry and strong London beer for the Flemish flagship. Of course there was a formal complaint in due course through the Spanish ambassador and a mild reprimand from the Queen, to which Hawkins replied, 'I had rather Her Highness found fault with me for keeping her ships and people to her honour, than to lose them to the glory of others'. To both English and Spanish seamen who witnessed the affair it appeared that the gloves were off though none presaged that the expedition would end in a fierce action on the Spanish Main.

The two mysterious Portuguese with their tales of an El Dorado in Africa had fled – had probably been expected to flee – and on 17 September Hawkins wrote to the Queen proposing a fresh enterprise, for bringing home 'with God's help 40,000 marks gained without the offence of the least of Your Highness's allies or friends'. He intended to sail to Guinea to take aboard slaves 'and sell them in the West Indies in truck of gold, pearls and emeralds', but he would not undertake this venture without her personal consent. His messenger, George Fitzwilliam, returned with her approval signified in a letter from Cecil after she had consulted Lord Admiral Clinton and at last the six vessels carrying some four hundred men left the Sound on 2 October 1567. In a gale off Brest the *Jesus of Lubeck* began leaking badly and the crew were kept busy stopping gaping holes in the stern planking with great pieces of baize. At one time Hawkins expected the great ship to founder and he cleared the lower deck to lead the men in prayers, which somewhat dismayed his men for 'it seemed such words could not issue out from so invincible a mind without great care'. Then the storm abated and by a miracle the *Jesus* was still afloat, though she remained a liability. The rest of the squadron had scattered, though they met up again at Teneriffe where Pedro de Ponte came out to the anchorage for a secret conversation, for Hawkins could not risk going ashore. Indeed, after dusk the Spanish ships lying in the roadstead between the English squadron and the shore weighed anchor so that Hawkins would be in direct line of fire from the castle's guns; but realizing the danger he moved out of range and as dawn broke the Spaniards found they had been cheated of an easy target. If Hawkins had had any doubts about the incident with the Flemish admiral in Plymouth Sound, they were now cleared, for it was obvious that he must expect Spanish hostility at every stage; licence to trade, achieved with difficulty in the past, could only be obtained now by strong-arm methods and might involve bloodshed. Some might have decided to abandon the voyage, but Hawkins would not be deflected from his course and he cocked a snook at the governor of Teneriffe by firing a salute as he sailed for the Portuguese settlement at Cape Blanco.

A little while before they made their landfall some French privateers had attacked that coast and, as luck would have it, Hawkins found a number of abandoned craft, from which he took the best caravel. By the last week in November he was at Cape Verde where he landed two hundred men to round up negroes, yet they met with strong resistance and eight of his party died from poisoned arrows. Working southwards they came up with the French vessels that had raided Cape Blanco and the captains of two of them agreed to join forces with Hawkins, including Captain Bland, whose presence was to be of great assistance to the English in their subsequent adventures. Besides searching the estuaries of Guinea for slaves, Hawkins was on the look out for small craft to use as pinnaces, since the *Jesus* had lost some of its ship's boats in the gale, and he also bought a larger bark from a Portuguese merchant. Conditions for trading were, however, much less favourable than

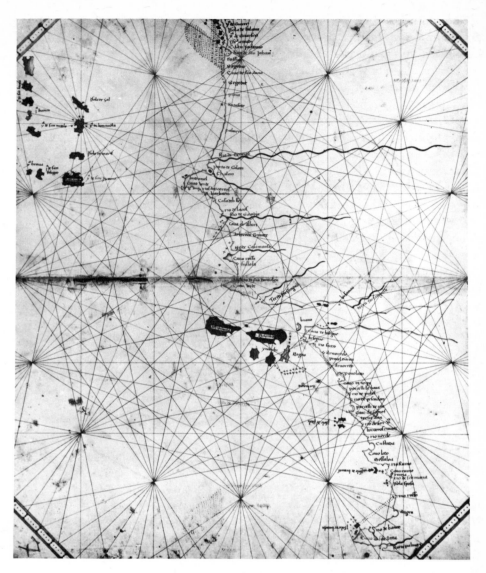

The earliest known map of the Cape Verde Islands drawn by Grazioso Benincasa in 1468.

earlier, for the Portuguese authorities were trying to defend their monopoly of the slave trade and the surest way of proceeding was to try and capture caravels already laden with Negroes. Hawkins was about to sail further afield, to the Gold Coast, when he received word from the King of Sierra Leone who begged his assistance in attacking a town of some eight thousand inhabitants called Conga, belonging to a rival chief; if he could succeed in forcing its surrender, he could have sufficient prisoners to make up his numbers of slaves. This seemed a sensible deal yet it involved some fierce fighting, resulting in the loss of nine English sailors. The troops of the King of Sierra Leone massacred most of their prisoners, leaving only two hundred and sixty Negroes for Hawkins to enslave.

50

The ten ships left Africa for the middle passage early in February, with Drake enjoying his first command in the Portuguese caravel, which he was later to exchange for the *Judith*. It was a lengthy voyage, for the fleet did not reach Dominica to water until nearly eight weeks after leaving Sierra Leone. At Cubagna, the port of Margarita, the Spaniards thought they were French raiders and were about to abandon the town when they heard their visitor was 'Juan Haquines'. He wrote to the governor asking leave to buy provisions, assuring him no Englishman would do any damage – 'the which also the Queen's Majesty of England, my mistress, at my departure out of England commanded me to have great care of, and to serve with my navy the King's Majesty of Spain, my old master, if in places where I came any of his stood in need'. The governor, who had in the past been so awkward, welcomed the English and showed them the damage the French freebooters had done, especially to the church, which provoked Hawkins to swear he would never allow his men to plunder sacred buildings.

At Borburata, the first place on the Main where trade seemed promising, the new governor was away but Hawkins wrote him a long letter in which he was at pains to point out that he sailed under the Queen's commission and that she required him to offer his services to all Spaniards against French interlopers. Disingenuously he told the governor his fleet had been prepared for quite a different part of the globe, but with that project abandoned he had come to the Main 'to seek here another traffic with the wares I already had and Negroes which I should procure in Guinea, to lighten the great charges hazarded in the setting out of this navy'. He admitted that he knew of King Philip's prohibition on trade, said he would not dream of asking for a special licence and in the next sentence promptly demanded one! – 'to sell sixty Negroes only and a parcel of my wares' to defray the wages of the fighting men he had brought. While awaiting the governor's answer he acted as if he already had a licence, setting up booths ashore for displaying a variety of merchandise which soon attracted eager customers. Hawkins also wrote to the local bishop, asking him to use his influence with the governor and inviting him to visit the English ships. The bishop excused himself from journeying, but undertook to speak with the governor and he assured Hawkins that all the colonists were anxious to trade with him. When the governor regretted, in most polite terms, that he could not grant the English party a licence, there was talk of another collusive 'battle'. If Hawkins would send a body of soldiers to the provincial capital of Valencia he could capture a number of leading merchants, setting them free on condition that they purchased Negroes from him; yet the Spaniards did not keep their side of the bargain, for when the English reached Valencia they found the town deserted. Then a compromise was reached: although no licence to trade would be issued, trading would be winked at. For two months they stayed at Borburata 'selling every day some wares for gold and silver' and the Spanish were sorry when at last Hawkins moved on, since the guns of his fleet had protected the colonists from French marauders.

No one in the fleet expected conditions to be quite as easy at Rio de la Hacha after Lovell's sad experience in 1567, so Drake was sent ahead in the *Judith* to prospect. When the treasurer, Miguel de Castellanos, refused him leave to fill his water-casks, Drake sent two shots through his house – an act of defiance of which Lovell had been incapable – and then achored out of range of the guns of the fort until Hawkins brought along the rest of his fleet five days later. The admiral was not going to take no for an answer this time, but he began negotiations in strict formality. As at Borburata he explained his presence in those waters under the Queen's instructions and asked permission to sell just sixty slaves, to pay his soldiers and help towards the charges of the voyage. Then he showed a fist: 'If you see in the morning armed men a'land, let it nothing trouble you, for as you shall command they shall return aboard again.' Castellanos would not be bluffed, nor would he be party to a collusive battle, so he told Hawkins the townsmen were well-armed and ready for the English whose soldiers would purchase their wages dearly if they dared to land.

Next day Hawkins put two hundred men ashore about two miles from the town, but before ordering them to march he gave the treasurer a final chance of reversing his decision. When he refused, the invaders moved in, rendering a bulwark by the shore defenceless through deft use of pinnaces. Further on they faced ninety arquebusiers, who fired one volley only, before fleeing to the woods, though their shots killed two Englishmen. Castellanos and some twenty horsemen retreated, with the English chasing them through the town of Rio and out the other side. The town and port were now in Hawkins' hands – the first Spanish settlement in the New World to be attacked by English sea dogs. A revised grant of arms to John Hawkins subsequently issued by the Heralds makes mention of his capture of Rio de la Hacha and his removal of the treasurer's ensign. This action made nonsense of the fiction that an English fleet was in the Caribbean to defend the Spaniards against French rovers, and at last Hawkins had been revealed in his true colours.

Rio de la Hacha was now a ghost town, not a soul remained and all possessions of any worth had been removed inland. A Spaniard from Borburata who had accompanied Hawkins was sent to those in hiding to warn the treasurer that unless the English could now trade freely they would set fire to the houses. Castellanos answered that he would see 'all the India afire' before he gave in. Against Hawkins' orders some of his crew started burning property, and when the treasurer saw the smoke he sent messengers under a flag of truce to say how much the fire pleased him, for if his town were destroyed Philip II would build them a far better one. Hawkins took the opportunity of undermining the treasurer's position by speaking to some of the merchants in this delegation, offering to pay for the damage done once he had been given a permit to trade; this was the solution that everyone except Castellanos wanted. Then a Negro defected to the English and offered, if he were freed, to show where the valuables – some of them being

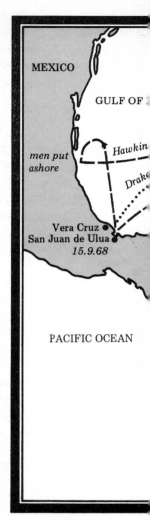

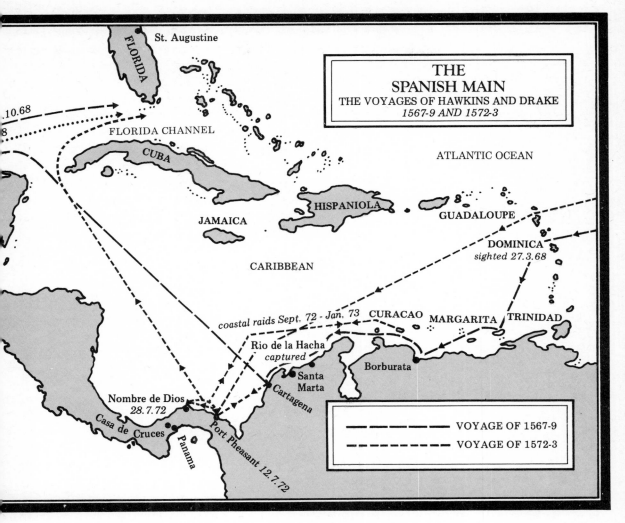

THE
SPANISH MAIN
THE VOYAGES OF HAWKINS AND DRAKE
1567-9 AND 1572-3

St. Augustine

FLORIDA

.10.68

8

FLORIDA CHANNEL

CUBA

ATLANTIC OCEAN

JAMAICA

HISPANIOLA

GUADALOUPE

DOMINICA
sighted 27.3.68

CARIBBEAN

coastal raids Sept. 72 - Jan. 73 CURACAO MARGARITA TRINIDAD

Rio de la Hacha
captured

Borburata

Santa
Marta

Cartagena

Nombre de Dios
28.7.72

Casa de Cruces

Panama

Port Pheasant *12.7.72*

————— VOYAGE OF 1567-9
- - - - - VOYAGE OF 1572-3

the crown's property – had been buried and this precipitated an angry demand from the colonists that Castellanos must negotiate. Indeed, he had no option, but before giving way he made a *cri de coeur*: 'There is not one of you that knoweth John Hawkins. He is such a man that any man talking with him hath no power to deny him anything he doth request. This hath made me hitherto to be careful to well keep myself far from him, and not any villainy that I know in him, but great nobility. . . .' An accommodation was reached. For 4000 gold pesos from the King's treasure, Castellanos acquired sixty Negroes and with 1000 pesos of his own money he bought a further twenty, and then the trade was open to all. Over the next month Spanish planters purchased some hundred and fifty slaves and much English merchandise. Admiral and treasurer now exchanged rich presents and gave the appearance of becoming warm friends. In his official report to Spain Castellanos wove an ingenious yarn that the 4000 pesos of royal money had been used to pay a ransom for what still stood of the town, including the church. Before the English sailed away, he wrote, they landed a number of Negroes they could no longer afford to feed and said this was in recompense for the damage caused to houses and accordingly he distributed them among the planters who had suffered. Hawkins felt he had got even with Castellanos at last, and it would have spoiled his satisfaction to have learnt that the individual really out-of-pocket in the whole affair was his 'old master', the King of Spain.

The visit to Santa Marta was much less complicated, for the governor was from the outset an amicable fellow. Hawkins was required to stage the capture of the town, which capitulated after the English had demolished an old house specially chosen by the governor. Over a 'truce', the man pleaded with his 'victors': if Hawkins burnt their town he must out of common humanity carry everyone off in his ships, for they would otherwise be massacred by the Indians. A week's profitable trading followed, at the end of which the governor gave the English officers a splendid banquet. There was no such traffic at Cartagena, where the governor was straitlaced. Unlike Rio de la Hacha, it was heavily defended as well as populous. Hawkins at first sought leave to provision his ships, for if this were granted he would be in a strong position for organizing sales of the rest of his cargo, including about sixty Negroes. But the governor was adamant; he would not accept the letter Hawkins had written and then, fearing that silence might be construed as consent, he sent a blank refusal to his request to buy victuals – 'a thing not denied unto infidels' as Hawkins later reproached him. Fortunately he found some wines and other goods on a neighbouring island. Shots were exchanged but for the English to have attempted to sack Cartagena would have been utter folly, so Hawkins decided to prepare for the homeward voyage, reducing his fleet to eight ships, anxious to leave the Caribbean before the hurricane season. He had enough water and provisions for eight weeks, which would have been the average time for the easterly passage if conditions were fair. At the outset, however, the fleet failed to meet with favourable winds in the Caribbean and after twenty days they were only approaching the west of Cuba, still far from the Florida Channel. Then they encountered a heavy storm which again threatened the decrepit *Jesus of Lubeck*; in the stern she 'had leaks so big as the thickness of a man's arm – the living fish did swim upon the ballast as in the sea'. All except the *William and John* turned about to run before the wind, and that small vessel, holding to her course, was not seen again. The *Jesus* remained a liability, yet Hawkins decided against sinking her off Cartagena, because as he put it 'she was the Queen's Majesty's ship and that it should not perish under his hand'. He was determined to find a harbour in which repairs could be made to render her sufficiently seaworthy for the Atlantic crossing. Moreover the dawdling in the Caribbean had made it vital for the whole fleet to take on further supplies. In the Gulf of Mexico, near the Florida coast, Hawkins sent pinnaces to search for a suitable creek, but they found no break in the

OPPOSITE Philip II
painted by Titian in 1556.

54

shoaling. A Spanish captain he met with advised him against making for Campeche, the nearest port, as the approaches were dangerous and it had inadequate facilities. There remained only San Juan de Ulua, the port for Vera Cruz, which the Spanish treasure fleets regularly visited to take aboard the output of the Mexican mines, and Hawkins decided to risk using San Juan, aiming to complete his repairs before the Spaniards should arrive.

As things stood, he could scarcely expect a welcome in the port but he feared a confrontation with the heavily-armed *flota*. So that the governor of San Juan de Ulua should be unprepared for him, Hawkins forced two Spanish vessels he came across to stay in company and on the third day, as they approached the port he formed his squadron into line ahead, with the *Jesus* in the lead. All the vessels struck their crosses of St George, leaving the only identifying marks the royal ensigns borne by the Queen's two ships. The officials of San Juan, thinking the approaching vessels must be the plate fleet, took to their boats to welcome them and a salute came from the harbour guns. It was later reported that 'the Queen's arms were so dim with their colours through wearing in the foul weather that they [the Spaniards] never perceived the lions and flowers de luces till they were hard aboard the *Jesus*'. There was a shingle bank parallel to the coast, some five hundred yards from it, where there were gun emplacements commanding the anchorage. Hawkins at once took possession of this island bank, but assured the governor of San Juan, Antonio Delgadillo, that his purposes were entirely peaceful. He was granted full facilities for repairing his vessels and for obtaining provisions and it was taken for granted that he would not attack the Spanish merchantmen in harbour, laden with treasure, awaiting the arrival of the *flota*.

It was Hawkins' misfortune that the plate fleet had made a record crossing from Spain and appeared on the horizon the morning after his arrival — eleven large vessels, escorted by two men-of-war. To add further tension to an awkward situation, aboard the admiral's ship was the viceroy of New Spain, Don Martin Enriquez, coming out to take up his appointment, under strict instructions from King Philip to defend Spain's colonial trade from English interlopers. Once Don Martin heard that the English were in port he took over command of the fleet from the admiral, Francisco de Luxan. Hawkins was placed in a fearful dilemma: if he allowed the Spaniards to enter San Juan de Ulua he would be completely at their mercy, for he was outclassed in numbers and armament, and while the Spanish fleet was trim and in first-rate condition, the English vessels were battered, the *Jesus* a lame duck. Yet if he refused them entry so that they had to anchor outside their own harbour, where they would be at the mercy of the winds, he would be perpetrating a diplomatic incident that might well lead to open war in Europe, for he was still 'the Queen's Officer'. Don Martin at first contemplated forcing an entry, but was told that because the English held the island bank he would be asking for trouble. At length an agreement was patched up; Hawkins would allow them to take refuge in the harbour on the understanding that the English ships would not be molested and should leave as soon as they were ready for sea. The viceroy had, perforce, to accept, but he was determined to break the agreement as soon as he could and before entering port took aboard a number of soldiers sent down by pinnaces from Vera Cruz. Each side provided hostages and little did Hawkins suspect that the men the Spaniards sent him were ordinary seamen, dressed in fineries, with the exception of one man, who at a critical moment would attempt to stab him.

As at Teneriffe months earlier, he noticed the suspicious movement of ships during the night, and he sent one of his trusted men, Robert Barrett who spoke Spanish fluently, to complain that the truce was being broken; when he came aboard the Spanish flagship he was put in irons. As dawn broke the English party controlling the guns on the island was surprised by a strong force, while the Spanish Vice-Admiral Ubilla was warping his vessel to close in, hard by the *Jesus*, and ordering the gun-ports to be opened. From the deck Hawkins shouted to him that such trickery was not what he expected of a gentleman, but Ubilla retorted that he was only doing his duty. An arrow was shot at him while Hawkins contrived to move the *Jesus* a little further to safety on his warps, having cut the head-fasts, holding her to the island. A confused battle followed, lasting from 10 am for at least six hours, fought in the confined space of the harbour, with the guns of the adversaries firing at point-blank range. One Spanish vessel came alongside the *Minion* and sent a party to board her, crying 'the Lutherans are upon us', but Hawkins in stentorian tones commanded, 'God and St George! Upon those traitorous villains and rescue the *Minion*. I trust in God the day shall be ours'. At this a body of men from the *Jesus* clambered aboard the *Minion* and in fierce hand-to-hand fighting drove off the Spaniards. English guns sank the Spanish flagship, started a devastating fire on the vice-admirals' ship and rendered several of the merchantmen useless. But since the Spaniards commanded the shore batteries, Hawkins could not hope to rig his sails and move the *Jesus* to safety and so he shifted as much of the cargo, equipment and stores as he could from the *Jesus* to the *Judith* and the *Minion*. Amidst the cannonade Hawkins 'courageously cheered up his soldiers and gunners and called to Samuel, his page, for a cup of beer, who brought it to him in a silver cup; and he drinking to all men, willed the gunners to stand by their ordnance lustily like men'. As soon as he had finished his beer and set down the cup it was carried away by a shot, at which he exclaimed, 'Fear nothing, for God who hath preserved me from this shot will also deliver us from these traitorous villains'.

As the action continued, the Spaniards sank the *Angel* and captured both the *Swallow* and the Portuguese caravel from Cape Blanco. Captain Bland, the French privateer, did valiant service until his mainmast was carried away, when he decided to fire the vessel and transfer his men to other ships. In the later afternoon the Spaniards sent down two fire ships on the tide and in the ensuing panic the great *Jesus of Lubeck* had to be abandoned, though

Perspectiua de vn qvarto de el fuerte y pobla[ci]on de san juan de vlua
la dicha poblacion tendra como digo a dios espar[?]te[c] [?] su[?] de[?]
numeros en cuyos de suma y dichas casas son de made[ra] de mauuio[s]
que e[s]tan atraues[?] fundadas y fabricadas sobre palos y debaxo
la agua — de san juan de vlua A veinte y siete de enero de mil
y quinientos y Nouenta Año [?]

Baptista Antonelli

Por el Caja que se me nota con la pesta sen te da

Aguja en los a[r]cos de la muralla y otra cin[?]ora

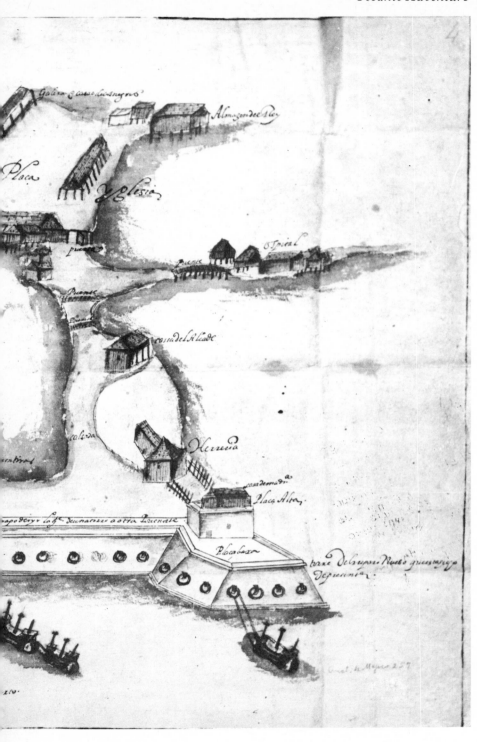

The moorings at San
Juan de Ulua where
Hawkins and Drake were
attacked by the Spanish
fleet; a contemporary
sketch.

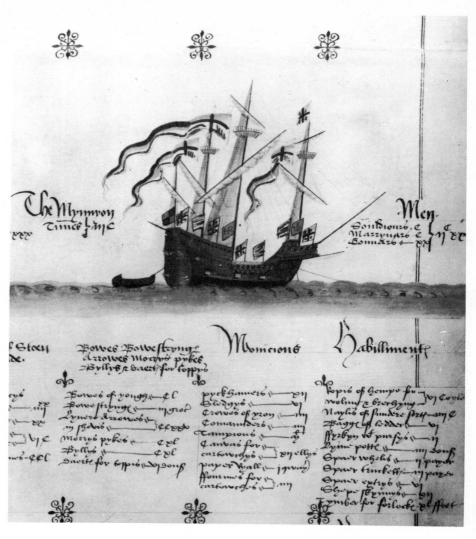

The *Minion* arrived back in England, her crew decimated by disease and starvation; a detail from the Anthony Roll.

Hawkins (we are told) 'tarried so long aboard . . . that he was almost left behind' – perhaps the first recorded case of the captain being the last to leave his sinking ship. Most of his men had escaped to the *Minion* or the *Judith*, though some perished in the attempt to scramble to safety. Of the fleet that had left the Main only those two ships remained, the one under Hawkins, the other commanded by Drake, and under cover of darkness they moved out of range of the remaining Spanish guns. By one account, Hawkins 'then willed Master Drake to come [alongside the *Minion*] to take in men and other things needful; and so he did'. Later there was misunderstanding between the two, for during the night Drake weighed anchor to start on the long homeward journey; as Hawkins put it, the *Judith* 'forsook us in our great misery'. It seems that Drake had lost contact with his admiral and, believing the *Minion* had suffered a similar fate to the *Jesus of Lubeck*, he decided to

60

save his ship, his men and his cargo by leaving San Juan de Ulua. Years afterwards, William Borough taunted Francis for deserting his compatriots. Certainly Hawkins, in the aftermath of his tribulations on the Mexican coast, felt that his cousin had abandoned him. Yet Drake's character, especially his imperturbable courage, and the whole of his subsequent career make it seem most unlikely that he knowingly left a ship in difficulty to fend unaided against the enemy and the elements. The most reasonable explanation is that, with deteriorating weather and the problems of making his provisions go round the extra men he had already taken aboard, he felt it his duty to make his way home independently, where he arrived with sixty-five men on 20 January 1569, after a far from comfortable passage. This return voyage was his first command and it was no mean feat to have come through the ordeal. He was appalled when late in the spring he learnt from John Hawkins of 'all the miseries and troublesome affairs of this sorrowful voyage'. Because of a dire shortage of food and water, a hundred men in the *Minion* pleaded with Hawkins to be put ashore on the Mexican coast; many of them died from sickness, brought on by malnutrition; others having no choice but to surrender themselves to the authorities at Tampico suffered at the hands of the Inquisition. Only two were condemned to death at the *auto de fé*, but the rest had to endure two hundred lashes apiece and serve in the galleys for an average of eight years. Hawkins and Drake kept special remembrance of Robert Barrett, the messenger sent to the Spanish flagship, who steadfastly refused to recant his Protestantism and was burned alive in the market place of Seville. The numbers of those aboard the *Minion* gradually dwindled from starvation and exhaustion so that Hawkins landed in England with only fourteen survivors. With hindsight, perhaps we may think that Drake had acted with more circumspection than had the expedition's commander.

For Francis Drake, no less than for John Hawkins, the battle of San Juan de Ulua was a watershed. It showed the merchant adventurers beyond question that honest and peaceful trade with the Spanish Indies was no longer possible, except illicitly on a small scale. There were to be no further English slaving voyages to the Guinea Coast for acquiring Negroes to trade with the Spaniards of the West Indies for many years to come, since the Spanish had now made it abundantly clear that they would not stoop to trading with interloping heretics; and so Drake embarked on a career as a privateer in the waters of the New World. Denied the chance of peaceful trade, he would plunder. Henceforth there was to be no peace beyond the line and each year the peace with Spain in Europe was to become more uncertain until, finally, relations deteriorated into open war in 1586. Drake himself never forgot the treacherous conduct of the viceroy of New Spain, Don Martin Enriquez.

3 THE NORTH WEST

The northern regions, 1570.

ENVY OF SPAIN'S MINERAL WEALTH and the search for new markets which the trade recession dictated brought about the revival of the project for discovering a northerly passage to Asia, which had in turn fascinated Sebastian Cabot, Robert Thorne and Roger Barlow. The challenge Thorne had made in 1527 that 'there is no land uninhabitable, nor sea unnavigable' was to be taken up in earnest by an ardent patriot, Humphrey Gilbert, who reckoned a man was 'not worthy to live at all that for fear, or danger of death, shunneth his country's service and his own honour, seeing death is inevitable and the fame of virtue immortal'. Gilbert boasted towards his end that he had devotedly served his Queen 'in wars and peace above seven and twenty years . . . from a boy to the age of white hairs'. A Devonian, his father, Otto Gilbert, had died when he was eight and his mother, a Champernowne, became the third wife of the elder Walter Raleigh; thus it came about that Humphrey and his brothers, John and Adrian Gilbert, were to be half-brothers of Walter and Carew Raleigh, so that the Raleigh house at Hayes Barton was to be a veritable home of English seamen. It was through his aunt, Kate Ashley, once the governess of Princess Elizabeth, that Humphrey Gilbert, after a formal education at Eton and Oxford, entered the Princess's household and later, when the courtier had become a man of action, we are told that the Queen 'had a special good liking to him and very oftentimes would familiarly discourse with him'.

It was Gilbert's ambition to devote his talents to the study of navigation, but the inroads which public service made on his leisure meant that his interests often had to be pushed aside. He had fought in Normandy with the army sent to aid the Huguenots in the first of the Wars of Religion and here he was wounded. Before long he was serving under Sir Henry Sidney in Ireland in his attempts to quell O'Neil's rebellion, yet his mind was still on exploration and in 1566 he presented a petition to the Queen 'for the discovery of a passage by the north west to go to Catonia'. The tract in support of his petition was to remain unpublished for a decade, but even in its earliest form it shows him as a born nationalist and an incorrigible opportunist. The north-west passage to Catonia (or Cathay), he wrote, was 'the only way for our princes to possess the wealth of all the east parts of the world, which is infinite'. He was convinced it was timidity alone that had prevented his countrymen from taking their rightful share in the 'great abundance of gold, silver, precious stones, cloth of gold, silks, all manner of spices, grocery wares and other kinds of merchandise of an inestimable price'. Yet there was a secondary benefit in his proposed operations, since the very search for this passage would lead mariners to discover the still hidden resources of North America, those virgin lands in temperate climates containing less exotic minerals and vegetables than the Far East, but still a worthy prize because they would be ripe for colonization. 'We might inhabit some part of those countries and settle there such needy people of our country which now trouble the commonwealth . . .'; though Gilbert was not thinking of transporting convicts, but of tempting younger sons of Catholic families to try

Sir Francis Walsingham; a portrait attributed to Jan de Critz the elder. As Secretary of State, Walsingham, an ardent Protestant and advocate of commercial expansion, actively encouraged the activities of men like Gilbert, Frobisher and Drake.

their fortunes overseas, aided by sturdy beggars who could find no work in England.

The Queen disregarded Gilbert's petition, for it was presented to her at a time when there was renewed interest in a north-east passage, fostered by the Muscovy Company, which in 1566 had its monopoly of trading to Russia confirmed by an act of Parliament and its title changed to 'The Fellowship of English Merchants for the Discovery of New Trades'. Elizabeth asked the company for a report on Gilbert's proposal and the city merchants, anxious to defend their considerable trading privileges, decried its merits. Michael Lok, not content with the exclusive rights which the Tsar had accorded to the company in the north of his dominions, dreamt of opening up a land route through Russia and Persia to India. If such were accomplished, London would with Russian help become the *entrepôt* for the spice trade and 'the whole traffic of the King of Portugal, now used to his East India, in short time would be utterly overthrown'. Anthony Jenkinson had since 1561 been attempting to establish commercial relations with India, but the route was hazardous and, in due course, bowing to the stark facts of geography, Englishmen were to penetrate the near east by way of the Mediterranean. Meanwhile Jenkinson was placing his faith in a northern sea route to the east, bent on finding a north-east passage rather as those pioneer Muscovy merchants, Chancellor and Borough had done. He told Queen Elizabeth in May 1565: 'I am persuaded there is no doubt of a passage to be found'. Gilbert and Jenkinson debated their rival routes before Queen and council, but as the outcome was necessarily uncertain the two decided it would be sensible to agree on a joint exploration – the north west was selected, to Gilbert's delight, but in the event nothing became of this, through lack of royal support. Gilbert's forceful advocacy of his project had, however, alarmed the Spanish ambassador who reported, 'There is here an English gentleman, as they say a great cosmographer, who thinks he has found a way, shorter than that which the Portuguese make, for the east India'. By then the Queen had found further work for Gilbert in Ireland in the colonization of Munster and then in dealing with the rebellion that developed.

For his energetic discharge of his duties Sidney knighted Gilbert on the field of Drogheda. Returning to England with a reputation for ferocity, he was elected an MP for Plymouth – John Hawkins was the other member – and he at once became caught up in the ambitions of the West Country navigators. He worked hard at his tracts for explorations and colonization, but soon he was leading a contingent of 1500 raw volunteers who crossed to Zeeland to assist the men of the Northern Provinces in their struggle against Spain. Personal gallantry was no substitute for disciplined leadership and the English volunteers were outwitted by the trained Spanish troops.

Back in London Gilbert revised his schemes, in particular the 1566 'Discourse on the North-West Passage'. He wrote to his brother John: 'You might justly have charged me with an unsettled head if I had at any time taken in hand to discover Utopia, or any country fained by imagination. But Catonia is none such; it is a country well known to be described and set forth by all modern Geographers, whose authority in this art (contrary to all other) bearest most credit, and the passage thereunto, by the Northwest from us, through a sea which lieth on the north side of Labrador, mentioned and proved, by no small number of the most expert and best learned amongst them.' One day the poet George Gascoigne enquired of him 'how he spent his time in this loitering vacation from martial strategems'. Gilbert took him to his study and showed him 'sundry profitable and very commendable exercises', as Gascoigne put it. In 1575 Gilbert was again thick in discussions with Michael Lok and also with Martin Frobisher, a relative of Gascoigne's. The poet walked off with the Catonia manuscript, introduced various changes and saw it through the press. This appeared the following year, probably without Gilbert's authority, and caused a stir in court and city. Humphrey Gilbert's elder brother, Sir John, who had no child to succeed to his estates, was opposed to him risking his life in such an enterprise and

Sir Martin Frobisher; a portrait by Cornelius Ketel dated 1577.

succeeded in arranging that the licence for the voyage should be in the name of Martin Frobisher.

A year or so older than Gilbert, Frobisher was the odd man out amongst the English sea dogs, for he was not a West Countryman and spent his apprenticeship with the chartered trading companies. Born in Yorkshire of Welsh extraction, when his father died he had been placed in the care of a distant relative in London, Sir John York, who, seeing his appetite for adventure, sent him on a voyage to Guinea when still very young. Thereafter

Ambrose Dudley, Earl of Warwick, sponsored Frobisher's voyage of 1576.

he regularly sailed on the vessels which Sir John Lok and his brother Thomas sent to the Barbary Coast and the Levant. The first reference to his independent activities is an examination in the Admiralty Court in 1566 on suspicion of having fitted out a vessel for piracy, but he cleared his name and was soon employed by the Queen in the Irish Sea. Through his connections with the Lok family Frobisher became involved with the affairs of the Muscovy Company and it was that company which licensed him in February 1575 to undertake a series of voyages in search of the north-west passage. Michael Lok was a man after Frobisher's heart, for he 'spent more than £500 in books, voyages, charts and instruments'. Among the men who put up money for his first voyage were Ambrose, Earl of Warwick, and Philip Sidney.

By June 1576 Frobisher was ready to set sail from Greenwich with a fleet of five vessels, the *Gabriel*, the *Michael*, two small barks and a pinnace of ten tons. They fired a salvo to salute the Queen as they left, which she acknowledged by waving from a window in the palace, but she herself had not invested any money in the venture. Frobisher passed through the North Sea, beyond the Shetlands and Faroes, and after four weeks sighted the most southerly point of Greenland. In a gale he lost the pinnace and parted company from the *Michael* which returned to Bristol. Frobisher persisted and crossed over to Baffin Island finding what he took to be a westward passage, later named Frobisher Bay. He then crossed to the northern shore and sailed westward 'above 50 leagues having upon either hand a great main', which he took to be the extremities of Asia and America respectively. He exchanged bells, looking-glasses and toys with the Esquimaux for seal and bear skins, but tragedy befell five of his company who had ventured in a small boat in the Sound; on a subsequent voyage he came across their clothing and drew the conclusion that the natives were cannibals – 'a loathsome thing to the beholders or hearers'. When he reached Harwich he brought with him a sample of black pyrite, an ore that an Italian alchemist named Agnello pronounced to contain gold, even if the goldsmiths of London were not encouraging. The Queen led the rush to take out shares in Frobisher's next voyage, the following year, for which Elizabeth contributed a man-of-war of 200 tons. Michael Lok chose this favourable moment to launch the Cathay Company of which he was appointed governor and Frobisher captain-general. A German mining expert in London, Burchard Cranich, gave his opinion that there was an excellent chance of extracting a good yield of precious metal from the sample shown him and a 'North-West Bubble' developed. Probably Frobisher was acting in accordance with the shareholders' wishes in 1577 when he abandoned serious attempts to search for the passage to Cathay and concentrated on excavating and removing black ore, though he fully claimed the land in the Queen's name. He did venture into Jackson's Sound where he found the horn of a sea unicorn, which was reserved as a curiosity for the Queen. At the Countess of Warwick's Island he discovered a 'good store of gold, to our thinking' and here he loaded his ships with 200 tons of it. On returning to England in September 1577 some of the cargo was placed in Bristol Castle for safety, the rest in the Tower of London. There were difficulties in extracting the supposed treasure since the furnace used could not be made sufficiently hot for the ore to yield its secrets. Those in the know said it was a mineral of poor quality compared with the sample brought back on the first voyage and men put their faith in Frobisher being more successful in 1578.

The captain-general was honoured by Queen Elizabeth at Greenwich and given a chain of gold in earnest of what was expected of him. She agreed to subscribe handsomely for the third voyage and even the cautious Burghley put up £100. Fifteen ships were in company and this time they proceeded down the Channel, taking aboard a number of miners at Plymouth. Skirting southern Ireland they sailed north west for a fortnight to make a landfall in Greenland, where Frobisher landed and loyally named the area 'West Eng-

An illustration from Frobisher's report of his travels to Greenland and Baffin Island which provided the first detailed account of Esquimaux.

land'. The last promontory he saw as he left Greenland he called 'Charing Cross'. As they passed by icebergs and faced gales, the fleet became separated and Frobisher lost himself in what he ironically called 'Mistake Strait' (probably Hudson's Strait). He wasted precious time waiting for stragglers to reach the rendezvous in Countess of Warwick's Sound and this left him little opportunity for further exploration. The more seaworthy vessels, fully laden with the ore, reached England in October. All appreciated that 'Her Majesty hath very great expectations of the same'. This time the Italian and German experts were hedging their bets. Captain Fenton went to Cornwall to look for various nuggets that might be mixed with the black ore in the crucible, there were arguments about the refining process, and then the truth emerged: Captain Frobisher's 'treasure' from the frozen north was not after all a precious metal, but was worthless, except 'to mend the highways'. The bubble of the Cathay Company had been pricked and fortunes were lost; Michael Lok was reduced to poverty and Mrs Frobisher and her children were found starving in a room in Hampstead. Despite this terrible blow, Martin Frobisher did not give up hope. Next year he was serving as captain of one of the Queen's ships, his head full of fresh ideas for a further voyage to 'Meta Incognita' under the Earl of Leicester's patronage, though when the objectives of that voyage were changed from discovery to trading, he withdrew, leaving it to Edward Fenton to take command.

Humphrey Gilbert, denied a part in those north-western expeditions that he felt were being badly mishandled, presented the Queen in November 1577 with a further discourse, 'How Her Majesty may annoy the King of Spain by fitting out a fleet of warships under pretence of a voyage of discovery'. By now Gilbert was quite certain about the menace of Spain and had reluctantly come round to regarding attack as the best means of defence for England. 'I hold it as lawful in Christian policy', he wrote, 'to prevent a mischief betimes as to revenge it too late.' He planned a surprise attack on the Newfoundland fishing fleets of Spain and Portugal and then, under the guise of planting a colony in St Lawrence Island, to swoop down the coast of North America into the West Indies. These proposals did not commend themselves to Elizabeth, so Gilbert penned a further petition, this time for settling new lands 'not actually possessed of any Christian Prince or people'. This was presented to the Queen when she was still very hopeful of Frobisher's success, but the fact that Gilbert secured a royal charter in June 1578 was principally due to the

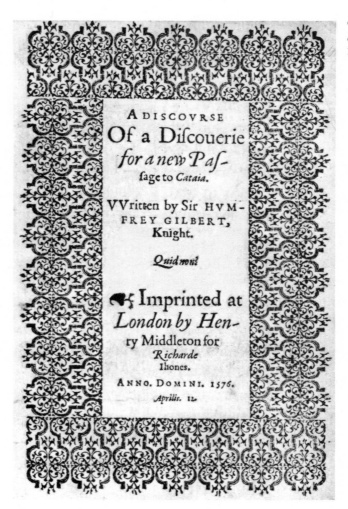

The title-page of Gilbert's discourse published in 1576.

cogent reasoning of Richard Hakluyt. He was to have exclusive rights for six years and was to become the first governor of England's first colony. No one was absolutely sure about Gilbert's original destination, for great secrecy was maintained and even his sailing instructions were obscure. Mendoza, the Spanish ambassador, could not be more specific than that he was bound for some place between the Hudson River and Florida, though he knew all the vessels were heavily armed.

Gilbert invested all his own and most of his wife's money in the venture, persuaded his brothers, Sir John and Adrian, to subscribe and secured the support of his Raleigh kinsmen, Walter and his elder brother Carew. Though the Queen had no direct financial interest, her court was represented in the person of Henry Knollys, the son of Sir Francis Knollys, Treasurer of the Royal Household and a militant Puritan, though in the outcome young Knollys detached himself from the main fleet and went off with three ships to rove the English Channel, indiscriminately looking for prizes. This augured ill for the voyage. Raleigh himself commanded the *Falcon*, belonging to William Hawkins, which was soon leaking so badly that Gilbert brought his fleet into an Irish port for essential repairs to be done. Aboard her was a Portuguese pilot, Simon Fernandez, who was to undertake many

A map of the world by Gilbert published in his discourse of 1576.

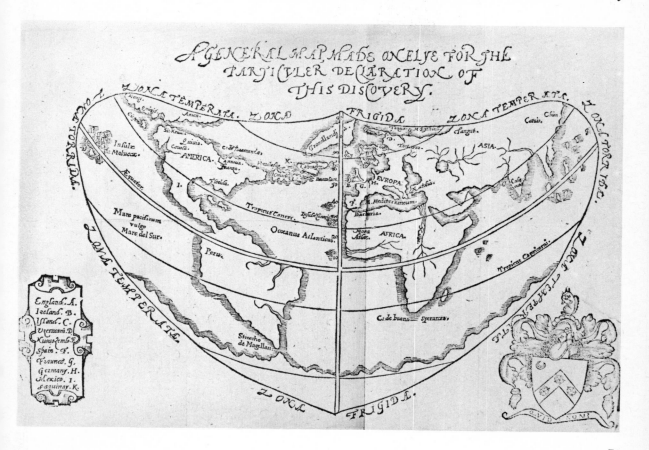

71

John Dee, the astrologer of Mortlake, was one of the leading exponents of the search for the north-west passage.

voyages in the company of English sea dogs. Gilbert was in the *Anne Aucher* and proposed following the route that John Hawkins had pioneered in the sixties but off the Cape Verde Islands he had to face an action with superior Spanish vessels, and he limped home, for the present abandoning his cherished project. All involved in this voyage became tarred with the brush of Knollys' piracies, yet Gilbert made it plain that he had not allowed any ships in his company 'to do anything contrary to my word given Her Majesty'. He, for once, appreciated the difference between privateering and piracy and, perhaps, found that honesty had not been the best policy; not only had he nothing to show for his heavy investment, but he was utterly bankrupt and being pressured to settle the debts of others. What a miserable thing it was, he complained, that after twenty-seven years' service to the Queen he should be daily subject to arrest for debt and had even been forced to sell his wife's clothes. He once more returned to service in Ireland, and Raleigh went with him, yet neither could get the twin problems of exploration and colonization out of their minds and Gilbert knew the best chance of rescuing his wretched finances was to exploit his 1578 patent.

As a preliminary measure Gilbert sent out his frigate, the *Squirrel*, of a mere eight tons burden, under Simon Fernandez to work down the American coast. He probably landed in what would later be known as New England and he was soon back in Dartmouth telling encouraging stories about the Indians and exhibiting the hide of a buffalo. The same year John Walker, probably infringing Gilbert's patent, made a lone trip to 'the river of Norumbega', claiming he had found an area that promised much in the way of cultivation as well as a silver mine. All idea of a further search for a north-west passage was being forgotten, as Gilbert pursued the theme of colonization in a temperate climate. He recognized that there was still acute interest in finding such a passage, despite the fiasco of Frobisher's voyages. The protagonists were now John Dee, the astrologer of Mortlake, who had the Queen's ear, and John Davys, a fellow Devonian, who had sailed on various occasions with Gilbert's brother, Adrian. While Gilbert was still in Ireland, Adrian, Davys and Dee had several conversations and at the beginning of 1583 they were closeted with Robert Beale, Walsingham's Assistant Secretary of State. As Dee recorded, 'only we four were secret and we made Mr Secretary privy of the north-west passage and all charts and rutters were agreed upon in general'. Through Adrian Gilbert's tactful approach, his brother assigned to them his own claims to exploration north of 50° – that is approximately to the north of the Gulf of St Lawrence. As a result of

LEFT The title page of John Dee's treatise, the *Art of Navigation*. Dee was a brilliant mathematician, a geographer and an expert in navigation. BELOW The design for his personal seal.

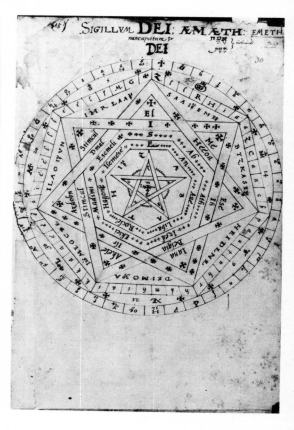

this renunciation Davys was to make three remarkable voyages between 1585 and 1587.

Meanwhile Gilbert was eagerly arousing interest in a further attempt at colonization and looking for financial backing. On the model of the Irish plantation he worked out a vast paper scheme for conveying property in his new colony to land-hungry younger sons and Catholic recusants who were feeling the pinch of the penal taxation of the early 1580s. Some nine million acres were to be notionally available to the undertakers. In April 1582 one reported that 'there is a muttering among the papists that Sir Humphrey Gilbert goeth to seek a new found land'; among these Catholics mentioned were Sir George Peckham and Sir Thomas Garrard who 'hope it will prove the best journey for England that was made these forty years'. Unfortunately the seminary priests were aghast at the idea of the faithful deserting the true cause and as a result of their propaganda men such as Garrard backed out of the scheme. There was also a rival project which Christopher Carleill, Secretary Walsingham's stepson, was trying to promote with the help of the Muscovy Company and the merchants of Bristol. The Queen was holding

The title page of Richard Hakluyt's first book, *Divers Voyages Touching the Discoverie of America,* published in 1582.

DIVERS

voyages touching the diſcouerie of America, *and the Ilands adiacent* vnto the ſame, made firſt of all by our *Engliſhmen, and afterward by the French-men and Britons:*

And certaine notes of aduertiſements for obſeruations, neceſſarie for ſuch as ſhall heereafter make the like attempt,

With two mappes annexed heereunto for the plainer vnderſtanding of the whole matter.

By Richard Hakluyt

Imprinted at London for Thomas VVoodcocke,

dwelling in paules Church-yard,
at the ſigne of the blacke beare.
1582.

back from Gilbert's scheme for in her view he was 'a man noted for no good hap at sea', and if the expedition sailed she would insist that he did not accompany it. Gilbert was becoming desperate for his patent had only one more year to run so in February 1583 he again set out for Elizabeth's consideration all the likely benefits of his proposed voyage, protesting that 'no man living shall serve Her Majesty more faithfully and dutifully during my life with all the good fortune that God shall bestow on me'. John Dee's advocacy counted for much with Elizabeth, and Richard Hakluyt provided invaluable support in his *Divers Voyages Touching the Discoverie of America*, an early draft of his *Principal Navigations*. 'The time approacheth and now is', he wrote with superb confidence, 'that we of England may share and part stakes (if we will ourselves) both with the Spaniard and with the Portugal in part of America and other regions as yet undiscovered.' There was certainly great topicality in the theme of expansion and colonization; the staid Walsingham, for instance, closely questioned a man who said he had walked unhindered from the Gulf of Mexico to Cape Breton. But it was Walter Raleigh, the new favourite, who succeeded in overcoming the Queen's

Michael Lok's map of the northern hemisphere dedicated to Philip Sidney and published in Hakluyt's *Divers Voyages* in 1582. Of particular interest is the siting of the mysterious 'Norumbega' which Gilbert strove to find.

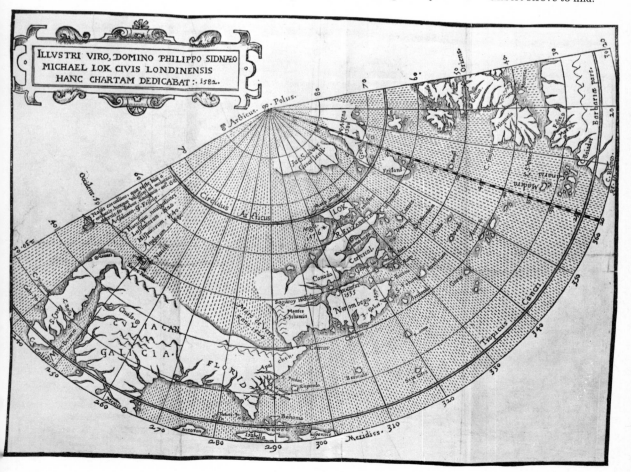

objections; the expedition could sail with her full permission and Richard Grenville could command it. She sent him a jewelled token in the form of 'an anchor guided by a lady', with a note asking for his portrait and wishing 'great good hap and safety to your ships' as if she too were aboard. Though Raleigh had spent £2000 in fitting out the *Bark Raleigh*, a fine ship of 200 tons, Elizabeth could not spare him from her side.

The fleet of five vessels left Plymouth Sound on 11 June 1583, with Gilbert in the *Delight* (120 tons); besides Raleigh's vessel and the little *Squirrel*, now on her third trans-Atlantic voyage, there were two craft that each had a piratical past, the *Golden Hind* – not Drake's ship, but a forty-ton frigate owned by Edward Hayes, who commanded her – and the *Swallow* of similar size, which Gilbert had recently taken from the notorious Studland pirate John Callice. Hayes, who kept a narrative of the expedition, described the men aboard:

We were in number in all about 260 men, among whom we had of every faculty good choice, as shipwrights, masons, carpenters, smiths, and such like, requisite to such an action: also mineral men and refiners. Besides for solace of our people, and allurement of the savages, we were provided of music in good variety: not omitting the least toys, as morris dancers, hobby horses, and Maylike conceits to delight the savage people, whom we intended to win by all fair means possible.

A fair westerly wind set them on their course, but after two days at sea the *Bark Raleigh* turned back on account, some said, of sickness aboard, others, that the crew had discovered there were insufficient provisions for the voyage. This faint-hearted attitude made Gilbert furious; he regarded the ship's return as a stab in the back and when he reached Newfoundland he wrote to Sir George Peckham: 'The *Bark Raleigh* ran from me in fair and clear weather, having a large wind. I pray you solicit my brother Raleigh to make them an example to all knaves.'

On 20 July there was 'much fog and mists' and the four ships lost contact with each other, but ten days later Gilbert sighted through the haze the coast of Newfoundland and, realizing they were too far to the north, he decided to follow the coast south, leaving the 'hideous rocks and mountains, bare of trees and void of any green herb'. In Conception Bay, to his relief, he found the *Swallow* and then moving on towards the entrance to St John's harbour there was the *Squirrel* safely at anchor, amidst various fishing craft from northern Europe. They were all in jubilant mood and on Monday 5 August Gilbert led his party ashore to take possession of the harbour and island in the name of the Queen. His royal commission was read and interpreted to the assembled fishermen and it was made clear to them that for the future rent would be demanded of them for drying their nets and that if any man should speak dishonourably of Her Majesty he would lose his ears. This was England's first colony and the royal arms, engraved in lead, were set up on a wooden post. Gilbert stayed here for a fortnight exploring the neighbourhood of St John's while a 'mineral man and refiner' named Daniel reckoned

OPPOSITE A skirmish with Eskimaux off Baffin Island; a watercolour by John White.

he had found traces of silver ore. Altogether it seemed an ideal place for development. The vessels were well stocked with provisions 'as if we had been in a country or some city populous and plentiful of all things'. Unfortunately there was sickness aboard the ships and an undercurrent of dissatisfaction with Gilbert's proceedings, so he put aboard the *Swallow* those in poor health and others eager to return to England, while he led the remaining ships to explore the coast to the south, trying to reach 'Norumbega'.

Attempting to make Sable Island, they encountered the treacherous shoals between the Newfoundland Bank and Cape Breton Island, feeling their way in the shallows. The weather improved at sunset on 28 August and the men's spirits rose, for the worst of their difficulties seemed over and so they celebrated with trumpet, fife and drum. But the next day an unheralded gale blew up, south-by-east, 'bringing withal rain and thick mist, so that we could not see a cable length before us'. The *Delight* went aground, was soon dashed in pieces and lost all hands – certainly a hundred men, among them Daniel the refiner and Stephen Parmenius, the Hungarian scholar who had written so many elegant Latin verses in praise of Gilbert. As she was the largest of the remaining ships the *Delight* had been laden with the bulk of the stores needed and her disaster took the heart out of the expedition, for the survivors were united in demanding that Humphrey Gilbert should call off his proposed survey of the American coast and make for home. He gave way, though he told the others that he was greatly satisfied with what had already been achieved: 'Be content, we have seen enough and take no care of expensive past. I will set you forth royally the next spring, if God send us safe home.'

As they altered to an easterly course they saw what Hayes, the chronicler of the exploration, called 'a fish in the shape of a lion' (perhaps a walrus) come 'to bid us a horrid farewell'. Everyone else was terrified, but Gilbert was thankful for the monster's appearance, 'rejoicing that he was to war against such an enemy, if it were the devil'. With the prospects of a rough crossing during the autumn gales it was suggested to Gilbert that he should transfer from the tiny *Squirrel* to the more seaworthy *Golden Hind*, but he refused, saying, 'I will not forsake my little company going homewards, with whom I have passed so many storms and perils'. Edward Hayes noted Gilbert's concern at the loss of his books and the specimens of silver ore that had been put aboard the *Delight*, yet he also detected Sir Humphrey's confidence that the Queen would be overjoyed at their endeavours and would readily be persuaded to subscribe £10,000 for next year's voyage. What was quite clear to Hayes was that Sir Humphrey had put out of his mind the idea of a colony to the south, in 'Norumbega', and was 'now become a northern man altogether'. St John's, Newfoundland, he reckoned could be a worthy starting-point for English overseas expansion.

They made good progress and on 8 September came near the Azores, but here they found 'terrible seas, breaking short and high pyramid-wise'. Hayes wrote that not one of his companions aboard the *Golden Hind* had ever

Theodore de Bry's map of Virginia, 1590.

The Indian village of Secotan near Roanoke drawn by John White who accompanied the first expedition of colonization to Virginia in 1585.

experienced so bad a storm, 'though many had spent their lives at sea'. That night he saw upon the mainyard a little fire 'which seamen do call Castor and Pollux. But we had only one, which they took as an evil sign of more tempests'. Indeed, the next day both craft seemed completely out of control, tossed about relentlessly and likely to founder, yet amidst the storm Gilbert seemed assured and inwardly at peace. Once Captain Hayes was quite certain the *Squirrel* had been lost, but she reappeared on the crest of the next gigantic wave and he saw Sir Humphrey sitting in the stern with a book in his hand. As the *Golden Hind* approached within shouting distance the admiral cried out to him: 'We are as near to heaven by sea as by land'. Such were words, Hayes later commented, 'well beseeming a soldier, resolute in Jesus Christ, as I can testify he was.' When the sun went down the *Golden Hind* continued to follow in the wake of the admiral, but about midnight the

OPPOSITE Sir Humphrey Gilbert painted by an unknown artist.

BELOW Gilbert's own chart of the polar regions with which he tried to prove the existence of the north-west passage; it is dated 1582.

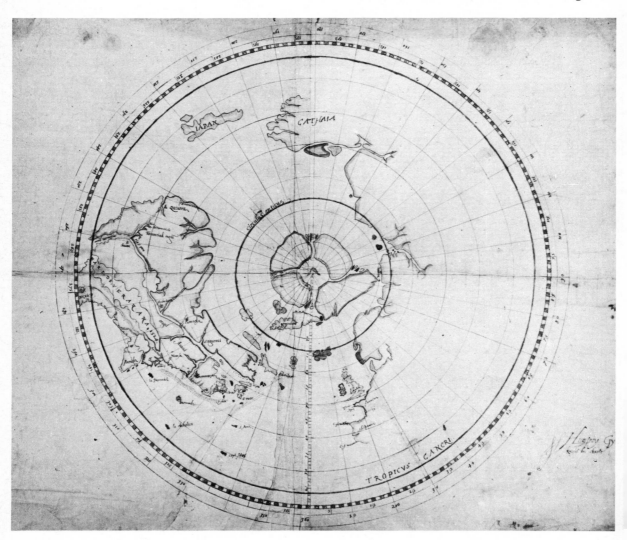

watch could no longer see the stern lights of the *Squirrel*, for the seas had swallowed her.

Humphrey Gilbert was undoubtedly courageous and single-minded yet he lacked powers of leadership and his shipmates found him irritable. There was some truth in the Queen's taunt that he was a man of 'no good hap at sea'; in a superstitious age he was unlucky too often. Moreover compared with Drake, Hawkins and Frobisher he was inexperienced in practical seamanship. Though a persuasive author who took infinite pains with his writings about exploration and colonization, when it came to putting them into practice he displayed impatience and when afloat showed surprising lack of judgement. Edward Hayes, who was on the whole a kindly critic in his memorial of the final voyage, could not but write that Gilbert thrust himself into action 'for which he was not fit, presuming the cause pretended in God's behalf would carry him to the desired end'. He presumed rather too much, and went to a watery grave. Yet more than any Elizabethan he had seen the possibilities of colonization which after his death would be actively pursued by Grenville and Raleigh. A generation later Englishmen would settle at St John's, Newfoundland.

While interest in the area Gilbert had called 'Norumbega' would be taken up by Grenville and his friends in their Virginian venture, the search for the north-west passage passed to Adrian Gilbert and John Davys, aided by Dr Dee and William Sanderson, a wealthy London merchant and amateur geographer who had married a niece of Raleigh's. In 1585 Davys sailed to the east coast of Greenland and, finding a great barrier of ice, moved south to round Cape Farewell and explored the west coast, which he named 'Desolation', though once past the ice he found 'many green and pleasant isles bordering upon the shore'. After pausing in a favourable anchorage, Davys steered west-north-west, 'thinking thereby to pass for China, but in the latitude of 60° we fell with another shore and there found another passage of 20 leagues broad, directly west [Northumberland Inlet] which we supposed to be our hoped strait'. As they penetrated this sound for some thirty leagues, 'finding it neither to widen or straighten' he deemed it provident to make for home before winter set in.

Davys returned next year to find he had been mistaken about the passage and again in 1587, when he sailed through Davis Strait into Baffin Bay. As he reported, he hoped to see 'America west from me and Desolation [west Greenland] east; then, when I saw the land of both sides I began to distrust it would prove but a gulf. Notwithstanding, desirous to know the full certainty [the mark of the true explorer] I proceeded and in 68° the passage enlarged so that I could not see the western shore'. He carried on to the latitude of 73°N, keeping near to the coast of Greenland where the waters were entirely free from ice. Here men came out in canoes to intimate as best they could to their unexpected visitors that there was a great sea even further to the north. 'Thinking to discover the north parts of America' Davys sailed towards this sea for another forty leagues finding the water to be 'very salt, blue and of inscrutible depth'. Then he came to a great bank of ice and decided he must make his way south. He failed to find two ships he had left to fish for cod and made his course for Devon. John Davys was active at sea for another eighteen years, yet he never made another Arctic voyage, for his energies were used in other waters. He remained convinced that a north-west passage existed and in his subsequent writings tried to prove that every sea is navigable, no region too cold for human existence. The activities of the 'father of Arctic discovery' left on the map of the north west a goodly crop of Elizabethan names, many of them with West Country connections. There is Gilbert Sound, Mount Raleigh, Exeter Bay and Totness Road; there is Queen Elizabeth Headland, Hatton Headland, Cape Walsingham, Cape Dyer, Cumberland Sound, Warwick's Foreland, Darcy's Island, and Sanderson's Hope. Above all there is Davis Strait.

H AWKINS HAD FORGIVEN HIS KINSMAN DRAKE for not standing by the *Minion* in the aftermath of the battle of San Juan de Ulua in 1568. Where Lovell never recovered from Hawkins' displeasure, Drake's apparent lack of judgement was put down to inexperience, for the older man had seen enough of his ability to realize that he was a born sea dog and he gave him every encouragement when he decided to return to the Spanish Main to settle old scores by plundering ships and settlements. The battle that the *Minion* and the *Judith* had survived showed unmistakably that open, peaceful trade with the Spanish Indies was impossible. There could be no more slaving voyages from Plymouth to Guinea and the West and the chance of selling English manufactures in Central America and the Caribbean had vanished. Spain had shown she would fight to preserve her trading monopoly with her colonial empire and keep in her own hands the precious metals from the mines of Mexico and Peru. Drake and other bold spirits in consequence took to privateering beyond the line.

Even in Europe envy of Spanish treasure was pushing England to the brink of war. In November 1568 three small Spanish vessels took refuge in Plymouth Sound, a fourth in Southampton, to elude a swarm of French pirates. They carried money which the Duke of Alva needed for paying his troops in the Netherlands – no less than 800,000 ducats, which had been loaned to the King of Spain by Genoese bankers. A pretext was found for detaining these ships and then came news of Hawkins' troubles in Mexico. Elizabeth was advised that the money was not technically Philip's, as had at first been thought, so she decided to borrow the sum herself and had it removed to the Tower of London for safety. The Spanish ambassador, de Spes, had written to Alva in a panic, advocating immediate reprisals and the Duke placed an embargo on trade, arrested English ships in Antwerp and the other ports and confiscated merchants' property. Elizabeth had no choice but to retaliate. The next few months showed that if England chose to be unfriendly to King Philip, Spanish vessels could not risk using the English Channel. Privateers under letters of marque brought in many prizes to the south coast ports, while the 'Sea Beggars' from Flushing and Brill, using English harbours, took their toll. The embargo effectively lasted until the summer of 1574.

This new political climate meant that Elizabeth was no longer embarrassed

OPPOSITE The American mainland drawn by Guillaume Le Testu, the Huguenot privateer who joined Drake in his Caribbean venture of 1572.

THE AMERICAN MAINLAND 🐾

The Dutch 'Sea Beggars',
using English ports as a
base, harrassed Spanish
shipping in the Channel.

by her seamen's depredations in the New World. Philip II could thunder
about the heretics' iniquities, but he would not risk a war in Europe. In 1571
Drake made his first voyage to the Main on his own account in the *Swan*. He
aimed at reconnoitring the waters of the Panama Isthmus and learning all
he could about the route taken by the mule trains bringing the treasure from
Peru which crossed from Panama to the Caribbean port of Nombre de Dios.
With careful planning he could ambush the treasure in the jungle and also
intercept the small craft that brought less valuable goods down the Chagres
River. He could remove this plunder by pinnaces to his vessels, hidden in an
out-of-the-way creek, and make for Plymouth. This design showed imagination and incredible boldness. He envisaged a series of combined operations
in which soldiers landed from pinnaces would work ashore in conjunction
with guns from ships, and over the years he would develop this novel tech-

nique of surprise 'commando' raids on Spanish ports. No corsair had taken such pains with his plans, for he knew there would be little chance of success without detailed knowledge of the terrain. Drake even visited Nombre de Dios, disguised as a Spanish merchant, so he could find his way about the harbour and the town in the dark and became as familiar with the neighbouring creeks and shoals as if this were the Devonshire coastline. He discovered an ideal lair which he called Port Pheasant, a landlocked harbour sheltered from all winds and sufficiently deep for anchoring his vessels at all states of the tide. Here there were plenty of fish, freshwater streams and fruit. We cannot be sure of its exact location, but it lay on the Acla coast, on the western side of the Gulf of Darien. Nearly as important he made contact with the Cimaroons dwelling in the jungle. These were Negro slaves who had escaped from their masters to form communities which the Spaniards could never subdue. According to the Bishop of Panama, of the thousand Negroes who arrived each year from West Africa, over three hundred managed to run for freedom. Drake was assured of their help in his land operations against the Spanish. Before returning to Plymouth he buried his surplus stores at Port Pheasant, ready for the next voyage on which he was determined to inflict a terrible blow against Spain and bring himself fame and fortune.

With formal relations between England and Spain still broken, Drake had no difficulty in securing financial backing and no problem about obtaining authority to sail west. De Spes had been expelled from England for his part in the Ridolfi Plot, just as news arrived of Don John of Austria's decisive victory over the Turkish fleet at Lepanto. Spain seemed invincible in Europe, but Drake knew that her colonial empire was extremely vulnerable. For his attack on 'the Treasure House of the World' he had no more than seventy-three men and two ships, the *Pasco* of seventy tons, John Hawkins' ship and his own *Swan*, much smaller, commanded by his brother John Drake. They crossed the Atlantic in five weeks and, after watering at Guadaloupe, made for Port Pheasant. Drake was alarmed to find that the stores he had hidden the previous summer had been rifled and when he went ashore to investigate a tell-tale wisp of smoke, he discovered a message from John Garrett, a Plymouth captain, written only five days before: 'Captain Drake, if you fortune to come to this port make haste away, for the [slaves of the] Spaniards which you had with you here last year have betrayed the place and taken away all that you left here.' Garrett, expecting Drake to return, had nailed his letter to a tree and lit a fire nearby, now in its last embers, to attract attention. It was a severe blow that the Spaniards had discovered his hide-out, but at least they had no idea exactly when he would be returning. Instead of being scared off, he built a stockade and had his men assemble the pinnaces which he had brought in sections from Plymouth for using in the shallows where not even the *Swan* could sail. Next day there arrived in the harbour a privateering bark belonging to Sir Edward Horsey which was commanded by James Ranse, and he had with him two prizes he had taken.

Drake began to think that his secret lair was becoming common knowledge. He made the best of an awkward situation for he persuaded Ranse to join forces with him in his projected attack on Nombre de Dios. At the Isle of Pines, Drake met with two frigates manned by Negro slaves who were taking aboard timber. He questioned them closely to find out the latest news from Nombre de Dios and then set them free ashore to join the Cimaroons, making it plain that no one must reveal his presence in those waters to the Spanish – as his account of the voyage dryly puts it, 'he was loath to put the town to too much expense, which he knew they would willingly bestow, in providing beforehand for his entertainment!'

The fleet came to anchor at night in a secluded bay, behind a promontory to the east of Nombre de Dios harbour. Ranse and his crew were left to guard the ships while Drake and his company set off in the pinnaces by moonlight in the small hours of 28 July. Stealthily they came ashore at about 3 am while the town slept. Some of the men thought it a foolhardy enterprise, but Drake spurred them on to what he said would be a famous victory. He knew the darkened town as well as he did the streets of Plymouth; he knew exactly where the shore battery was and the lone gunner and his six cannons were soon silenced. To create a diversion, John Drake and John Oxenham were sent off with a party to attack the town from the west side. Having placed twelve men to guard the pinnaces, Francis led his main force to a hill on the east, from which he would march on the King's treasure house down by the waterside.

Bells were rung to alarm the townsfolk still abed and the Spaniards were deceived by the division of the English into two bands into thinking them a much more powerful force than they were. As Drake brought his men to the market-place, however, with drums beating and trumpets sounding, enough soldiers had mustered to bar his approach to the Panama Gate. In a sharp clash, an English trumpeter fell and Drake himself was wounded by a shot in the thigh, though he concealed his pain, and the enemy were answered by fierce musket fire and some well-directed arrows. They took to their heels when John Drake's small party entered the fray, shouting the traditional war cry 'St George'. Two prisoners were compelled to lead the Englishmen to the governor's house where they found an enormous quantity of silver in heavy bars. Drake decided that valuable though this was, it was too heavy a prize to be burdened with while there was still strong hope of a hoard of gold; he forbade his men to touch the silver, for if they could force the doors of the King's treasure house they would find more gold than their pinnaces could possibly carry. At this juncture a messenger from the boats on the shore warned Drake that he must be clear of the town by dawn for they understood that reinforcements were on the way. As luck would have it, before they could force the treasure house, there was a tropical thunderstorm which not only wasted a valuable half-hour but soaked much of their powder and match and damaged their bow strings. Despondency set in, but Drake never had room for craven cowards, and would not tolerate waverers at such a

OPPOSITE A portrait of Drake by M. Cheeraerts.

time and in such a place. 'I have brought you to the treasure house of the world', he barked at them. 'If you leave without it you may henceforth blame nobody but yourselves.' Oxenham and young Drake were soon forcing their way into the building, while their captain said that he would see that the market-place was held. Simultaneously there were two disasters: it was found that the treasure house was quite empty and Drake collapsed from loss of blood. Despite his careful enquiries, he had not known of the new instruc-

tions that for greater security treasure was now to be sent from Panama only when the vessels forming the plate fleet had anchored at Nombre de Dios – and as the last fleet had left for Spain a mere six weeks earlier, the treasure house would remain empty for many months. Drake's collapse was no less unnerving, especially since not a man was aware of his injury; now his wound was known, people belatedly observed that his blood had been filling the prints of his footsteps for some time and they 'thought it not credible that one man should be able to spare so much blood and live'. Thoroughly disheartened, the Englishmen carried Drake to the pinnaces.

The attack on Nombre de Dios had failed inasmuch as they returned without gold, without silver even (though the more daring had pickings of one kind or another), with a trumpeter dead and their captain injured. Yet their exploit had shown how easily a Spanish stronghold could be surprised and, but for the tropical storm and the chance wounding of their leader, the English would have made a significant haul. As it was, they still managed to seize a wine ship from the Canaries as they left the bay, and made a temporary base on a small island where Drake rapidly recovered his strength and his spirits.

The governor of Nombre de Dios sent a messenger to him to try and fathom his intentions, under cover of offering food and asking advice on how to treat wounds received from poisoned arrows. Drake replied curtly that he was Francis Drake, an Englishman, and never poisoned his arrowheads. As to supplies, he said, the English party lacked nothing, apart, that is to say, from that 'special commodity which that country yieldeth' (meaning gold). He warned the man to advise his master to keep on the alert because he intended to reap some of the 'harvest which they get out of the earth and send to Spain to trouble all the earth'. Before he left, the messenger was entertained to an English dinner and loaded with presents so that he said that he had never been so much honoured in all his life. After a while, Captain Ranse decided that there was no point in remaining any longer in the Caribbean; he had his own prizes and a share of the ship with the Canary wine, so he made for home, but Drake was determined to wait for the next plate fleet. In future he would plan the details of a raid less rigidly and from experience learn to improvise and make snap decisions. It is clear that detailed planning was a matter which John Hawkins had inculcated in him but from now on Drake was to be very much his own strategist and his methods were ideally suited to the warfare and conditions of the Spanish Main. In a way, he had outstripped his tutor, born into a different world. Drake could not believe that the new type of warfare he represented – making use of soldiers ashore and artillery afloat in combined operations – would not succeed. In Oliver Cromwell's day admirals, such as Robert Blake, were officially termed 'generals at sea' but their role had been fashioned by Francis Drake's own experience.

The months of waiting in the Spanish Main were filled with exploits to keep up his men's morale. But life was far from easy. Fever was endemic and

The mines of Potosi in Bolivia, one of the richest deposits of silver found in the New World; an anonymous late sixteenth-century drawing from an atlas of sea charts.

91

there was poignancy in the death of Drake's brother Joseph – one of twenty-eight casualties – in January 1573; despite the risk of infection, Francis comforted him in his arms at the end. The little force of seventy-three was becoming seriously depleted and, a heart-rending decision to have to make, Drake came to the conclusion that he must scuttle his *Swan* for lack of men to work her. He ordered the ship's carpenter, Tom Moone, to bore gimlet holes through her bottom at night, though the man pleaded in vain to have the ship saved from this fate. Next day the crew, led by John Drake, who was not in the secret, slaved away at the pumps for hours, but, realizing that she could not be saved, removed everything from her hold and decks before firing her.

Off Cartagena and Santa Marta Drake made successful raids, using his pinnaces in shallow water, still a manner of campaigning that caught the Spanish unawares. Another personal tragedy was the death of his other brother, John, whom Francis had left in command of the *Pasco* while he was exploring the Chagres River. When a Spanish frigate hove in sight, the men were eager to plunder her, but John Drake cautiously advised them she was probably well armed, whereas the English party were poorly provided with weapons. The others remained anxious to make the attempt, however risky it might prove, and in the end John assented. 'It shall never be said that I will be hindmost, neither shall you report to my brother that you lost your

A Spanish treasure frigate designed by Pero Menéndez Marquez to carry treasure from the West Indies to Spain.

voyage by any cowardice of mine.' As he feared, the frigate was heavily defended and the boarding party he led ran into immediate trouble, having shot discharged in its face. John was mortally wounded and died within the hour, having dictated a rough will calling on Francis to see that his wife was paid the profits on the £30 he had invested in the voyage.

Much time was spent exploring the rivers and tracks of the entire Panama Isthmus with the aid of Drake's Cimaroon allies, while others saw to the careening of the ships and putting the pinnaces in first-rate order. With eighteen men Drake went with native guides far into the tropical forest. On 11 February 1573 they reached a ridge from where Drake first saw the Pacific Ocean and prayed that he might himself adventure there in time. Then they came near to Panama and could see the treasure ships arriving from Peru. When the gold had been checked and packed on mules to follow the secret path across the Isthmus, Drake would strike.

At last Cimaroon scouts reported that the caravans were ready to move across the pampas and Drake waited in the deep undergrowth with his little force, not far from Panama, ready to pounce as soon as they heard the bells on the mules. But the Spaniards sensed that there was danger and were very much on the alert, fearing not so much English hijackers as Cimaroons, who were a far more deadly foe. The first caravan of mules bore not packs of gold but bales of taffeta and silk. Everything went wrong. A seaman who was the worse for liquor ignored Drake's orders and attacked a small convoy of donkeys coming from Venta Cruces bearing nothing of value. The treasurer of Lima, who was riding along the track with his daughter and his own very valuable belongings, gave the Englishmen the slip and warned the treasure-train. The Cimaroons appeared to some as faithless allies, more interested in bloodshed than in booty. So the ambush for which Drake had waited for five months ended in a fiasco. But for him that glimpse of the Pacific was a marvellous compensation for the treasure that had slipped through his fingers.

The Spaniards now knew that Drake was in the jungle, and, though they could not pin down his exact whereabouts, they were thoroughly alerted. He took his band, augmented by Cimaroons, to attack Venta Cruces on the Sagres River and in the woods outside the township a Spanish captain challenged him. 'What people are you?' 'We are Englishmen.' 'Surrender in the name of King Philip; on the word of a gentleman and a soldier I will use you with all courtesy.' To this Francis replied, 'For the honour of the Queen of England, my mistress, I must pass this way', and he fired at him. His fire was answered by a volley from muskets which mortally wounded John Harris and injured Drake, though not seriously. Venta Cruces was soon his, but it yielded little treasure. The Spaniards were amazed at the benevolent courtesy with which the English treated the women, who had been frightened out of their wits by the sight of Cimaroon warriors. So the tide had begun to turn in Drake's favour. At about this time also, Drake fell in with a Huguenot privateer, Le Testu from Le Havre, who brought him the news of the Massacre of St Bartholomew's Eve, and his blood boiled at the horrifying details of the persecution of fellow Protestants. They made a joint operation in the jungle near Nombre de Dios to intercept three caravans of 190 mules, each bearing 300 lbs of silver. They took as much as they could carry and buried the rest. Near the mouth of the Rio Francisco, twenty miles from Nombre de Dios, Drake made a rich haul with the help of his Huguenot and Cimaroon allies, although Le Testu was wounded, and the English pinnaces were forced to put to sea in heavy weather to escape from a Spanish flotilla. It was a desperate situation, for if the pinnaces were captured or sunk he would never reach the *Pasco*. Drake buried the gold plate which they had seized and encouraged his stranded party to construct a raft from young trees brought down by the storm, rigged it with a makeshift sail from a biscuit sack and put to sea accompanied by only one Englishman, two men from Le Testu's crew and a few Cimaroons. The sea was running high and the little craft was often completely submerged during the six hours in which they battled in the blazing heat, with salt and sun blistering their bodies; and yet the men had absolute confidence in him. 'If it pleases God that I should put my foot aboard my frigate', he assured them, 'by one means or another I will get you all aboard too, in spite of all the Spaniards in the Indies.' At last they were sighted by the pinnaces, but their rescuers, while amazed at their courage, grieved when they saw how few Englishmen were on the raft. Drake cheered them by pulling from under his shirt a specimen of the most recent booty – a plate of gold – declaring, 'Thank God our voyage is made.'

That same night they went back in the pinnaces to rescue the wounded Le Testu and the Englishmen who had remained with him, and retrieved the treasure they had buried. Soon they were sharing out the spoils with the Frenchmen, vowing to meet again. Drake decided that the *Pasco* was by now too damaged to withstand an Atlantic crossing, so he captured a Spanish frigate and transferred his flag to her. Before leaving the Caribbean, he broke up the pinnaces and presented his Cimaroon friends with all the spare ironwork to use for their arrow-heads. With typical bravado, he passed close to Cartagena and then by the Florida passage found the Gulf Stream to bring him home.

A man on Plymouth Hoe recognized Drake's personal ensign as the strange frigate dropped anchor in the Sound on 9 April 1573 and answering the captain's wave darted off to the parish church to interrupt the sermon with the news that after fifteen months at sea, Drake was home, and (we are told) 'few or none remained with the preacher'. He was eager to report to John Hawkins his success in bringing home perhaps £30,000 in booty, and to tell all England of the terror which he had struck at Nombre de Dios and along the coast. For Drake this remarkable voyage was, he felt, only a beginning. From Port Pheasant or a similar isolated haven, he could repeat his devastation of Spanish settlements and shipping any time that he chose, and the next time, pray God, would not have the ill luck of a tropical storm or the unpleasantness of a leg injury at a crucial moment, so that he could

Le Testu's map of
southern Africa.

succeed in emptying the gold from a full treasure house at Nombre de Dios.
The seas, the Spaniards and the jungle of the Isthmus had no terror for him.
He could afford to be arrogant, for he had something to boast about, yet
almost at once friends warned him of the changed political scene. Negotiations with Spain were now in full train to end the embargo on trade and settle
damages, so this was no time to be bringing ashore plunder from the Spanish
Main which could well be impounded by the government in the interests of
wider commercial considerations, and Drake learned that he could well be a
marked man, who might if necessary be disowned by his sovereign. He went

95

to ground with his treasure until more favourable times and next emerged
fighting in Ireland.

Even before Sir Humphrey Gilbert's fate was known, Sir George Peckham
and Christopher Carleill had preparations in train for a further expedition
to North America for establishing colonies in New England, since Gilbert's
licence was running out. Long before they were in a position to sail Walter
Raleigh had received a patent in March 1584 which assigned to him his half-
brother's rights to found colonies but excepted control over the Newfoundland fishery. He was to have exclusive rights over territories 600 miles north
and south of his settlement for six years.

Raleigh was by now thirty-two. For an absolute outsider to the court, with
no hint of noble blood, his rise to favour had been meteoric. Elizabeth had
immediately taken to him and was soon regarding him as 'a kind of oracle,
which nettled them all'. To account for his extraordinary success incidents
were invented, such as the affair of his throwing his cloak in the mire for
the Queen to walk upon. He was tall, handsome, bore himself superbly and
had the kind of intelligence his sovereign appreciated. He, more than any
other courtier, 'carried his estate upon his back' and rivals whispered that
his pair of jewelled shoes cost him £6000. With Leicester again married and
the Queen's match with the French Duke of Alençon at an end, Raleigh
carried all before him in the 1580s. Compared with him, both Drake and
Hawkins were rough-mannered and provincial, while Lord Admiral Howard
of Effingham was pompous and out of his depth in the Privy Chamber.
Elizabeth was fascinated by Raleigh's Devonian speech and mimicking his
pronunciation nicknamed him 'Warter'. Approving of his ambitions at sea
she teasingly called him 'the Shepherd of the Ocean'. Damnably proud, high-
spirited and impetuous, he would be a sea dog with a difference; he had no
desire 'to run from cape to cape, and from place to place, for the pillage of
ordinary prizes'. He was highly critical of Drake's plans to raid Spanish
settlements, for Philip ii, he wrote, 'is not so impoverished by taking three
or four port towns in America as we may suppose, neither are the riches of
Peru or Nueva España so left by the seaside as it can be easily washed away
with a great flood, or spring tide, or left dry upon the sand in a low ebb'.
Raleigh, it was noted, had been 'trained in martial discipline, both by land
and sea, and [was] well inclined to all virtuous and honourable adventures'.
He would regard the name 'corsair' as an insult, yet he still had a zest for
visiting distant places and used to say 'there are stranger things to be seen
in the world than are between London and Staines'. The one snag was that
Elizabeth, having taken him up, was reluctant to lose his company, so that
he could never be sure whether or not she would allow him to take part in the
expeditions that were so dear to his heart.

Within five weeks of receiving his patent Raleigh sent out a small reconnaissance party under Philip Amadas of Plymouth, aided by Arthur Barlow
and the invaluable pilot Fernandez. After watering in the West Indies they

sailed north by the Florida Channel and came to Hatteras on the Carolina Banks. On landing, the island was formally taken on Raleigh's behalf for the Queen. They were encouraged by their expedition, for the natives were friendly (living 'after the manner of the golden age') and the country fertile 'for the earth bringeth forth all things in abundance, without toil or labour', noted Barlow. The English also explored Roanoke, an island lying inside a great reef, close to the entrance to Albemarle Sound. They returned to England in the autumn of 1584 with two Indians and samples of skins, pearls and other products.

That summer, while Barlow was drafting a glowing report on the future of Roanoke, Richard Hakluyt, the embassy chaplain in Paris, had come to London to discuss with Raleigh the problem of promoting interest in colonization so there might be adequate financial backing for making a settlement. They agreed that advance sales of tracts of land, on the model of Gilbert, were impracticable, but a forceful tract could point out the marvellous opportunities for investors to reap their fortunes. As a result Hakluyt wrote his *Discourse of Western Planting* which proved successful propaganda. He began loyally by asserting that 'the Queen of England's title to all the West Indies, or at least to as much as is from Florida to the Arctic Circle, is more lawful and right than the Spaniards or any other Christian Princes', and this somewhat questionable statement was well-attuned to the mood of the day. An English settlement towards the south, properly nurtured, could outstrip Spanish colonial power and thus England would have a firm base from which ships could prey on Philip's treasure fleets, and once old Spain was cut off from her western colonies she would wither away. As a churchman Hakluyt underlined the missionary element in colonial enterprise, since western discovery 'will be greatly for the enlargement of the gospel of Christ'. But what most struck readers – as Raleigh intended – was the optimistic account of the actual resources of that earthly paradise. In October Hakluyt presented his *Discourse* to the Queen and it was soon supported by Barlow's first-hand report. Raleigh introduced a bill into the Commons to confirm his title, not because parliamentary approval was necessary but as propaganda for his main expedition. He told the House that the lands explored by Amadas and Barlow had been wrongly called 'Wyngandacoia' since when they asked the Indians at their first encounter the name of the country 'one of the savages answered "Wyngandacon", which is as much to say "You wear gay clothes"'. On Twelfth Night 1585 the Queen knighted Raleigh and subsequently allowed him to call his colony 'Virginia' in her honour, as he had wanted. For the 1585 expedition she provided the *Tyger* of 160 tons and among subscribers were Sir Francis Walsingham and Sir Christopher Hatton. Raleigh's relations rallied round, with William Sanderson securing backing in the city and Sir Richard Grenville anxious to lead the expedition himself. The costs were to be recouped by plundering Spanish vessels.

Grenville sailed from Plymouth on 9 April 1585 in the *Tyger*, the largest of the five vessels. Amadas was to be appointed 'admiral of the country' in

Virginia once Grenville had returned, while Ralph Lane, another Devonian, was designated leader of the settlers. Lane was an equerry to the Queen and had seen much service in Ireland. Once again Fernandez was to pilot the vessels in those barely known waters, but Raleigh himself was not accompanying them. There were some remarkable men on the expedition; Thomas Cavendish, who would be the second Englishman to circumnavigate the globe, commanded the *Elizabeth*, while the 107 first settlers included Thomas Hariot, mathematician and scientist, and John White, a cartographer and artist with a keen eye as a naturalist. The ships parted company during a storm and Grenville spent a fortnight in an isolated part of Puerto Rico repairing damage to the *Tyger* and building a pinnace to replace one they had lost. The *Elizabeth* met up with them and after taking various prizes they came to Isabela in Hispaniola to trade openly for cattle and livestock and acquire seeds and plant cuttings. The Spaniards were unusually friendly and invited the Englishmen to Puerto de Plata where they bought further provisions and watched a bull fight.

The two ships were now well stocked with supplies and on 20 June sighted the mainland of North America, but in searching for a passage through the Carolina Banks they went aground and the *Tyger* was so badly damaged that her stores were ruined by salt water. The only ray of hope was the arrival of the *Lion* and the *Dorothy* which they had not seen for two months. Parties

John White made detailed studies of the wildlife of Virginia; two of his watercolours.

were landed and the waters were carefully explored from the pinnace and ship's boats, yet nowhere could be found that was safe for anchoring large vessels. Grenville blamed Simon Fernandez for their misfortune and Lane became testy. Hariot realized the problems that would face the settlement if they were denied a good harbour: 'The sea coasts of Virginia [he wrote] are full of islands whereby the entrance into the main land is hard to find. For although they be separated with divers and sundry large divisions, which seem to yield convenient entrance, yet to our great peril we proved that they were shallow and full of dangerous flats, and could never pierce up into the

Thomas Hariot, the Oxford mathematician and cartographer, compiled a huge scientific catalogue of the climate, geography, vegetation and wildlife of Virginia.

99

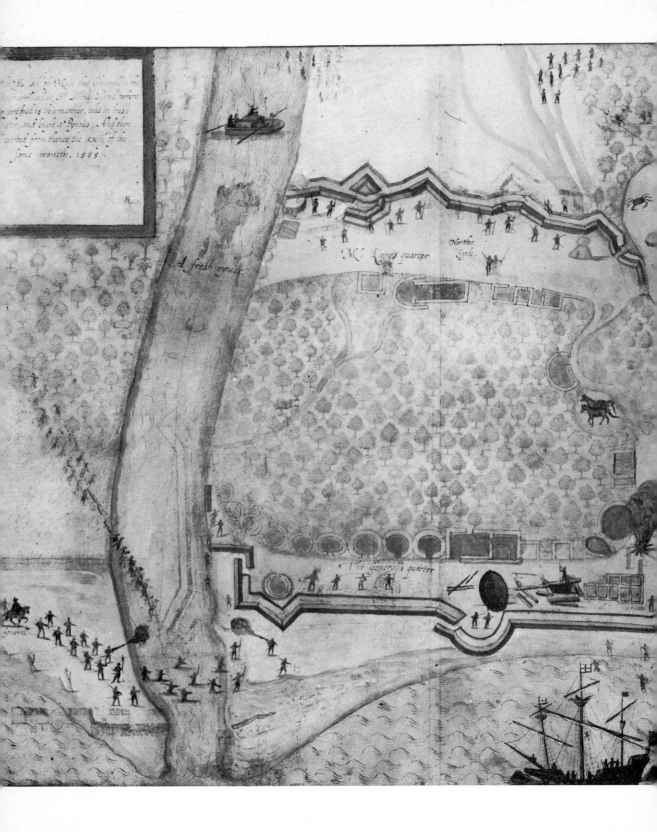

The Generall ... arrived at S.t John Lland where ... fortified in this manner, toke in freshe water, and such a Pynnes. And then ... from thence the xxiij of the same month. 1585.

A fresh ryver.

Mr. Lanes quarter

Northe Syde

The generalls quarter

Generall

mainland, until we made trials in many places with our small pinnace.' At last they found an opening in the reef near the southern end of Roanoke Island that was deep enough for all but the *Tyger* and in consequence the colony was established on the island instead of the mainland. Before the end of August Grenville had decided to sail for home to arrange for further supplies to be brought out and so Lane was left with only the pinnace. Off Bermuda Sir Richard captured the *Santa Maria* with a valuable cargo of sugar, spices and ivory that gladdened his heart. Raleigh had come to Plymouth to meet him, anxious to learn of the progress of the infant colony and to look over the spoils which, it was reckoned, would more than defray the costs of setting out the expedition. A 'cabinet of pearls' from one of the prizes taken in the Caribbean was reserved for Her Majesty.

We need not dwell on the difficulties experienced by Lane and his fellows in their first winter. Morale became low as supplies dwindled; some resented

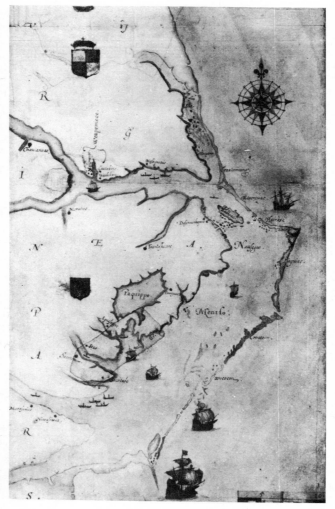

OPPOSITE A plan of Grenville's encampment in Puerto Rico drawn by White in May 1585. The 'Generall's' (Grenville's) quarters and those of Ralph Lane are identified.

LEFT White's map of Virginia.

101

The title page of Hariot's remarkable book, *A Brief and True Report of the New Found Land of Virginia*, published in 1588.

OPPOSITE Sir Walter Raleigh and his son, Wat, painted in 1602.

&: A briefe and true re-
port of the new found land of Virginia: of
the commodities there found and to be rayfed, as well mar-
chantable, as others for victuall, building and other neceffa-
rie vfes for thofe that are and fhalbe the planters there, and of the na-
ture and manners of the naturall inhabitants : Difcouered by the
Englifh Colony there feated by Sir Richard Greinuile *Knight in the*
yeere 1 5 8 5. which remained vnder the gouernment of Rafe Lane Efqui-
er, one of her Maiefties Equieres, during the fpace of twelue monethes : at
the fpeciall charge and direction of the Honourable S I R
WALTER RALEIGH Knight, Lord Warden of
the ftanneries ; who therein hath beene fauou-
red and authorifed by her Maieftie and
her letters patents:

Directed to the Aduenturers, Fauourers,
and Welwillers of the action, for the inhabi-
ting and planting there:

By *Thomas Hariot*; feruant to the abouenamed
Sir Walter, a member of the Colony, and
there imployed in difcouering.

Imprinted at London 1588.

Lane's dictatorial methods and others, who had imagined they would easily stumble across a gold mine, became disillusioned and (in Hariot's words) now had 'no care for any other thing but to pamper their bellies', wishing they were back in comfortable England. Yet despite the bickerings the first Roanoke colony of 1585–6 survived. It was ironical that the provisions sent out by Raleigh in April and the fleet taken by Grenville should have arrived too late and when Drake, at the end of a season's campaigning in the West Indies, called in at Roanoke to offer help, all that the colonists wanted was a passage home. Tradition has it that tobacco was first introduced to England with the return of Hariot and his companions.

During his voyage round the world (which is separately described in the chapter which follows) Drake had made his name feared throughout the Americas and he was eager to be afloat once more. Despite those exploits to humble Spanish maritime power, the Protestant cause in Europe was sinking. On the death of Henry, the Cardinal King of Portugal, Philip II, as

1602

S.ʳ Waller Raleigh Knight Lord Warden of
the Stanerees   of the
   & of the Isle of Jarsey & ber M. Lieute
nant generall of the counties of Devonshyre & Cornwall:

The forme of a fort wch was made by Mr.
Ralfe Lane in a parte of St Johns Jlande
neere Caproß where we toke in salt
the xxvj[th] of May. 1585.

the most obvious candidate to the throne, had ordered Alva to invade the kingdom and at the battle of Alcántana near Lisbon had routed the supporters of Don Antonio, the pretender to the Portuguese crown. As a result Spain had doubled her colonial empire and acquired very considerable shipping and important harbours in the Peninsula. For all the leadership of William the Silent, Elizabeth's subsidies and English volunteers, the Dutch Protestants had steadily lost ground to successive Spanish commanders. The death of the Duke of Alençon from a fever brought the House of Guise to consolidate the various Catholic factions in France into a league to oppose the Protestant Henry of Navarre, now heir to the throne. Parma, Philip's new governor of the Spanish Netherlands, went from strength to strength in his campaigns and in July 1584 William the Silent was assassinated. In England the Queen was in constant danger from assassins. The discovery of the Throckmorton Plot hastened the expulsion of Mendoza from England at the beginning of 1584; he was the last Spanish ambassador during Elizabeth's reign. His parting shot was: 'As I have apparently failed to please the Queen as a minister of peace, she would in future force me to try and satisfy her in war.'

Open war with Spain now seemed inevitable, much as the Queen clung to peace. Drake was called to the Privy Council for discussions on naval policy and on the day before the opening of Parliament he was named as leading member of a syndicate undertaking 'the charge of the navy to the Moluccas'. The sum of £40,000 was being put up by the Queen, Leicester, the Hawkins family, Raleigh, Hatton and Drake himself to equip a fleet to go to the Spice Islands, not as a trading venture but as a military operation. This was a plan which clearly stemmed from Drake's visit to the Moluccas on his voyage round the world and was intended as a blow at a rich corner of the old Portuguese Empire that was far from the main centres of Spanish colonial power. The preparations went forward throughout the resumed parliamentary session of the early spring of 1585, but before Drake's fleet was ready to sail, the political situation had changed and he was, instead, ordered to the West Indies. Like Richard Hakluyt, Drake was convinced that the surest way of crippling Spain would be to cut off her supplies of precious metals from the Indies, but Elizabeth was cautious about approving a grand strategic plan that would cost her money or leave the English Channel undefended.

Even while Grenville's ships were still in Hispaniola Philip II ordered the arrest of all English merchant ships in Spanish and Portuguese ports, as a reprisal for the English corsairs' depredations across the line. This was taken in England as a declaration of war, and so instead of striking at the Moluccas, Drake's fleet was first to rescue English merchants stranded in the Peninsula and then to aim for the West Indies, where the admiral's expertise was indisputable. Twenty-nine warships were ready, the largest being the *Elizabeth Bonaventure* of 600 tons in which Drake flew his flag. Martin Frobisher was vice-admiral and among the captains were Richard Hawkins (John's son), Edmund Wynter (a son of Sir William), Drake's youngest brother Thomas, Leicester's brother-in-law Francis Knollys, a

OPPOSITE Plan of the entrenchments built by Ralph Lane and his party near Cape Rojo in Puerto Rico where they stopped to take on salt in May 1585; a John White watercolour.

A seventeenth-century cartoon depicting the expulsion of Mendoza, the Spanish ambassador, in 1584, after the discovery of the Throckmorton Plot.

grandson of Burghley's, William Cecil, and a West Countryman Thomas Fenner, whom Drake highly regarded; Fenner was to work closely with him in the 1588 campaign. This was to be a military as much as a naval operation, for there were twelve companies of soldiers – about 2300 men – under the command of Christopher Carleill, Walsingham's son-in-law. There was keen competition between young men at court to take part in the adventure, among them Sir Philip Sidney, who escaped from Whitehall to join Drake's ship at Plymouth, but the latter realized the Queen would be furious and warned her of his plans to embark. Moreover, he had no room for an inexperienced sailor whose sole idea seemed to be that they should seize and hold a base in the Americas. Royal messengers came to Plymouth to order his return and in the event Sidney was given the post of governor of Flushing, one of the Dutch cautionary towns to be handed over to English garrisons under the terms of the Treaty of Nonsuch of August 1585, when Elizabeth agreed to send an army under Leicester to aid the Dutch in the fight with Parma. Here Sidney would earn an immortal name.

After many delays Drake's fleet sailed from the Sound on 14 September and made for Vigo Bay. In case the Queen should change her mind and summon him to London, as she had summoned Sidney, he did not wait to complete the victualling of his ships once his sailing-orders arrived. He landed parties at Vigo and Bayona in search of booty and to evacuate any English merchants, but all of them chose to stay, unaware that an irrevocable breach in relations with Spain was taking place, as they had their accounts to settle; for them business was business, for Drake there could be nothing but action. He left the Spanish coast with colours flying, triumphant, and no Spanish man-of-war was sent to pursue him. 'If the influence of sea-power on history is what has been claimed for it', wrote Sir Julian Corbett seventy-five years ago, 'then this moment marks an epoch.' Drake had cocked a snook at Spain and was off to the West Indies, the next objective. He had planned to sack San Domingo, La Hacha and Santa Marta in turn, rendering them defenceless, and then to take Cartagena. Afterwards he would deal with Nombre de Dios and Panama, both for Drake of famous memory, and perhaps raid Havana. This was a grandiose scheme and in the event a number of factors prevented the Spanish colonial empire from being crippled on such a scale.

They made first for the Canary Islands to commandeer provisions, but the seas were too rough to make a landing at Las Palmas. Drake then made for the Cape Verde Islands – somewhat off his main route – where he sacked the towns of Santiago and Porto Praya, but then, after a promising beginning, things began to go wrong, for a violent fever took a heavy toll of his men; some three hundred of them died and a great many more were to remain seriously ill for the rest of the expedition. By the middle of December, they were in the Antilles and at St Christopher thoroughly cleansed the ships and prepared the soldiers for campaigning. Drake sent men to reconnoitre

LEFT Sir Philip Sidney; a contemporary portrait by an unknown artist.

BELOW Sir Francis Knollys who served under Drake in the expedition of 1585.

San Domingo, the capital of Hispaniola and the administrative centre of the Caribbean. He learned that though it was heavily defended, there was a beach suitable for landing men ten miles west of the port and on New Year's Day 1586 he put ashore Carleill and his soldiers, while the fleet made a show of force off the town. The Spaniards had been completely taken by surprise. Great quantities of guns and ammunition were captured, but no treasure could be found, so Drake opened negotiations with the inhabitants for a ransom to be paid, to save them from a holocaust. After the ceasefire,

Drake's attack on San Domingo; a contemporary engraving.

there was a strange contrast in the relations between victors and vanquished, veering from old-world courtesy to wanton brutality. Under the flag of truce, a Spaniard had killed a Negro servant belonging to Sir Francis, who felt provoked into hanging two friars and cursing that he would hang all prisoners in his hands unless the culprit was surrendered. The man was duly produced and ordered to be hanged by his fellows. While haggling over the ransom money, for which he had to reduce his demands to 25,000 ducats, Drake teased some of the Spaniards by asking them to translate a Latin inscription carved on a staircase over Philip II's royal arms. The words were *'Non sufficit orbis'* ('This world is not big enough for him'). They remained here four weeks to prepare for their next strike.

The port of Cartagena was much more heavily defended. The fleet anchored in the lagoon and under cover of darkness the troops were landed on the peninsula to approach the seaward defences of the city in dead ground, safe from enemy fire. It was Drake's own plan which Carleill so effectively carried out and, as at San Domingo, after a brief clash of arms the place surrendered. The governor was at a complete loss to understand how he had been outwitted by so small and inexperienced a band of warriors. They stayed here for seven weeks, during which fever was again rampant and any thoughts Drake might have had about holding the stronghold with an English garrison had to be abandoned, so the batteries were stripped of their guns and the other defences rendered useless. Once again, no significant amount of treasure was found and the terms of the ransom were finally

The attack on Cartagena in 1586; an engraving by Boazzio.

settled at the modest payment of 110,000 ducats, though this did not include a sum for the fort, which Drake thereupon demolished. With so many men still on the sick list, the dream of raiding Panama from across the Isthmus completedly faded, so Drake decided to make for home, bearing off sixty captured guns, bells and metal and the most valuable contents of merchants' dwellings. He also took with him Negroes and liberated galley slaves.

His plan was to return by way of Cuba and Florida, taking such prizes as he should meet with and he never ruled out the chance of intercepting the Mexican plate fleet. Perhaps, as he reported to Burghley on his return, he had missed the plate fleet by a mere twelve hours, because 'we had in that instant very foul weather'. If so, this was a great blow to the enterprise, but it seems that Drake was possibly referring to his operations the previous autumn off the Peninsula. We see the admiral in the thick of the heavy work, when the fleet was at Cape Antonia, with many of the men still suffering from the effects of fever. 'To encourage others and to hasten the getting of fresh water about the ships [he] took no less pains himself than the meanest; as also at San Domingo, Cartagena and other places ... with such wonderful travail of body as doubtless had he been the meanest person, as he was the chiefest', wrote Captain Biggs. Now he devastated the settlement of St Augustine on the coast of Florida, where the Spaniards had succeeded the first French Huguenot colonists, removing the great guns and taking off a chest or more of money. Thus a danger to the Roanoke settlers was removed.

His last port of call was the infant colony of Virginia, which he reached on 9 June. The main fleet anchored outside while Drake went ashore to meet Ralph Lane who had been facing serious difficulties since Grenville's departure the previous August. The admiral offered to transport all the settlers home, but if they wanted to stay, he would allot them a suitable vessel and as many provisions as he could spare. Courageously Lane decided to remain and so a ship was left with a considerable quantity of stores. That night, however, a violent storm arose and the vessel assigned to Lane was cast away. For three days the gale persisted and the ships were in great danger from the perilous anchorage. Lane's courage and confidence were badly sapped and, as a result, he decided to embark his settlers for a return to England with Drake on 19 June. So ended Raleigh's first Roanoke colony.

As luck would have it, a few days after they had sailed, Raleigh's relief ship arrived and after 'seeking our colony up in the country and not finding them' they returned with their provisions to England. Next month Sir Richard Grenville reached Roanoke with three stout ships carrying ample supplies and even additional recruits for the settlement.

His departure from Devon had been delayed when one of his craft had gone aground on Bideford Bar and then on the voyage he had been distracted by the chance of prizes; indeed, he seems to have lost all sense of urgency. Becalmed off Ushant, he greeted a Breton mariner returning from Cadiz and invited him aboard for a cup of wine. He asked him if he happened to know the French captain John Biddekin and the man said he did. Grenville with great amusement told his guest: 'Here is of his wines I took [from Biddekin] a few days past and if it had not been for an Englishman that was in his ship, I would have left him nothing.'

In Roanoke Grenville was dismayed to find Lane's fort and houses utterly deserted, so he explored the country in search of them. When it was clear not a man of Lane's party remained, he decided to land fifteen men with adequate stores for two years, to ensure continuity in English possession of Roanoke, not realizing they had negligible chance of surviving an Indian attack. The men were never seen again.

As there was much sickness among his men Grenville had taken them to Newfoundland to recuperate. Then he looked for prizes to pay for his voyage and took two, one a vessel from Puerto Rico laden with sugar, ginger and hides. A Spanish prisoner reported subsequently that he now knew the reason for Englishmen wanting to settle on the American continent: 'there is a waterway from the Atlantic to the Pacific, they say. They think it is near by.' Grenville was back in Bideford in December, almost five months after Drake had taken his fleet into Plymouth. Theirs were not the only expeditions in that crowded year 1586, for Raleigh had been instructed to fit out a small voyage to the Newfoundland Banks to seize Spanish and Portuguese fishing vessels and prevent English fishermen from selling them their surplus catches. The commander was Bernard Drake, a kinsman of Sir Francis, who took several prizes but caught a fatal fever from the Spanish prisoners.

Drake's operations at San Domingo and Cartagena had shown how vulnerable the strongholds of the Spanish Main were to a corsair extraordinary, and they ruined Philip II's credit with the banking houses of Europe. Not only was Parma in the Netherlands short of money for his troops who were fighting the Dutch, but the merchants of Old Spain were feeling the pinch. Englishmen at large began to realize that the tide had begun to turn, for if England was very far from being out of danger, her enemy was certainly no longer 'invincible' by land and sea. 'Truly', wrote Lord Burghley, 'Sir Francis Drake is a fearful man to the King of Spain.'

5 THE PACIFIC AND BEYOND

DURING HIS ADVENTURES IN THE PANAMA ISTHMUS in February 1573, Drake had been told by a Cimaroon guide that if he climbed a certain tree in the tropical forest, on which footholds had been cut, he would be able to see both the Caribbean that he knew so well and also, by turning his head, catch sight of 'the great South Sea', or Pacific Ocean. The Englishman climbed and saw the blue of the Pacific and was so impressed that on reaching ground again fervently prayed that 'Almighty God in his goodness would give me life and leave to sail once in an English bottom upon that sea'. His companion John Oxenham said a heartfelt 'Amen', then they followed the track towards Panama. Too soon their ways parted for on returning to England Drake lay low, fearing his depredations might lead to arrest under pressure from the Spanish ambassador, and then spent a period in Ireland, serving under Walter, Earl of Essex, against the rebels, until England's relations with Spain might again deteriorate and make it politic for him to make further forays against treasure ships and colonial settlements. John Oxenham, who had professed his eagerness to sail with Drake on any further voyage, was to grow tired of waiting.

The route into the Pacific pioneered by Magellan had been hazardous as well as slow. Many a Spanish or Portuguese vessel had since his day perished in the strait named after him and not a few had failed to find the entrance to the passage. By 1560, indeed, some were maintaining 'the Strait of Magellan no longer exists; either a landslide has blocked it or else an island has arisen out of the sea to dam up its channel'. This view, however, was not shared by Humphrey Gilbert, nor by Richard Grenville. So remarkable had been the series of discoveries over eighty years that armchair geographers like John Dee and Richard Hakluyt, practical surveyors such as Thomas Digges and experienced navigators of the calibre of Martin Frobisher were all convinced that many more secrets were yet to be revealed through careful planning and bold endeavour. Parallel with the writings advocating a search for the north-west passage to Cathay, serious thought was being given in England to penetrating the unknown 'southern seas'. Men were becoming fascinated by the idea of 'Terra Australis Incognita' – a vast continent that was believed to lie to the west and north west of the Strait of Magellan, balancing the land-mass of the northern hemisphere. The Spanish navigator Mendaña had left Callao in Peru in 1567, set on a course west-south-west to discover 'Terra Australis', but the weariness of the ocean seemingly stretching indefinitely had unnerved him, so he had altered to a north-westerly course, to reach the Solomon Islands. News of this discovery, of the expedition to the Philippines and of hopes of further enterprises in the great unknown Pacific reached England when Henry Hawkes, a prisoner of the Inquisition in Mexico, escaped and made his way home.

The key figure in promoting English interest in 'Terra Australis' was Richard Grenville. Born at Bideford in north Devon in 1542, when he was three years old he had lost his father who drowned when the *Mary Rose* capsized at Spithead. Young Grenville had read law at the Inner Temple as

OPPOSITE The silver cup made to encase the coconut presented to Elizabeth by Drake on his return from his voyage of circumnavigation.

the best training for running the family estates and of filling the role expected of him in the administration of the West Country. There was no hint in those early years of a zest for the sea, but in 1567 he went with an elder cousin, Henry Champernowne of Modbury, and other West Country friends to fight for the Emperor against the Turk for a season, before the Sultan sued for peace. After returning home he went to Ireland, to take up lands in the settlement of Munster, until these hopes of a peaceful plantation were dashed by rebellion. It is worth emphasizing that the pioneers to be most concerned with the later colonization of Virginia all had close connections in the plantation in Ireland.

At Buckland Abbey Grenville became aware of the great possibilities of oceanic exploration for, with the achievements of Hawkins and Drake, it was impossible in the West Country not to be caught up by the strong tide of nationalist, maritime adventure. Grenville was dismayed that a distant relative, his brother-in-law's uncle, Sir Thomas Stukeley, had not properly exploited his patent from the Queen in 1563 'to make a voyage to discover certain lands in the West towards Terra Florida', but had, true to his rumbustious nature, gone off hunting for prizes. It was not plunder that attracted Grenville, however, but discovery and he came under the spell of Humphrey Gilbert. With his cousin's help he drafted his various projects. Grenville became convinced that the best way to discover the north-west passage was to sail through the Strait of Magellan into the Pacific. With patience and fortitude he could find the 'Straits of Anian', which geographers were sure existed, considerably further to the south than the passage later to be known as Bering Strait. He presented a well-argued case and soon was combining with this proposal a second, his South Seas project. Having passed through Magellan's Strait he would find not only the Straits of Anian, but also 'Terra Australis'. 'Since the Portugal hath attained one part of the new found world to the east, the Spaniard another to the west, the French the third to the north, now the fourth to the south is by God's providence left for England, to whom the others have in times past been first offered.' (Henry VII *could* have patronized Columbus and his son *could* have developed trade, the fisheries and colonization in North America in the generation after Cabot's voyage, even if it is hard to see how English mariners could have been the first round the Cape to India and the Moluccas.)

The aim of Grenville's proposed voyage was 'the discovering, traffic and enjoying for the Queen's majesty and her subjects of all or any lands, islands and countries southward beyond the equinoctial, or where the Pole Antarctic hath any elevation above the horizon', that is to say, lands not already possessed by any Christian Prince, 'as by the charts and descriptions shall appear'. Such a passage betrays the hand of Gilbert. The adventurers would not enter any ports by force and they would only trade with any place under Spanish or Portuguese sway 'if occasion be free' and the traffic could be achieved without injury to the subjects of those crowns. The problem of prior claims could not be ignored and Gilbert tried to solve it as tactfully as he could. In the corresponding petition to the Lord Admiral the prospectors descended to detail. They announced they were 'certain gentlemen of the West Country, desirous to adventure ourselves and our goods' to the benefit of Queen and country 'by discovery of certain new trades of navigation and traffic'. Their voyage would enlarge the bounds of Christendom, bring gold, spices and other valuable commodities into England, provide new markets for English cloth and, in consequence, help to conquer unemployment. In case men should think they were bound for unhealthy, equatorial lands or might end up in inhospitable frozen wastes they argued that their 'course contriveth not near the line but, crossing the same, still hasteth directly to the temperature of our own regions'. The end of their enterprise was to be the establishment of a colonial settlement, an English empire in the south. 'Ships of our own are well prepared. The West Country being the aptest of all parts of England for navigation southward,' (the document becomes urgent) and the prospectors include mariners 'to whom the passage almost thither is known'. They asked for the Queen's letters patent as authority for their undertakings and also as an inducement for Elizabeth herself to take shares in the voyage. In the summer of 1574 such a patent was drafted for Grenville, Piers Edgcombe, Edmund Tremayne, Alexander Arundell (Sir Richard's half-brother), Thomas Digges, Martyn Dare and others. William Hawkins was involved but, significantly, Drake's name is not mentioned. Among the ships being rigged out was the *Castle of Comfort*, a well-founded vessel of 240 tons, with great fire power. In 1566 the *Castle*, in a memorable action under George Fenner in the Cape Verde Islands, had held out alone against seven Portuguese galleons. Preparations in the dockyards attracted the attention of de Guerras, the Spanish ambassador, who reported what he could glean about the intentions of 'Grenfield, a great pirate'. Some said they were going to the Strait of Magellan, but 'the real design is not yet known, as there are so many plans afoot, but as they are going in this guise they probably mean to sack some of the islands and lie in wait for the ships from the Indies and other merchantmen'.

Grenville had tried to persuade John Oxenham to accompany him, but for some reason – probably loyalty to Drake – he had declined and, as we shall see, was planning a venture of his own that would lead to his imprisonment. But Grenville's conversations with him had given Oxenham much information about his voyage and four years later he was to be cross-questioned by the Inquisition in Lima about the project and to make circumspect replies. Grenville, he said, had applied to Elizabeth for a licence to pass through the Strait of Magellan into the South Sea 'in order to search for land or some islands, where to found settlements, because in England there are many inhabitants and but little land'. The Queen gave him the licence and Oxenham himself saw it. Grenville now acquired various ships 'when the Queen rescinded the licence, because she had heard that beyond the Strait of Magellan there were settlements made by the Spaniards, who might do them harm'. A fellow prisoner with Oxenham underlined that Elizabeth revoked the patent 'for fear that he might do harm in the possessions of her brother, King Philip'.

It is clear that the *détente* with Spain leading to the Treaty of Bristol, signed at the end of August 1574, made Grenville's voyage totally unacceptable to English statesmen. That treaty settled the commercial disputes between English and Spanish merchants in the Peninsula, the Netherlands and England, arising from the mutual confiscations and embargoes following the seizure of the Spanish treasure ships in 1568. There was hope, too, of a political accommodation now that Requesens had replaced Alva as governor of the Netherlands. Had Grenville sailed he would have threatened the new understanding with Spain and so the royal licence was countermanded. Disappointed that he had missed the boat, Grenville busied himself in Devonshire and employed the *Castle of Comfort* in the western Channel as a privateer under letters of marque from the French Huguenots. His oceanic proposals were, however, postponed rather than abandoned, for they were to form essential elements in the instructions for Francis Drake's voyage of circumnavigation. Envious of Drake's success in winning the laurels that might have been his own, Grenville subsequently concerned himself with the planning of a colony in Virginia.

While Grenville was still hoping to sail for the South Seas, John Oxenham was fitting out a ship of 140 tons, with Devonshire backing, to sail for the Panama Isthmus in search of plunder. Instead of attempting to round South America, he would reach the Pacific by a bold dash across from Nombre de Dios. Spurred on by Drake's earlier exploits, he landed in 1576 with fifty of his men and set out through the jungle to reach the Pacific near Panama, where he built a pinnace and used it to cross to the Pearl Islands. Effectively he was the first Englishman to sail in Pacific waters. He lay in wait for treasure ships coming from Peru and succeeded in taking two vessels, one with 60 lb weight of gold, the other with 100,000 pesos of silver, but he was greedy for more and, in default of other craft passing his way, took a mass of pearls from the islands. He then hid his loot in the jungle until it could be carried by stages across the Isthmus to his ship, but the natives in the Pearl Islands, aghast at the plunder of their pearls, reported Oxenham's presence to the governor of Panama, who mounted search parties. Very probably they thought the expedition was being led by Drake. The Spaniards found the two prizes, then Oxenham's pinnace, and finally his hoard of treasure and provisions in a hut made of boughs. Then the Englishmen appeared, aided by two hundred Cimaroons, but in the fighting came off badly, for eleven English seamen were killed and seven taken prisoner. Oxenham led the remainder towards Nombre de Dios but found his ship in Spanish hands. For the moment they took to the mountain area, hoping their pursuers would abandon the hunt and then there would be the chance of taking a prize on the eastern coast. The viceroy of Peru had, however, given orders that they were to be rounded up at all costs and a company of 150 soldiers was sent to scour the

Isthmus. By ill fortune Oxenham and his fellows were betrayed by some of the Cimaroons and taken to Panama for examination. The ordinary seamen were hanged outright as pirates, but Oxenham and a few others were sent under guard to Lima for interminable questioning about English plans for penetrating the Pacific.

Drake returned to Plymouth early in 1576 to plan for his next adventure. His service in Ireland, far from being an unprofitable period in the wilderness, had helped to provide him with useful contacts at court. Essex, his commander, had given him a letter of introduction to Sir Francis Walsingham, leader of the war party on the Privy Council and a man whom the seaman

Sir Christopher Hatton, the future Lord High Chancellor and favourite of the Queen, became Drake's patron; an engraving after a painting by Ketel.

Hatton's coat of arms surmounted by a hind. In his patron's honour Drake renamed his ship the *Golden Hind* on entering the Pacific Ocean.

admired for his fervent Protestantism. A friend Drake had made in Ireland, Thomas Doughty, had now become secretary to Christopher Hatton, the rising favourite, and he was sure that his master would give their plans effective support and also enlist the Queen's patronage. The list of shareholders in the joint-stock company formed for financing the new voyage was a distinguished one. Besides Walsingham and Hatton, there were Leicester, Lincoln, the Lord Admiral, John Hawkins, and Sir William Wynter of the Navy Board. We shall probably never be certain of the real intentions behind the voyage. Everyone appreciated that this was to be no ordinary adventure and so it was given out as a blind that Drake was to sail to Alexandria and most of the crew believed this to be their destination. There is no reason to think that he had reached an understanding with Elizabeth, kept a close secret from other promoters, that the main object of the voyage was to attack Spain's shipping and settlements. Of course, everyone in the venture knew from Drake's past performance and his character that he would take every opportunity that came his way for plundering, but these were to be fringe benefits. Circumnavigation of the globe, the discovery of 'Terra Australis' (a project of Grenville's so recently abandoned by royal com-

118

mand), the annexation of New Albion on the coast of California and the foundation of English interests in the Spice Islands were not all in the minds of the Queen, Hatton or the others; they knew that the opportunist captain would not overlook any course of action that would be advantageous to his shareholders or bring credit to his sovereign. Basically, his instructions were to reconnoitre the coast of South America from the River Plate right round Cape Horn to the regions in Chile at which Spanish occupation stopped; settlement and a long-term conquest of Spanish Peru was envisaged and in the view of at least one man (the younger Hakluyt) this would 'subject to England all the golden mines of Peru and all the coast' of America upon that sea.

In the event, Francis Drake did not deflect the voyage from its agreed purpose and was to spend two months on the east coast of South America south of 32° South, and two further months at Port St Julian. Then, after enduring a terrific gale in the region of the Strait of Magellan, he was to spend two months on the west coast, between 39° and 28°South. What happened afterwards depended on the weather and the state of his ship and crew, but 'was finally justified by the dangerous weather conditions on the recommended return route and by the generally unpromising results of his reconnaissance'. In the surviving fragment of his draft instructions, Drake was empowered to decide how far north to proceed along the coast of Chile, and he must have had full discretion to amend his route thereafter.

On 15 November 1577 the fleet sailed from Plymouth, with Drake flying his flag in the *Pelican*, later to be renamed the *Golden Hind*. Though no exact drawings or measurements of the vessel survive, a great many details about her have come down to us. She was a small galleon, small even by sixteenth-century standards, being not more than 140 tons. She carried three masts – the main and the foremast being square rigged, with topsails, spritsails and top-gallants, and a lateen sail on the mizzen; the total sail area was 4,150 square feet. There was a low forecastle and an after-castle which was higher, so that head-on the ship seemed unstable to a landlubber. The *Pelican* was well-armed, with seven guns under hatches on each side, two in the poop and a number of smaller cannon. She was about a hundred feet long, eighteen feet in the beam and had a draught, fully-laden, of thirteen feet.

The Portuguese pilot, Nuño da Silva, who spent fifteen months aboard, noted with a practised eye: 'Drake's ship is very stout and very strong, with double sheathings. ... She is a French ship, well-fitted with good masts, tackle and good sails, and is a good sailer, answering the helm well. She is neither new, nor is her bottom covered with lead. ... She is staunch when sailing with the wind astern if it is not very strong, but in a sea which makes her labour she makes no little water.' It was a vessel of which da Silva was indeed envious, and he was fascinated by the stores and facilities provided, not least the forge for making nails. The Portuguese probably meant that the *Pelican* was built 'after the French fashion', not that she had been constructed in France. The crew numbered ninety, of whom nine were 'gentlemen,

The *Golden Hind*; a detail from a world map engraved by Jodocus Hondius *c.* 1590.

younger sons of English land-owning families'. There was room in the small forecastle for only a few of the crew, and most seamen slept on the gun deck. The officers slept in cabins aft, as was customary, and fed together in the great cabin, while the musicians played, with the captain's chair at the head of the table. Drake intended to live in style afloat, with goodly provision 'for ornament and delight carrying to this purpose with him expert musicians, rich furniture ... whereby the civility and magnificence of his native country might amongst all nations, whithersoever he should come, be the more admired'. His own cabin was panelled in oak. Besides a bed and a chair, there was a desk and a table on which he kept charts, books and instruments, and also his sea-chest covered in leather, with the inside of the lid painted with views of his vessel. Here, too, was the captain's drum, on which was painted his arms, of which he was intensely proud, for they decorated his plates and some of his guns; da Silva noted that on one bronze

120

cannon 'was sculptured the globe of the world with a north star over it, passing over. He [Drake] said these were his arms and that the Queen had conferred them upon him, commanding him to encompass the world'; Drake had acted rather impetuously if he spoke as da Silva reported, for his grant to bear arms was not issued until after his return home! Among his books was a commentary on Magellan's voyages. 'Francis Drake', wrote da Silva, 'kept a book in which he entered his navigations and in which he delineated birds, trees and sea-lions. He is adept at painting, and with him [his nephew John] who is a great painter. When they both shut themselves up in his cabin they are always painting.' There was a practical purpose in this recreation, for uncle and nephew sketched coastlines, harbours and islands not as imaginative seascapes, but as a faithful record to illustrate 'sailing directions'.

Five ships sailed in company, manned by 164 men, but only the *Pelican* completed the circumnavigation. When Magellan had set out on his voyage in September 1519, there had also been a fleet of five, and then, too, only the flagship returned safely to port, though without the admiral. In 1577 the other four English craft were the *Elizabeth* of eighty tons under John Wynter, vice-admiral, the *Swan*, a fly-boat of fifty tons under John Chester, the *Marigold*, a bark of thirty tons under John Thomas, and the tiny *Christopher*, a pinnace of perhaps only fifteen tons, under Thomas Moone. It seems incredible that such small vessels were journeying into such distant, unknown waters, but as yet only Drake knew the destination. When they were off the Lizard there was a howling gale so the ships had to take shelter in Falmouth. Despite the protection of the harbour, both the *Pelican* and the *Marigold* were in trouble, especially with their masts, and after the storm had abated, Drake decided to return to Plymouth, arriving there thirteen days after he had originally set out. It was an inauspicious beginning. During the next fortnight, repairs were successfully completed and then, on 13 December, the fleet made a second attempt, 'holding on with a prosperous wind and

An astrolabe, used to measure the altitude of the stars, made for Drake by Humphrey Cole.

121

good success in all things', bound for the Barbary Coast in North Africa. The only mishap was when a ship's boy was lost overboard from the *Christopher* off Portugal.

On Christmas Day they arrived at the island of Mogadore, in the Moorish kingdom of Fez, that had not so long before been under Portuguese rule. Here one of the men, John Fry, who had picked up something of the local language from an earlier trading voyage, indiscreetly went ashore and was taken captive. Drake led a posse to try to rescue the unfortunate man, but had to give him up for lost; Fry was subsequently released and sent home in a Mediterranean trader. The fleet passed on south, taking two Spanish caravels near the Tropic of Cancer, and raced towards Cape Blanco on the Moroccan Coast, with 'every sail at command, as if Neptune had been present'. At the Cape, Drake stayed for six days to water and clean his ships and here he left behind the pinnace *Christopher*, which he replaced by one of the captured caravels, renamed *Christopher II* out of deference to Sir Christopher Hatton's interest in the expedition. The Cape Verde Islands were the next port of call and here, early in February, they took a Portuguese ship, bound for Brazil with a cargo of wine and cloth, which Drake added to his fleet as the *Mary*. Portuguese vessels had been fair game for English privateers over the line, but hitherto there had been an uneasy peace in other waters. Drake had no qualms about taking the prize and before he could return to England, Portugal would be invaded and conquered by Spain.

Drake pressed into his service Nuño da Silva, the *Mary*'s pilot, for he was a most experienced navigator and the English captain was fascinated by his collection of charts and nautical instruments. Nuño was to stay aboard the

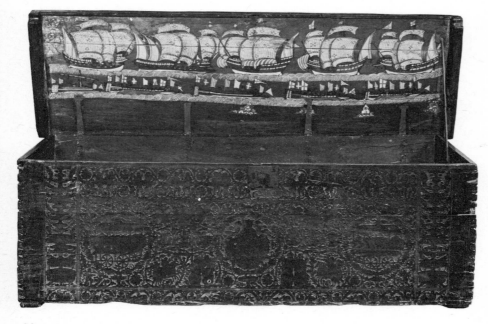

Drake's wooden sea chest: the underside of the lid is decorated with ships, in the centre, the *Golden Hind*.

Pelican, where he was honourably treated, for some fifteen months. By now Drake had divulged to his officers that he intended to sail into the Pacific, and the Portuguese pilot caught the adventurous spirit of his captor 'to travel unto the new-discovered parts of the world'. Da Silva's experience of the South Atlantic was considerable and once they reached the South American coast he displayed detailed knowledge.

In the southern seas, when they had crossed the Equator, conditions were eerie; the climate was fickle and in the Doldrums a flat calm under the burning sun could be followed without warning by a sudden tempest. The sight of strange birds and tropical fish alarmed the superstitious, while crossing the line itself was something that made many feel uneasy. Some of the crew were on edge, questioning the route, the destination and even the ability of their admiral. Thomas Doughty, the courtier, had been placed in command of the Portuguese prize, but from the first there had been trouble, when he falsely accused Drake's youngest brother, serving as an ordinary mariner, of tampering with the cargo. Later, Doughty and Francis Drake exchanged commands. When the ships were in the Doldrums, Drake learned from the trumpeter, John Brewer, that Doughty had made a seditious speech attempting to persuade his crew to desert, and so he made him a prisoner in the *Swan* on charges of mutiny and witchcraft. Doughty certainly believed in the occult. Some feared that he was a spy in Spanish pay, others that he was an agent of Lord Burghley's, a few that he was a coward as well as a land-lubber. Naturally he found supporters who either shared his lack of confidence in Drake or were lukewarm about the great adventure on which they had embarked without being aware of the secret plans.

After two months without sight of land, the fleet reached the South

Superstitious seamen believed the southern seas to be inhabited by strange exotic monsters; an early seventeenth-century engraving.

American coast, to the north of the River Plate. Then suddenly the ships were engulfed by a thick fog 'with the palpable darkness of Egypt' and this was followed by the most terrific storm Drake had ever known. The *Pelican* was in danger of being driven on to a lee shore and only the Portuguese pilot's skill and local knowledge of shoals saved her. So near a disaster had provoked Thomas Doughty into stirring up fresh trouble in the *Swan*. He told the crew that but for his own influence with important investors, Drake would never have succeeded in sailing. Dinner-table talk about mutineers led one officer to aver that Drake should deal with such as Magellan did, 'which was to hang them up to be an example'. 'Nay, soft!' Doughty retorted. 'His authority is none such as Magellan's was, for I know his authority so well as he himself doth.' As the discussions continued, it was clear that the troublemaker was endeavouring to undermine Drake's position and even to stir men to mutiny.

It proved impossible to keep the little fleet together and Drake spent many days sailing up and down the coast of Brazil to find stragglers, or those who had parted company; he would not rest until he had found them all. The *Swan* was becoming too much of a liability (quite apart from Doughty) and so the crew and provisions were transferred to the *Pelican*, and the flyboat, after the cannons and ironwork had been removed, was abandoned in Seal Bay in Patagonia. Later on, Drake laid up the *Christopher II*. Near Port St Julian, not so far from the Strait of Magellan, the missing ship, the *Mary* at last came into sight on 18 June 1578 and Drake decided that it would be wisest to abandon her. There was still an ominous undercurrent of sedition, yet everyone knew that St Julian was the place at which Magellan had executed his mutineers in 1520. Ashore the Englishmen found the remains of the firewood gibbet and, with a devilish sense of the macabre, a cooper from the *Pelican* made tankards from the gibbet's wood.

During archery practice ashore, two Patagonians joined in, but a fight developed when other natives arrived, and two Englishmen were killed. These casualties were a further blow for morale, and Drake felt that he could no longer turn a blind eye to the behaviour of Thomas Doughty. His drum summoned every man ashore for a traditional trial and, before a jury of forty, various witnesses were heard and the prisoner was given leave to address the court. In his speech, Doughty claimed that he was the real architect of the expedition, in persuading the Queen of its feasibility, and shared equal authority with Drake, who had consistently ignored him and had not even been straightforward with him about the true destination of the fleet. Drake answered these points briefly and made known to all that Queen Elizabeth had given him a sword, to use for his personal safety, telling him, 'We do account that he which striketh at thee, Drake, striketh at us'. The jury pronounced the prisoner guilty and deserving of death as a mutineer, and Drake thereupon gave him the customary choice – to be marooned ashore, to be executed forthwith or to be taken home in chains to appear in due course before the Privy Council. Next day Doughty made it

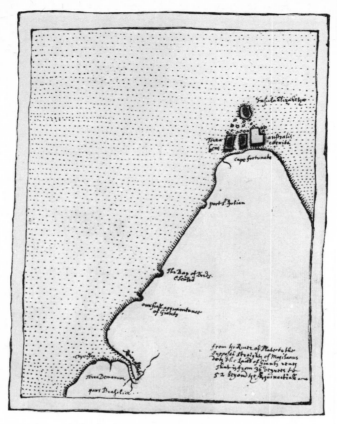

The southern tip of South America and the Strait of Magellan; a drawing by the chaplain, Francis Fletcher, whose report of the voyage was later published.

known that he chose execution, as befitting a gentleman. Before sentence, at his request, Drake and he took the sacrament together and then, as was customary, all the officers entertained him to a banquet. Afterwards the two protagonists talked together in secret in Drake's cabin and we may assume that Doughty made confession of his faults. Certainly, the fact that he deliberately chose not to face trial in England, despite his contacts with men in high places, suggests that his conduct had been indefensible. Although we shall never know the extent of his crime, for all contemporary accounts are partial, we can readily appreciate the strain under which Drake was placed, for Doughty had been his friend. Doughty's conduct had in his view put the entire expedition in jeopardy and there could be no hope of success while he lived. He had to be sacrificed for the sake of naval discipline. As the severed head fell from the block, Drake picked it up, exclaiming: 'Look, this is the end of traitors.' Doughty was buried ashore.

There were still murmurings, and to silence any further factions Drake's drum rolled out once more to summon every man ashore. They stood in ranks in front of a tent, set up at Port St Julian, with Drake flanked by Captain Thomas of the *Marigold* and Captain Wynter of the *Elizabeth*. In a forceful, emotional speech, Drake talked of the dangers that lay ahead and rather than making a plea for unity, threatened any who made for disunity.

125

From papers in his hand, he scotched the theory which Doughty had put forward about the origins of the voyage, and about his own authority as commander. He told them of the Queen's summons to her presence: '"Drake, so it is that I would gladly be revenged on the King of Spain for divers injuries I have received", and said further that I was the only man [who] might do the exploit.' Doughty, he said, was not alone in his treachery and he now named others who knelt for pardon; they were assured that 'there shall be no more deaths'. He then astounded his hearers by announcing that all his officers were dismissed from their posts. They protested in vain, for this son of a Devonshire nobody made it plain to them that he would stomach no class distinctions at sea. In this adventure the ordinary seaman and the courtier were of equal rank, and they must share in the dirty jobs, be equally subject to the hazards of the waves and the dangers from enemies, and learn to pull together in every way. 'My masters, I must have it left. I must have the gentleman to haul and draw with the mariner, and the mariner with the gentleman, I would know him that would refuse to set his hand to a rope.' They had sailed of their own free will, they were not pressed men and if any now wanted to change his mind he would do his best to find him a passage home; but if any such crossed his course he would send him to the bottom. This sermon went home and they left the 'Island of Blood' in better spirits on 17 August, 'being now in great hope of a happy issue to our enterprise'. His personal magnetism no less than his preaching had made every member of the crew conscious of his superb leadership.

Three days later, as they passed Cape Virgins, almost at the entrance to the Strait of Magellan, the perilous gateway to the unknown, Drake stage-managed a ceremony which raised his men's spirits. He caused his little fleet, now reduced to three vessels, to strike their topsails as an act of homage to the Queen, in token of their obedience to her and their recognition of her personal interest in their exploits. At the same time, in honour of his friend and sponsor, Sir Christopher Hatton, Drake changed the name of his ship from the *Pelican* to the *Golden Hind*, taken from Hatton's coat of arms. He instructed his nephew John to embellish the vessel with Hatton's arms and to paint the stern in the red and yellow of his livery, while the ship's carpenter made a figurehead of a hind to take the place of the pelican.

It had taken Magellan thirty-seven days to traverse his strait, but Drake took only sixteen. On the fourth day, they named an island they came to after St George, their patron saint. Here they felled a massive tree and stored it in the hold as ballast, with the intention of presenting it to the Queen, 'as a sign they had passed the strait'. The ships faced a strong headwind in the second half of the passage, because the high shores acted as a tunnel for the wind. Once they entered the South Sea on 6 September, Drake intended mustering his company ashore and, after preaching to them, to have set up on the land 'a monument of her majesty engraven in metal', yet there was no hope of the vessels finding a safe anchorage. Coming into the South Sea, the little ships faced a terrific gale which lasted a full month and, before it had blown itself out, the *Marigold* became detached from the others and was lost. As Wynter put it, 'that night was the most tempestuous night that ever was seen in this outrageous weather'. During this gale, Drake was beaten well to the south of Cape Horn, much to his dismay, yet this enabled him to make the discovery that there was no continent stretching from the Antarctic, as had been supposed, and instead there was open sea to the south of South America, a merger of Atlantic and Pacific. Coming again along the coast, Drake anchored but lost his cable, and then the *Golden Hind* lost touch with the *Elizabeth*, Wynter's ship. Fires were lit ashore to attract attention, but to no avail. Wynter himself feared that Drake's vessel may have been wrecked and decided that the best plan would be for him to re-enter Magellan's Strait and turn eastwards towards the Moluccas, where he might happily rendezvous with his admiral, for Drake had told him that they would eventually make for the Spice Islands. As it happened, Wynter had difficulty in persuading his crew not to return from their hazardous voyage and instead of sailing east he made for England, arriving in June 1579 to announce that the *Marigold* had been wrecked and perhaps the *Golden Hind* as well.

After repairing the *Golden Hind* Drake found fairer weather. He made his way up the coast of Chile and stopped at the island of Mocha, a most fruitful place, but the Indian inhabitants, mostly refugees from Spanish colonial rule, attacked the English party as they were admiring the ostriches. Drake was shot by arrows in the right cheek, under his right eye and close

On the island of Mocha Drake and his crew were attacked by Indians and the admiral was wounded; an engraving by de Bry.

by his nose – a very narrow escape. Four of the crew had fallen in the Indians' attack and another ten were badly wounded. As soon as they were able, they continued their northerly cruise, for Drake fervently hoped that he might make contact with John Oxenham and his surviving companions for an eventual attack on Panama. But *en route* there came all kinds of opportunities and the attack on Valparaiso was like old times for they took 25,000 gold pesos from a Chilean vessel in the port on 5 December.

The next four weeks were spent in a series of raids on Spanish settlements ashore and craft afloat, varied only by a short period of careening in a safe bay. Early in February 1579 he took a quantity of silver at Arica, and a day or so later reached Callao, the chief port of Peru, taking the *Golden Hind* into harbour towards midnight to anchor in the middle of some thirty vessels. No warning had been sent to the viceroy about the likelihood of Drake's descent, but at first light the terrified Spanish realized the identity of their companion. As the ships cut their moorings, Drake concentrated on boarding the largest vessel from his pinnace in search of treasure. Aboard they found a black leathern chest crammed full of 'royals of plate'. Next they attacked the *San Cristobel* newly arrived from Panama and easily seized her. But Drake had to abandon the plan dear to his heart for rescuing his old

Callao, the port of Lima; a sixteenth-century engraving.

128

The capture of the
Cacafuego, the richest
prize of Drake's voyage;
an engraving by Levinius
Hulsius, 1603.

shipmate, Oxenham, from Lima, not far in land from Callao. Had he possessed a stronger force (including Wynter's men), he would have marched inland but now he could only hope that his show of strength in the harbour would lead the Inquisition to spare John Oxenham's life, and he wrote to the viceroy to the effect that the man's execution would lead to terrible reprisals. Drake was anxious to be away, partly because he knew it could not be long before a Spanish fleet was sent after him, but even more because he had information that on those coasts was a large vessel with a fabulous cargo – none other than the *Cacafuego*, *en route* from Lima to Panama. He put out all his canvas to give chase and a fortnight later, on the afternoon of St David's Day, he came up with her.

The vessel's true name was the *Nuestra Señora de la Concepćion*; for *Cacafuego* was a somewhat obscene nickname coined in the lower deck of a Spanish galleon. Drake knew that she was a floating treasure house and offered a gold chain to the man who should spot her first; the winner was his hawk-eyed nephew John, who was in the crows-nest. Young Drake subsequently wore his prize chain from his neck. By a masterful ruse, the admiral succeeded in giving the Spaniards the impression that the *Golden Hind* was not a fast ship. He left all her sail unfurled, but towed astern cables, mattresses and even heavy pots. When it got dark, he cut adrift these tows, quickly

129

overtook the great ship, which had never considered herself in danger, and lowering his sails, was ready to come alongside. To the Spanish captain's question, 'What ship is this?' came the shout, '*Nuestra Señora de la Concepćion*, we are English! Strike sail, or we send you to the bottom!' 'What English? Who does bid me strike sail? Never. Come aboard and strike sail yourself.' Drake opened fire. His first shot carried away the mizzen mast, his second damaged the rigging by the mainmast. Under cover of a volley of musket shots, the pinnace came alongside the *Cacafuego* and the English boarding-party soon took command of the vessel. The captain, San Juan de Anton, and his boatswain were brought aboard the *Golden Hind* as Drake was removing his helmet and coat of mail; 'Be patient,' he told the Spaniards, 'for such is the usage of war' and then took them to his cabin. Aboard the prize, all crew and passengers were closely guarded while the great ship was moved well away from prying eyes ashore to an isolated stretch of sheltered water. Here, over six days, the rich cargo was transferred to the hold of the *Golden Hind*. It comprised, runs the Englishmen's report, 'fruits, conserves, sugars and a great quantity of jewels and precious stones, 13 chests of royals of plate, 80 lb of gold [and] 26 tons of uncoined silver'. It was a staggering array of booty. Drake talked freely with San Juan de Anton, telling him that he had come 'to rob by command of the Queen of England and carried the arms she had given him and her commission'. He also made plain his concern for Oxenham and his fellow-prisoners at Lima: 'Tell the viceroy of Peru not to hang them, for if he does I swear it will cost the heads of 3000 men of Peru, all of which heads I will cast into the port of Callao.' This message was in fact delivered and prolonged Oxenham's life, though the next year, when Drake had left American waters, the prisoners were executed. Drake had been bent on showing the Spaniards an Englishman's clemency to captives and put the men from the *Cacafuego* ashore, even providing Anton with credentials to show to Wynter, should he meet with him. The Spanish authorities had no idea where Drake would strike next as they perused maps trying to anticipate his movements once he had left the Peruvian coast. One thought that he would navigate 'very far north' to look for the north-west passage home, since 'a man who has had the spirit to do what he has done will not be lacking in courage to persevere in his attempt'. Such was, indeed, Drake's long-term plan, but immediately he looked to Nicaragua. Off that coast he took a bark bound for Panama and though he set the crew ashore, he kept the pilot, who had with him a fine collection of charts, including some for the China route, since the man was to pick up a vessel at Panama to navigate her to the Moluccas. Next he captured the *Espirito Santo* off Guatemala, as the result of a classic boarding action. The captain was Don Francisco de Zarate, cousin of the Duke of Medina Sidonia. There was no gold or silver aboard but bales of taffeta and silks, and quantities of 'fine earthern dishes ... from the country of China'. Zarate was treated so courteously aboard that when he was released he gave Drake a falcon made of gold with an emerald in the beak as a memento of their meeting. Drake asked him if he personally knew the viceroy of New Spain, Martin Enriquez, and he answered that he did. 'It would give me greater joy to come across him than all the gold and silver of the Indies,' the Englishman commented. He could never forget the old score which he had to settle with Enriquez for his treachery to his comrades at San Juan de Ulua.

Like the Portuguese da Silva, the Spaniard Zarate had nothing but praise for the *Golden Hind* – in every way she was 'a perfect sailer'. He also envied the way in which Drake exercised his command of the crew, showing that Doughty's execution and the vigorous speeches had had a marked effect on discipline. 'He treats them with affection and they treat him with respect. He carries with him nine or ten cavaliers, cadets of English noblemen. These form part of his council which he calls together for even the most trivial matter, although he takes advice from no one. But he enjoys hearing what they say and afterwards issues his orders. He has no favourites.' Drake punished the least fault. Those who dined at the captain's table were served on silver dishes with gold borders, reported Zarate: 'He dines and sups with viols.' On Sunday, as usual, Drake ordered the ship to be dressed with her flags and banners, while the crew donned their best rig for devotions. Another Spaniard aboard noted the regular reading of the Bible and Chaplain Fletcher's sermons. The Spaniard was much alarmed at the beautiful, accurate paintings of the coast which Drake and his nephew had been making, 'for everything is depicted so naturally that anyone who uses these paintings as a guide cannot possibly go astray'.

On Maundy Thursday the English raided Guatulco in Guatemala. Twenty men were put in the pinnace as a landing-party to sack the little town, plundering the church of crucifixes and rich ornaments, and entering the town hall where judges were hearing a case against three Negroes who were charged with plotting to burn the settlement; the prisoners were released, two of them joining Drake's crew for a spell. In a conversation with a local merchant, Drake said, 'you will be saying now that this man is a devil, who robs by day and prays by night'. Yet he was merely obeying his own sovereign's orders and personally regretted taking any property which belonged neither to King Philip nor his viceroy. 'I am not going to stop until I have collected the two million crowns that my cousin John Hawkins lost for certain at San Juan de Ulua.' Another Spaniard taken prisoner at Guatulco reported that Drake was proud of being Hawkins' cousin, though he 'is so boastful of himself as a mariner and man of learning that he told him there was no one in the whole world who understood the art [of navigation] better than he'.

On the day he was leaving the Guatemalan coast, Drake dropped the old Portuguese pilot. Drake and Nuño da Silva had become very close. Some have accused Drake of callously abandoning Nuño to a wretched fate, though he could hardly have known that the man would be taken into custody by the Spaniards and sent to the viceroy at Mexico City who would, after cross-questioning him about the English corsair's intentions, hand him

Plymouth

ATLANTIC OCEAN

CANARY ISLANDS

Mogador
25.12.77

TROPIC OF CANCER Cape St Lucas

Cape Blanco

CAPE VERDE ISLANDS

New Albion
17.6. - 23.7.79

Point Reyes Peninsula
(Drake's Bay)

Guatemala

San Domingo

Guatulco

SIERRA LE

CANO ISLAND

EQUATOR

Cape Francisco

Guayaquil

PERU

Callao

Arica

St HEL

TROPIC OF CAPRICORN

CHILE

SAN SEBASTIAN
31.10.86

PACIFIC OCEAN

Coquimbo

Valparaiso

Santiago

River Plate

MOCHA

Cavendish enters Pacific
24.2.87

Drake enters Pacific
6.9.78

Port Desire

Port St Julian *17.8.78*

Cape Virgins *20.8.78*

Strait of Magellan

Cape Horn

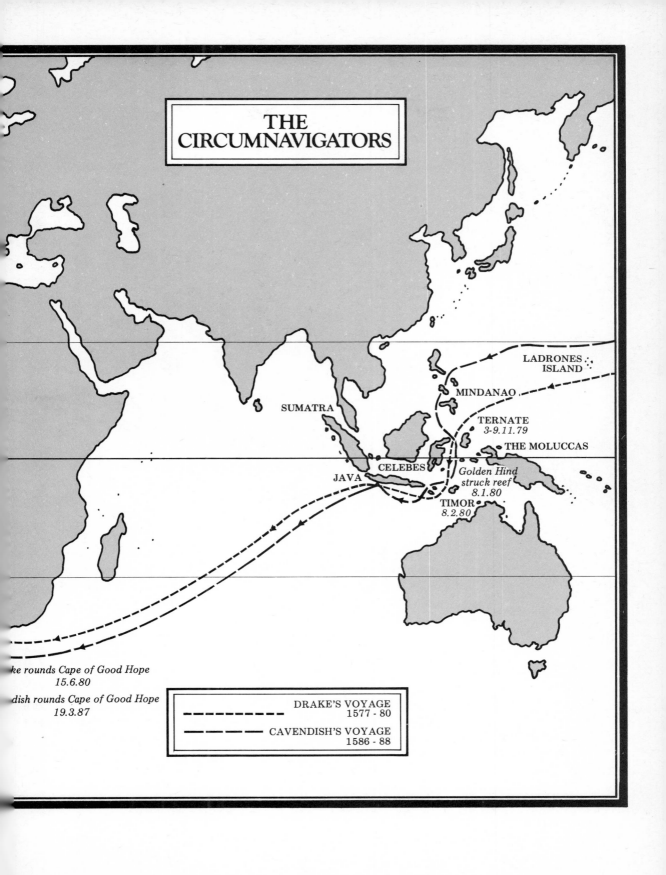

THE CIRCUMNAVIGATORS

LADRONES
ISLAND

MINDANAO

SUMATRA

TERNATE
3-9.11.79

THE MOLUCCAS

CELEBES

*Golden Hind
struck reef
8.1.80*

JAVA

TIMOR
8.2.80

*ke rounds Cape of Good Hope
15.6.80*

*dish rounds Cape of Good Hope
19.3.87*

	DRAKE'S VOYAGE 1577 - 80
	CAVENDISH'S VOYAGE 1586 - 88

Drake's arrival in New Albion; an engraving by de Bry.

over to the Inquisition on suspicion of having turned heretic; (he was to be put on the rack, then kept in prison for four years until released on Philip II's personal orders). Drake was now leaving for the north to seek a passage that would, he hoped, take him directly home and since there would be no further chance of putting Nuño ashore, he would have to run the not inconsiderable risk of landing in a hostile, Protestant country.

As far as the Spanish could tell, Drake had completely vanished, for the *Golden Hind* was sailing off the west coast of North America. Gradually during their seven-week voyage, the men complained of the cold, for it seemed 'the frozen zone, rather than in any way near unto the sun' and there were also days of heavy mist. The mapmakers had believed that the coast ran in a north-easterly direction until the north-west passage was reached, but having reached the latitude of 40° North, near what was to be called Vancouver Island, the English pioneers concluded that there was no such passage, 'or if there be, that yet it is unnavigable'. The Straits of Anian were a pipedream after all. Though they patiently searched, wrote Francis Fletcher,

134

'yet we found not the land to trend so much as one point in any place towards the East, but rather running continually North-West, as if it went directly to meet with Africa'. At 48°North, they went about and sailed down the coast to find a suitable haven in a warmer climate and came to anchor in California on 17 June, somewhere near the modern San Francisco. The most likely spot is a bay in the Point Reyes Peninsula, since named Drake's Bay. Because the *Golden Hind* was leaking badly, she was moved near the shore and her valuable cargo was landed so that repairs could be made. The Indians in the district were overjoyed at the arrival of the English party, taking Drake to be a god, and insisting that he become their overlord (or *Hich*). He named the country New Albion, partly from the white banks and cliffs lying towards the sea, partly because he wanted some affinity with his native land, the Albion of old. Ashore he set up a metal plaque, which read:

Be it known unto all men by these present, June 17, 1579, by the Grace of God, in the name of Her Majesty Queen Elizabeth of England and Her successors for ever, I take possession of this Kingdon, whose King and people freely resign their right and title in the whole land unto Her Majesty's keeping, now named by me and to be known unto all men as Nova Albion.

Francis Drake

This was six years before Raleigh's Roanoke colony was established. They spent five weeks in careening their vessel, caulking the timbers and other repairs and then again put to sea, to the dismay of the Indians.

Drake now planned to cross the Pacific Ocean, sailing in the belt of the north-east Trade Winds, to reach the Moluccas. After two months, they sighted a small group of islands, but the natives were unfriendly and came out in their canoes to pelt the ship with stones. Drake discharged a single

The 'plate of brasse' bearing Drake's inscription dated June 17, 1579. It was found on the shore of San Francisco Bay in 1936.

135

The island of Ladrones which Drake renamed the 'Isle of Thieves'; an engraving by de Bry.

cannon to scare them away. A similar experience in these waters had led Magellan to name an island 'Ladrones' and Drake followed suit by renaming the place the 'Isle of Thieves'. Once through the archipelago, they continued on their course and by 21 October were passing by the southern Philippines; the northerly wind prevented the *Golden Hind* from coming close to the land, though a number of canoes, full of warlike natives, came out to investigate the great ship. They reached the Spice Islands, or Moluccas, on 3 November, finding them 'very fruitful and yielding abundance of cloves', of which they purchased six tons very cheaply. The islands were under Portuguese rule, but the colonists were at this time engaged in a fitful war with the Sultan of the neighbouring Malaysian island of Ternate. Coming to that island, the Englishmen were given a warmer welcome. The Sultan made it known that he would like to see the *Golden Hind* at closer range and came out in a canoe to the anchorage. Drake invited him aboard, but the Sultan preferred after all to stay in his canoe. He liked the English music he heard and asked the musicians to come into his boat, to play for him for an hour. During his stay at Ternate, Drake made an agreement with the Sultan by which his people undertook to sell their spices exclusively to English merchants. While Drake was still at the island a Chinese merchant came to the ship with an interpreter to question him about his voyage and to invite him to visit China before sailing home, but the captain told him that he was already well behind schedule. Although the ship badly needed further careening and a general

overhaul, the English preferred to seek a more isolated spot than Ternate and they moved on to a small uninhabited island, to the south of Celebes, which became their base for four weeks; they called it Crab Island. The forge was set up ashore to assist with repairs and make fresh iron hoops for the water-casks, while the timbers were recaulked and all the rigging checked. On 12 December 1579, almost two years to the day since leaving Plymouth, they left Crab Island by a westerly course.

Drake had taken the first English ship into the Pacific Ocean, and now he was about to be the first Englishman to enter the Indian Ocean, but he still had to pass through the string of scattered islands and reefs of Indonesia. The look-outs were on the alert for signs of shoaling as Drake searched for a safe passage in these difficult waters and when, after four weeks of tricky

Drake at the court of the Sultan of Ternate; an agreement was reached that gave English merchants the monopoly of the island's spice trade.

137

navigation, the way ahead seemed at last clear, the sails were fully set to take advantage of a stern wind. Suddenly, on the night of 9 January, the *Golden Hind* went aground on a submerged rock, making an ominous crunching sound, and listed heavily to starboard. The chaplain, Francis Fletcher, led the whole company in prayers and then the pumps were manned. They had tried to put out an anchor to windward, but could not find the seabed; with first light they made another attempt, again unsuccessfully, and then began to reduce the weight carried by the ship by casting overboard first the cloves bought at Ternate and then some of their cannon. It was no use; the *Golden Hind* would not move an inch and so the entire crew took the sacrament, most of them convinced that final destruction was only a few hours ahead. There was utter despondency, but Drake himself refused to jettison the richest portions of the cargo and thus admit defeat. And then, after they had been grounded about twenty-four hours, the danger was suddenly over. After the tide had begun to flood, the wind slackened and the vessel began heeling into deep water astern. The *Golden Hind*, which drew thirteen feet of water, had been stuck on a smooth ledge of a submerged reef; to leeward the sounding was only six feet, but to windward the lead could find no bottom. It was a miracle that the planking had escaped serious danger. 'Of all the dangers that in our whole voyage we met with, this was the greatest', wrote the chaplain.

After leaving Ternate the *Golden Hind* was grounded on rocks off the Celebes. Some of the ship's cannon and the consignment of cloves from Ternate had to be jettisoned; an engraving by Levinius Hulsius.

THE WORLD
Encompassed

By
Sir FRANCIS DRAKE,

Being his next voyage to that to *Nombre
de Dios* formerly imprinted;

Carefully collected out of the notes of Master
FRANCIS FLETCHER *Preacher in this im-
ployment, and diuers others his followers in
the same* :

Offered now at last to publique view, both for the honour of
the actor, but especially for the stirring vp of heroick spirits,
to benefit their Countrie, and eternize their names
by like noble attempts.

LONDON,
Printed for NICHOLAS BOVRNE
and are to be sold at his shop at the
Royall Exchange. 1628.

Drake pevorqti novit quem terminus orbis,
Et quem, bis mundi vidit vtera, Polus;
Si tacent homines, facient te Sidera notum,
Sol nescit comites non memor esse sui.

Afloat again and set on a safe course, Drake dealt with his insubordinate chaplain, who had been heard to remark when they were stranded on the reef, that their fate was divine judgement on the captain's sin in executing Thomas Doughty. Drake now cleared the lower deck and, sitting on a sea chest, had Fletcher brought before him, with shackles on his feet. 'Francis Fletcher', he solemnly announced, 'I do here excommunicate thee of the Church of God and from all the benefits and graces thereof, and denounce thee to the devil and all his angels.' He was forbidden on pain of death to come before the mast and ordered to wear a placard with the words, 'Francis Fletcher, the falsest knave that liveth'. It was a terrifying occasion, as Drake intended it should be. Morale was all important if they were to reach Devon again, and Drake had no time for the faint-hearted whose unspoken thoughts smacked of mutiny; above all, the excommunication was an object lesson in unquestioning obedience to a captain's commands. It was bizarre that a lay-man should excommunicate an ordained minister of the Church of England, yet Drake was, under his commission, the Queen's personal representative, and in consequence regarded himself as supreme governor in spiritual affairs on his ships no less than Queen Elizabeth herself did in her realm. Fletcher survived his humiliation. The Almighty had, after all, intervened to save them from certain destruction and he acknowledged his fault in

The journal of Francis Fletcher was published in 1628 by the admiral's nephew, another Sir Francis Drake, under the title *The World Encompassed*.

giving up hope too early. A few days afterwards, Drake completely absolved him and reinstated him in his pastoral duties. They were not yet out of difficulties, for after their terrifying experience in uncharted waters, they proceeded with extreme caution. At length, however, on 12 March they reached Java. Here Drake went ashore and his musicians gave a concert to the Rajah, who later came aboard the *Golden Hind* to return the compliment 'with his own courtly music'. Then they set sail across the Indian Ocean with a fair wind and enjoyed an uneventful passage to make their landfall near modern Durban.

They passed the Cape of Good Hope in mid-June and began the long journey north and west by the African coast. Five weeks later, when they sighted Sierra Leone, they were desperately short of water with no one's ration more than a sixth of a pint; but now, in the mouth of the Tagoine River, they replenished their stores. By 15 August they were crossing the Tropic of Cancer and in a week were off the Canaries. The end was almost in sight for the fifty-nine survivors of the original eighty-five men who had left England in the *Pelican*. At last, on 26 September, the *Golden Hind* reached Plymouth, two years, nine months and thirteen days since its departure in December 1577. The men's first question to the fishermen they passed was if Her Majesty were alive and well, and they loyally responded to the news that she was. They were also told that there was much sickness in Plymouth and so instead of berthing alongside came to anchor behind St Nicholas's Island, soon to be renamed Drake's Island. There were few people about to welcome them and then Drake realized why this was so. According to his careful log it was a Monday, but in encompassing the globe he had lost a day and so the people of Plymouth were at morning service. Soon the Mayor, Mary Drake and others were rowed out to the *Golden Hind*, overwhelmed at their safe return and amazed at the precious cargo aboard. Drake wrote at once to the Queen telling her briefly of his exploits for as chief shareholder in the voyage she had an absorbing interest in the treasure captured. Brewer, the trumpeter, took the letter to court. Already there were rumours that the Queen was 'displeased with him, for that by the way of Peru and Spain she had heard of the robberies he had committed'. He realized – as after Panama – that there might be merit in lying low if policy dictated that the Queen had to bow to criticisms which the corsair knew the Spanish ambassador, Mendoza, must be making about his exploits. He awaited news from court anxiously. Some of his crew joked that it would be the Tower or a trial in the Admiralty Court for him.

Then the royal message came: Elizabeth would receive him at court and inspect specimens of the gold and jewellery he had brought home; he had nothing to fear, she assured him. By the same messenger, the Queen sent secretly to Edmund Tremayne to see that the rest of the cargo was safely locked away in Trematon Castle. Mendoza had demanded an audience of the Queen as soon as he heard of Drake's return, but she had refused to see him until she knew more about Spanish aid to the Irish rebels. For some months

Two of de Bry's coloured engravings of the New World:

Negroes working the gold mines.

The brutality of the Spanish conquest was matched by the Indians' treatment of their Spanish prisoners.

FOLLOWING PAGES The Spanish lands in the Caribbean mapped by John Rotz in 1542; South America is at the top of the chart.

The grete occeane sey

Friendis

of the entillas

espagnola

The new fonde londe quhar men goeth a fisching

the cost of pezon

The Indis of occident quhar the spaniards
doith occupy

Cotiba

Lucatan

Londe of Florida

10 25 50 75 100 125 150 175 20
                                    200

6
7
8
9
10
11
12
13
14
15
16
17
18
19
20
21
22
23
24
25
26
27
28
29
30
31
32
33
34
35
36
37
38
39
40
41
42
43
44
45
46
47
48
49

the ambassador had been demanding reparation for 'the plunders committed by this vile corsair' and paying spies in western ports to give him news. He heard all about Brewer's ride to London and immediately sent men to Plymouth to find out what they could from members of Drake's crew about the route and the treasure, which he was convinced was being concealed. The haughty Spaniard felt sure that he could use English merchants' fears of reprisals to put pressure on the Queen to restore the booty, or at least to come to terms, but it was galling to have to tell Philip that he was so weak at sea that Englishmen could 'offend [him] with impunity'. Soon Drake was boasting that he had plans for returning to the Americas with six ships, offering his shareholders a return of seven hundred per cent. 'This has so great an influence over Englishmen that everybody wants to have a share in the expedition.'

Drake spent six hours at Richmond Palace closeted with the Queen while she questioned him, fascinated by his relation of the hazardous voyage as he pointed to the map he had brought, and overjoyed at the gold ducats and other specimens he offered. The two of them got on famously, though this was only the third time he had seen Elizabeth to talk to; she called him her 'pirate' and liked his Devonian speech. Soon Drake was riding back to Plymouth to make a full inventory of the treasure. She let him keep £10,000 for himself and share a similar sum among his crew, but the rest was to be placed for greater safety in the Tower of London, until grave decisions had been taken. In the end, despite wavering by some councillors, nothing was returned to Spain and the investors received a return on their money of 4700 per cent! No wonder Drake was a hero at court and in the city, no less than in the ports. The Queen's pickings, which she so badly needed to reduce the drain on her purse of the leaping costs of administration and defence, were probably not less than £300,000, for we know that besides her return on her shares she also took an independent 'bounty'. But for this reserve of 'chested treasure' in the Tower, her subjects would have had to have borne a far more pinching rate of direct taxation throughout the long naval war with Spain that dominated the last eighteen years of her reign.

Drake had caught the public imagination. England had badly needed a hero and now one had emerged deserving every ounce of the pent-up adulation that was voiced. His success story had all the ingredients of a first-class drama and the Devonian had not only proved himself an intrepid fighter and brilliant explorer, but had won untold riches. 'The people generally applauded his wonderful adventures and rich prizes', wrote John Stow. 'His name and fame became admirable in all places, the people swarming daily in the streets to behold him, swearing hatred to all that misliked him.' And at court his star was dominant. He had presented Elizabeth with a crown encrusted with five emeralds, 'three of them almost as long as a little finger, and two round ones'. She wore it on New Year's Day, when Drake gave her a further present of a diamond cross valued at five thousand crowns. 'She says she will knight him on the day she goes to see his ship, which she has

OPPOSITE A gold salamander pendant set with rubies and some of the many gold coins recovered from the wreck of the *Girona*, one of the four galleases that sailed with the Armada and which was wrecked off the Irish coast.

145

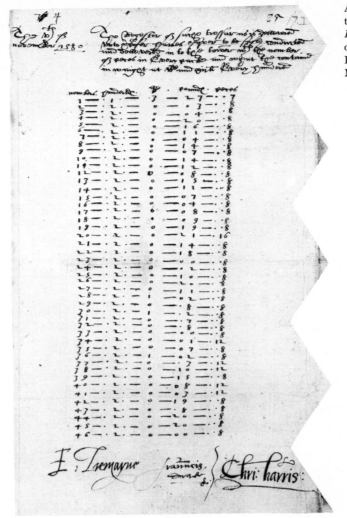

ordered to be brought ashore and placed [at Deptford] as a curiosity', reported the crestfallen Mendoza.

Before the crew was paid off, the *Golden Hind* was sailed on a triumphant final voyage from Plymouth round to Deptford, to berth near the building of the Trinity House pilots. Here came the Queen with a great entourage on 4 April. Everyone was in high spirits, though Drake's investiture was to be much more than a domestic event, for Elizabeth intended to make as much political capital out of it as she could. She slyly told the kneeling corsair that she had ready a gilded sword to strike off his head for turning pirate, and then she handed the sword to the Seigneur de Marchamont, the personal agent of the Duke of Alençon, asking him to perform the ceremony for her. This, indeed, foreshadowed an Anglo-French league against Spain. In view of the impending arrival in England of a great French delegation to hammer out the terms of a marriage treaty between Elizabeth and Alençon (whom she nicknamed her 'Frog'), Drake's present to the Queen of a frog encrusted with diamonds was in a pawkish vein of humour. Elizabeth asked to be introduced to Drake's wife, Mary, and then insisted on seeing over the entire ship. Her gifts to him on this occasion were a beautiful pendant jewel, enclosing her portrait in miniature by Nicholas Hilliard, and a scarf of green silk, bordered with gold lace and embroidery at both ends of which a motto was worked in fine gold threads: 'The Almighty be your Guide and your Protector to the End'. Mendoza (the only member of the diplomatic corps not to be invited to Deptford) was aghast. In his view, Drake was a pirate who deserved to be severely punished, probably executed, and now his sovereign had knighted him and blasphemously given him a holy text to preserve his life.

The chair made from the timbers of the *Golden Hind*.

Soon royal letters patent were issued stating that 'whereas Sir Francis Drake, Knight, has circumnavigated the globe from east to west and has discovered in the south part of the world many unknown places, Her Majesty to perpetuate his fame and valour doth grant unto him and his heirs' the manor of Sherford in Devon and smaller properties in the Midlands and North Country. The following New Year's Day, the Queen gave him a goblet of silver engraved with a representation of his ship which had made history. The vessel itself was to be laid up at Deptford, near to the spot at which he had been knighted. Here a special dock was constructed and for three generations sightseers came to marvel at the tiny craft and pay homage to the memory of the man who had sailed her. Two pieces of furniture made from the timbers survive – a table in the Inner Temple and a chair in the Bodleian Library, Oxford.

With his wealth and his title Drake required a country seat and coveted Buckland Abbey, near to his birthplace, which had been embellished by Sir Richard Grenville. Through intermediaries Sir Francis purchased the great house and its estate for £3400, a very considerable sum. He knew that Grenville regarded him as an upstart and envied him the opportunity of carrying out his own South Seas project. Sir Richard accordingly withdrew from the life of Plymouth and South Devon with silent disdain and returned to his native Bideford on the north coast. Drake had supplanted him at Buckland and at court, for nothing succeeded like success and it was understandable that his own triumph should be a bitter cup for Grenville.

6 THE ROVERS

THE MACHINERY FOR DEALING WITH PIRATES at the beginning of Elizabeth's reign was totally ineffective and many of the officials in the maritime counties charged with the task of enforcing the law were known to be in league with the worst culprits. The instructions to local vice-admirals included the charge 'to avoid the appearance of conniving at piracy', simply because such malpractices were an open secret. Thomas Lewis, mayor of Cardiff and a commissioner 'for the repression of piracy' had commercial dealings with a number of wanted men and was helpful in arranging for prisoners awaiting trial to be released. The Lord Admiral's representative in Lincolnshire had his own private harbour to which prizes were regularly brought by the rovers. The customs collector at Arundel in Sussex invested heavily in Captain Heynes' voyages and conveniently kept the booty locked away in the Queen's customs house. All round the coasts the law was being openly mocked by the men responsible for enforcing it. In some areas, such as east Dorset and the Helford River, there was an intricate network of investors, receivers of plunder and suppliers of provisions, gunpowder and naval stores, which was controlled by local magnates with the active help of mayors, justices of the peace and customs officers. Elsewhere men would turn a blind eye for a consideration, it was difficult to find a jury that would convict and whenever enquiries were afoot villagers near the coast maintained a stubborn silence.

Conditions in the English Channel, the North Sea and the Irish Sea were desperate and no ship was immune from attack. In the port of Hamburg there were rumours that the Queen of England herself was hiring pirates 'to spoil all merchants that traffic through the Narrow Seas'. Such an impression had arisen from the Lord Admiral's issue of licences to individuals to arm their ships and put to sea to capture 'men of war' of all nationalities, yet the temptations for gamekeepers to turn poachers were great and under cover of these letters some indulged in open piracy. Regularly proclamations were issued ordering 'all Sea Rovers commonly called Freebooters' to leave English ports, yet it proved impossible to enforce such orders. In the first dozen years of the reign the Privy Council spent more time – according to the evidence of its minutes – discussing pirates and the methods of suppressing them than any other single topic.

The navy had become reduced at the opening of the reign to twenty-one sea-going vessels and not all of these were in commission throughout the year. For some years, then, there was negligible protection of the busiest shipping routes and more isolated stretches of inshore waters were totally free from surveillance by naval craft. Protection was left to local initiative, such as the vessels fitted out by the Cinque Ports periodically 'to clear the seas', and the 'wafters' sent from Great Yarmouth to protect the herring fleet each autumn. The expectation of serious trouble led to most merchantmen being armed with cannon and free resort to guns and small arms bred lawlessness. When a pirate was caught red-handed the chances of his conviction and, following that, of his actually serving a sentence of imprison-

OPPOSITE A sixteenth-century warship; from a contemporary engraving.

ment or of paying with his life at Execution Dock were so slight that in 1564 the government prescribed much sterner treatment. Every condemned pirate was for the future to be hanged on cliffs near his home port 'to be example of others that shall presume hereafter to commit the like'. Yet pardons remained common. Between 1558 and 1578 a total of no more than 106 English rovers were hanged and even in 1578, when the authorities were particularly energetic, bringing over 900 men to trial, only three went to the gallows.

Special commissioners were appointed in 1565 for the first time in every maritime county of England and Wales to discover cases of piracy, and to report on receivers of plunder and identify all aiders and abettors, not least those selling the rovers essential supplies. In most counties these commissioners were already serving as justices of the peace, yet they were not empowered to try cases judicially, but only to attach offenders for appearing at the Admiralty Sessions. The commissioners were expected to make full and frequent reports to the Privy Council, but there was inevitably a good deal of friction between them and the local officials of the Admiralty Court. The theory was that if the rovers could be cut off from provisions on the mainland and denied markets for their wares the evil they embodied would be eradicated. The county commissioners were strengthened by additional appointments in 1578 to undertake extensive investigations and their drive was effective in providing the central government with a mass of detail about the ways in which victualling of pirate craft and receiving booty were conducted. Three years later a novel method of discovering 'the detestable doings' of the sea dogs and their shore-based protectors was introduced – analogous to the system of public informations – and met with some success. All subjects of the Queen were encouraged to prosecute suspects before a special panel of judges and London merchants and for their pains could claim two-thirds of the fines imposed as a result of their public-spirited action. But the real turning-point in the endless campaign against the rovers was in 1583, when Sir Julius Caesar was appointed judge of the High Court of Admiralty. Caesar was a man of enormous energy and sterling integrity, and he made his power felt. He made a clean sweep of inefficient and corrupt local officials and checked the worst abuses in franchises outside his jurisdiction. The weakness of the system of separate county commissions for dealing with pirates had long been painfully apparent and at Caesar's instigation in 1588 a central Admiralty Commission was appointed, at first with twenty-three members, empowered to search out cases of piracy throughout England and Wales. Within five years there were 120 central commissioners and great Caesar himself was going on circuit. The Queen disliked the scheme for itinerant Admiralty Court justices, as she feared the administrative costs would be high, but she withdrew her opposition when Sir Julius offered to pay all expenses out of his own pocket. For the first time in 1591 the West Country felt the full terror of the law. Pardons were less easy to acquire and the government was at last showing concern about the

The seal of the High Court of Admiralty in the reign of Elizabeth.

150

Sir Julius Caesar
reformed the Admiralty
Court in a determined
effort to suppress piracy.

routine acquittals of pirates by local juries. In certain flagrant cases jury-men were summoned to Westminster to answer for their conduct.

The crews manning the larger English pirate barks usually included at least one foreigner, often a Dutchman, sometimes a Frenchman, for besides their usefulness as interpreters they would be expected to have picked up a good deal about the habits of foreign captains in making for port, in the tactics of the chase, the stowage of cargoes and much else, since there were still regional variations in practical matters of seamanship. Some Turks served on English craft and even a few Africans, like 'the black fellow called Edward'. What is interesting is that half as many recruits came to piracy from distant inland places as were born into it from coastal towns and villages. The sea appeared to many adventurous youths as the obvious route to riches. In their dreams it was the quays of West Country ports, not the streets of London, that were paved with gold and so from gaining their sea-legs in a coasting vessel many drifted by way of service in a privateer to outright piracy. A man who had been a cowherd in Wiltshire rose to be boatswain under Clinton Atkinson and a lad from Abingdon who had learnt the trade of armourer put his skill to profitable use on the seas. There was always a shortage of experienced shipwrights and so some were kidnapped or induced to sign on under false pretences; a shipwright who had joined a vessel at London for a voyage to the Canaries discovered too late that his services were needed by the den of Welsh privateers at Beaumaris. Yet once aboard, every man had a specified number of shares in every prize to be taken and discipline was much less rigorous than in the Queen's ships.

It was at this period that pirates began to adopt flamboyant garb when they went ashore – a habit that would reach its zenith in the early eighteenth century. Some, of course, had more money than they knew how to use and to deck themselves out in gorgeous, extravagant clothes proudly advertised their successful exploits. Pirates felt that if courtiers wore their estates upon their backs, they had sounder finances to dazzle their beholders than a Raleigh or an Earl of Oxford. Dandies with their sword scabbards en-crusted with jewels, their satin-lined cloaks and outlandish hats, they attracted gaping crowds in provincial ports. This exhibitionism reached its height at Execution Dock, Wapping, since to see a pirate hanged was one of the sights of London. Thomas Walton's final performance to the crowd in August 1583 provided bizarre entertainment, for he 'rent his Venetian breeches of crimson taffeta and distributed the same to such of his old acquaintances as stood about him'. This apparel, complained the chronicler John Stow, was 'too sumptuous for sea rovers'. Clinton Atkinson of Stud-land had left Corfe Castle for the Tower of London in great state, boasting his 'murray velvet doublet with great gold buttons and his velvet Venetian breeches laid with fresh gold lace', yet he gave these fineries away to friends before going to his end at Wapping so the onlookers felt cheated of their entertainment.

All around the coasts the tales of the rovers' daring were much the same.

There was Charles Wilson, a Londoner, working from Holy Island, who did a brisk business with Edinburgh merchants, especially for sugar and sweetmeats. Wilson claimed to be acting under letters of marque from the King of Sweden and made such a nuisance of himself in the north-east that Queen Elizabeth told the governor of Berwick she would rather have him caught than any other pirate. When, however, he was taken, the Earl of Bedford, as governor of Berwick, upbraided his captor for being 'a naughty fellow' and pressed for Wilson's pardon. For weeks on end conditions were so bad between the Tees and the Humber that 'no man will dare to put to sea', and when the pirates took a prize 'they would come on land at any place and no man dared say anything to them, so [the local men] let them have what they listed for very little money and then continued banqueting on land with them for three or four days'. Further south in Lincolnshire the serjeant of the local Admiralty Court laid out £30 for a feast for pirates at his house at Ingoldmills. The most gruesome attack of the reign occurred at Great Yarmouth when a ship from Dort in Holland was boarded as it crossed the bar. In turn each member of the crew was bound and cast overboard until only the captain, Cornelius Williamson, remained and for him the attackers had reserved a special fate. 'They tied up the said Cornelius with a rope about his neck until he was nearly dead, and when he was come to his wits they stripped him all naked and cast him eight times tied with a rope in the sea till they knew where his money was.' After this rigorous keel-hauling it was not surprising that he broke down. He was left as bare as his ship to bring her alongside singlehanded. At Aldeburgh a new broom from the Admiralty Court locked up a rascal named Peter Lambert who had readily boasted of his contempt for the law of the land, of the sea and of the heavens; however his wife carried on acting as receiver of booty and succeeded in sending Peter a file in a meat pie, thanks to which he cut through the bars of his cell and returned to the seas.

In the Thames approaches lurked many small craft waiting to surprise ships on the last leg of their voyage to London, but it was unorganized, lone raiding, for large-scale operators could not by now be working so close to the capital. Piracy proper in the Thames and the Port of London was in fact degenerating into pilfering. Even so, there were carefully laid plans for disposing of plunder to shopkeepers in the city. A key receiver was Walter Darby, a scrivener with chambers in Barnard's Inn, who had once been to sea with Martin Frobisher and kept closely in touch with carriers and middlemen in the contraband trade. The sooner plundered goods changed hands the better and any dealer who hung on to such wares waiting for a more favourable price regretted it. We know that within no more than ten days following the attack on a Dutch vessel off Land's End, the greater part of her cargo of linen had passed into the stock of Cheapside drapers.

There were three particularly bad areas – eastern Dorset, the Falmouth area and South Wales. Lulworth Cove in Dorset, for centuries a haven for smugglers and pirates, was effectively a private harbour of Sir Richard

Rogers of Bryanston, who owned the manors of East and West Lulworth. The serjeant of the local Admiralty Court, Simon Lobley, was naturally a retainer of his, and his tenants if need be lodged storm-bound rovers in their cottages and hid booty in their barns. Sir Richard himself tended to remain in the background, though there is an account of him being rowed out one May morning to cut his personal mark with a knife on the mainmast of a Dutch pirate's craft 'for that no other should deal with her' and he later restored her to the pirate, the notorious Courte Higgenberte who operated for a decade with English brethren of the sea. For this service Sir Richard received a chest of sugar and a tun of wine. Francis Rogers, his brother, was more actively involved, supplying pirates with bread, beef and beer in return

The ruins of Corfe Castle; the castle was the centre of the activities of the pirates of the Isle of Purbeck.

for contraband wine and not a few desperate men were entertained in his house. He would take his armed pinnace to prowl off St Alban's Head. The Rogers brothers escaped undue attention from the government until the summer of 1578 when Francis was foolish enough to steal the mails, as well as everything else, from a Guernsey ship, and the packets included a batch of despatches from the governor of Guernsey for the Queen. Francis failed to answer his summons to appear before the Privy Council, but Sir Richard came up to Whitehall, where the Council, more in sorrow than in anger, admonished him, being a justice of the peace, for placing the law in disrepute. Henceforth he must 'use himself better in those cases' and was to send up his brother without delay to answer the serious charges against him. Yet Francis Rogers succeeded in lying low. Before long the Rogers' heyday was over, for Lord Howard of Bindon, vice-admiral of Dorset and a nephew of Lord Admiral Howard of Effingham, an unswerving opponent of the rovers, decided to build a castle at East Lulworth.

By one of those anomalies of jurisdiction that persisted in Elizabethan England, Lord Howard of Bindon's writ did not run in the Isle of Purbeck, a peninsula that extended east from Lulworth towards Poole Harbour, which formed a separate liberty, centred on Corfe Castle. Purbeck had time out of mind been a haunt of pirates and even when the courtier Sir Christopher Hatton became appointed titular Lord of the Admiralty there, men did not change their ways. Stephen Heynes, a prominent member of the Purbeck gang, boasted in his cups that he 'had better friends in England than any alderman or merchant of London', naming Sir Christopher Hatton. The absentee Hatton's deputy, Francis Hawley, was besieged in Corfe Castle by crews who had come ashore 'so strong and well-appointed as they cannot be of the sudden repulsed', he reported, yet there were too many tales of gifts of plunder accepted by Hawley 'for goodwill and favour in the Island of Purbeck' to believe that he was above corruption. Every day he sent his servants to the vessels anchored in Studland Bay 'to see what they would give him' and once he was so annoyed at not receiving a present he had expected from Clinton Atkinson that he offered money to a rival freebooter, Captain Porter, 'if he could betray him'.

Men came from far and wide to Studland in search of bargains. There was a strange novelty about so many of the items offered by pirates – wine from Crete, hawks from Norway, parrots from Brazil, ivory from West Africa, 'cunningly-worked bracelets of Barbary gold' and coins with unusual inscriptions, yet bearing the glint of gold. Much business was done by barter; for instance Henry Morris, the searcher of the port of Poole, obtained fine wines in return for powder and shot; butchers offered salt beef and bacon, hoping for silks and satins for their wives, and at times live bucks were exchanged at the water's edge for sugar and spices. It was not unknown for pirates to allow credit – a boastful way of exhibiting their self-confidence in being able to survive the next engagement at sea and eluding the authorities for a return to the Bay to collect their debts. Hard bargaining took place

The effrontery of the Studland Bay pirates ran the gamut from harmless indulgence of personal eccentricities to indiscriminate acts of brutality.

in the many unlicensed taverns that sprang up around Studland Bay. After a successful voyage and the division of spoils, the gentlemen of the sea would descend on these taverns and inns to celebrate noisily, make deals, engage new seamen and look for wenches. They were a bizarre crowd, for some would get themselves up in the clothes of men they had murdered, others would ape lawyers by dressing up in furred gowns and spectacles. Games of dice or cards would, as the liquor flowed, lead to fights, so these hostelries were not healthy spots for a lone traveller to patronize; indeed, the terrors to be met in the tavern kept by Will Mundy were summed up by a pirate – 'his house is the hell of the world and he the devil'. Publican Mundy needed to be tough to keep his end up when Stephen Heynes was in port, for Heynes had an unequalled reputation for torturing victims, being the first pirate to practise the abominable business of sticking lighted matches under a man's fingernails and he was not above breaking an opponent's bones over his capstan. Heynes's treatment of the master of the *Salvator* of Danzig, which he brought to Studland as a prize, in his attempt to make him reveal where treasure was stowed away, was so shocking that his own crew went down on their knees to beg him to spare them having to witness further atrocities.

Studland was reckoned to be the ideal place for a novice to join a pirate bark, for here before long he would be bound to meet with the principal captains. To Studland drifted the unemployed, the desperate and the dregs of the seaman's profession. Edward Proctor, a Londoner, had been pressed to sail with Sir Humphrey Gilbert, but because he was taken ill he had been put ashore at Dartmouth with no immediate hope of livelihood – 'and so he came', his deposition reads, 'from there by land to Studland'. An Irishman, William Ellis, fed up with fighting as a mercenary in the Netherlands, came by stages to Studland 'where he understood men of war had usual resort, to be entertained amongst them, for that he could do little good by law'. When privateering proved unrewarding many of the less law-abiding shipowners would make for Studland Bay to indulge in open piracy for a season, rather than remain idle. These Dorset rovers reckoned that they lived charmed lives and often took extraordinary liberties with the authorities. Clinton Atkinson, one of the half-dozen most wanted men, had the sheer effrontery to bring a civil action in the High Court of Admiralty against a merchant who owed him £200 and daringly appeared in the London court in person; yet the officers there allowed him to return to Dorset without as much as requiring bail!

The tide began to turn in 1581, when John Piers of Padstow was taken at Studland and at a special sessions held at Corfe Castle was condemned to death with most of his crew. He was hanged overlooking the bay, 'to the terrifying of others, for that the same place hath been much frequented and the inhabitants molested with pirates'. Two years later there was at last a carefully planned swoop on the anchorage, when two of the Queen's ships seized seventeen rovers' craft and three of their prizes. A great many pirates, including Captains Atkinson and Purser, were sent to the Tower to be examined by Sir Julius Caesar and his deputies, and as a result much evidence was extracted from them about owners, receivers and victuallers. A series of trials was conducted, but the Privy Council was against mass executions; partly because, with open war against Spain so near, it would have been foolhardy to have exterminated so great a reserve of skilled mariners who would be needed for the defence of the realm when the crisis came; partly because it was the leaders of the gangs who deserved to pay the extreme penalty, not the small fry. The council decided 'to have a convenient number for example to be executed and the rest to pass under Her Majesty's mercy and pardon'. Thomas Walton was among the nine hanged at Wapping; many others were imprisoned in the Marshalsea, but served only a month of their sentences, since they were 'ready to perish for want'. Studland, like Lulworth, was being brought under close supervision, yet in the final years of the century there was trouble at neighbouring Poole, where pirates took over Brownsea Castle, commanding the entrance to the harbour, which they fortified with cannon to use as a base for operations and threaten maritime trade.

The Killigrew family, hereditary captains of Pendennis Castle which guarded the entrance to Falmouth, was the mainspring of Cornish piracy. The Killigrews had had a long innings. In the 1550s they had wreaked havoc on shipping in the English Channel and further afield, for their ships came and went as they pleased in Brest and La Rochelle; the despatches from the English ambassador at Paris in 1555 sounded constant alarms: 'The Killigrews are at sea, with four or five barks, and have taken good prizes, trusting to take yet more, and in case the worst fall, the gains thereof will be able to find them all this next winter in some island.' By 1560 the head of the clan was Sir John Killigrew, who built Arwennack House near Pendennis, which was a well-defended storehouse for the rich plunder brought to the Helford River and Carrick Roads. At court Sir John was dubbed 'a landlord in name only', for it was an open secret that he and his whole kin lived by robbing ships approaching Falmouth, acting as a grand receiver of stolen goods from pirates of all nations as well as heavily investing in voyages of plunder. Quite apart from keeping south Cornwall under his thumb, Sir John's influence stretched from Munster to Dorset, through ties of kin and mutual interests and he numbered among his associates Sir John Wogan, vice-admiral of South Wales, and Sir John Perrot, whose word was law in Pembrokeshire. His payroll included Thomas Venables of Southampton, master of the *Dolphin*, who had his own contacts with men in the Isle of Wight, so that plunder passed to Penryn and Falmouth by way of Newport, and merchants had 'little hope to recover the same'. When questioned about

Pendennis Castle; from this vantage point at the entrance of Falmouth harbour, the Killigrews, captains of the castle in the sixteenth century, took their share of the spoils of piracy on the Cornish coast.

RIGHT The main gate of the castle, built by Henry VIII, is surmounted by the royal coat of arms.

his hospitality at Arwennack to a rough diamond named Captain Elliot, the knight grandly answered, 'It is hard for a common entertainer of strangers in his house to know all men's deserts'. His mother, old Lady Killigrew, was a tough and unprincipled businesswoman, whom we can see from the documents parcelling out looted Holland cloth to relatives, ordering goods to be buried in the garden and even herself leading a boarding-party to rifle a German ship at anchor, determined to lay her hands on the 'pieces of eight' she was told were concealed. The last episode was too flagrant to escape general knowledge and Lady Killigrew found herself before the judges at Launceston, though her son's bribes secured her acquittal. When later in the reign Sir John was unable to operate quite so openly on the Helford River, he diverted more and more of his cargoes to Irish ports. The acquittal by two Cornish juries on his instructions in 1588 of a pirate who had attacked two Danish vessels, despite the weight of telling evidence against him, reached the ears of the Council which professed amazement at the verdict. 'Those which so acquitted him shall be called in question in the Star Chamber and proceeded against with that extremity and the grave censure which that High Court may lay upon', came the order, but as usual the government's bark was far worse than its bite. As late as 1597 Sir John Killigrew was able to help a rover who had the bad luck to be returning to Falmouth with a prize in tow when the Queen's ships were at anchor in the harbour. The knight coolly had himself rowed out to present his compliments and £100 in coin to the senior naval officers, to ensure that no action was taken.

The principality of Wales was still a pirate's paradise and each haven had its small-time rovers who envied the success of John Callice of Tintern (whose career we shall examine), but lacked both his daring and the necessary financial backing for operations on more than a limited scale. A typical case was Captain Aristotle Tottle, who gave himself airs by assuming the name, as he understood it, of a famous seaman from classical mythology! Dr David Lewis, judge of the High Court of Admiralty in London, was well aware of the favourable conditions in which lawbreakers found themselves in his native Wales and he complained bitterly about local officials who never dared arrest a culprit for fear of upsetting his influential friends, 'but will play bo-peep, seest me, and seest me not'. An agent Lewis sent to gather material for a detailed report noted that 'the inhabitants are froward in accusing one another', and when a colleague approached Sir William Morgan, the local vice-admiral, for his help in making arrests, Morgan told him 'he did not care for the commission, nor me'. The pickings were, indeed, considerable. An attack on a small flotilla of vessels, mistakenly hugging the coast on their way round from Bristol to Milford Haven, produced a haul of silks, velvets and wine worth £10,000 in the currency of the day.

Sir John Perrot, perhaps a natural son of Henry VIII, never forgot the slight of dismissal from his post as vice-admiral of South Wales in 1565 and he made life unpleasant for Richard Vaughan, his successor, who was no more upright. There was an inquiry into how it had been possible for so well-known a pirate as Robert Hickes to remain at anchor for five whole weeks off Pembroke with a prize, doing brisk business, and each blamed the other for inaction and each accused the other of earning fat bribes. After that incident Vaughan was determined to put Perrot in his place and kept a close watch on Laugharne, the latter's private landing-place. When he tried to board a suspicious vessel lying nearby, the crew stood by 'with calivers ready, with fire in their cocks', saying 'none had to do there but Sir John Perrot'. Vaughan came to London in 1578 to complain of Perrot before the Privy Council and went round the town saying 'Sir John better deserved hanging than any thief', but the Council thought his accusations far too malicious, and after committing him to prison for a spell they deprived him of the vice-admiralty office. How Sir John chuckled! He now gave the appearance of a much reformed character, fitting out a man-of-war to cruise between the Isle of Wight and Ireland 'to rid the seas of pirates', as he claimed, yet the fact that on each trip the vessel called in at Falmouth so Perrot could enjoy the entertainment offered by the Killigrews rather suggests his heart was not entirely in the work. By the early 1580s, however, the heyday of South Wales piracy was passing and although Sir John Wogan made a bid to carry on Perrot's role by placing 'two great guns' to protect the water approaches to his house at Boulston, he does not emerge as a systematic organizer of piracy on the scale of his predecessor.

In North Wales the volume of contraband trade was much less and there were far fewer good harbours than in the south, yet it remained a lawless region; as one visitor put it, 'in very deed they be ignorant what piracy is'. As elsewhere the illicit trade was supported by powerful local interests and incidents would only come to light as a result of disputes between cousins and neighbours, who sought to blacken their opponents in the eyes of the government in order to acquire for themselves an even greater share in the running of the area and the pickings of piracy. Most of the rovers themselves

OPPOSITE Sir John Perrot, who may have been a natural son of Henry VIII, played a notable part in the contraband trade off the coast of South Wales. Perrot's activities centred on Laugharne; the castle was granted to him for services in Ireland.

BELOW An eighteenth-century engraving of Laugharne castle and the anchorage.

161

were small fry, utterly dependent on their relations with landowners, customs men and Admiralty Court officials. The only independent pirate was, perhaps, Nicholas Hookes of Aberconway, whom no one dared to cross; indeed nearly everyone in the town was related to him, because he was the twenty-fifth child of a local merchant and was himself the father of twenty-seven children in the port. Two islands off the Caernarvonshire coast were key places, Bardsey and St Tudwal. Bardsey Island was the personal domain of John Wyn ap Hugh, a reward for his military service under the Duke of Northumberland, and he had turned the old Augustinian priory into a vast warehouse for naval stores and provisions. His factor on the island was required to be 'at all times ready to deliver to all pirates ... victuals and necessaries, when and as often as they have need, receiving from them for the same large recompense, as wine, iron, salt and spices'. Such booty passed from Bardsey to market towns eighty miles away, it was said. John Wyn could be seen in action haranguing a local jury, which a few minutes earlier had convicted one of his captains; he told the good men and true to have more sense, or it would be their turn to face awkward charges next and, by and by, they would find themselves in the dock. St Tudwal was 'a wild road and landing-place', visited only by pirates and those intent on trafficking with them, but unlike Bardsey it was important to be able to speak Welsh on the island, or one was suspected of being an interloper and treated accordingly.

The most powerful man in Anglesey was Sir Richard Bulkeley, vice-admiral of North Wales, who contrived to keep in the background, though it was plain that illicit trade could only have prospered through his connivance. He had, in fact, set up his brothers Charles and David Bulkeley as pirates and had encouraged Irish, French and Dutch rovers to frequent Beaumaris, which many reckoned to be 'the safest haven in the west'. The Bulkeleys' brother-in-law Griffith John Griffith owned a man-of-war, which was captained by his son, and whenever the vessel returned to harbour with a prize a splendid dinner was given at the Bulkeley mansion where the booty was parcelled out. When one of the Queen's ships took in tow an abandoned pirate bark there was no choice but to have the vessel formally auctioned, yet Sir Richard succeeded in purchasing it from the Admiralty Court assessors at a nominal figure that made all Anglesey laugh.

One of the most colourful characters in the maritime fraternity was John Callice, the illegitimate son of a member of the Herbert family, headed by the powerful Earl of Pembroke. At the age of eleven Callice had left Tintern to be apprenticed to a London haberdasher, Alderman Bounds, but the sea was in his blood and he abandoned his apprenticeship for service as a hand in one of the Queen's ships under Sir William Wynter. His name first came to prominence in 1574 as master of the *Cost Me Noughte*, a most appropriately named prize, and for the next four years he was ubiquitous, being associated with every capture of note, whether it was off the Scillies, near Great Yarmouth, off Holy Island, in the Strait of Dover or near Lundy. He became master of the Bristol Channel and used Cardiff as his base for taking on supplies and unloading prize goods. Here he would lodge with his father-in-law, the sheriff of Glamorganshire, and seemed immune from prosecution. The Privy Council considered Callice the most dangerous pirate afloat and thought the south and west coast ports misguided in acknowledging him as their hero. And then by a stroke of good fortune Edward Horsey, the Captain of the Isle of Wight, succeeded in capturing Callice and his entire crew and sent them under strong guard to London. In the Tower awaiting trial, Callice received messages of goodwill from old associates such as Captain Hickes of Studland, who wrote offering to give the shirt from his back to save him and concluding, 'I pray God send us both our heart's desire and a merry meeting'. Dr Lewis, the Admiralty Court judge, patiently examined Callice to piece together his remarkable career as best he could, and the pirate insisted in the formal record on being described as 'gentleman'. This prompted the further question, for if he were a gentleman, what was his landed property that would escheat to the Crown on his condemnation? The reply came: 'After his mother's death he shall have £10 a year lands at Tintern'. Hanging from the gallows at Execution Dock seemed a foregone conclusion, yet John Callice threw himself on the sovereign's mercy, hoping for a pardon in

The Tower of London in the early seventeenth century drawn by a Dutch traveller.

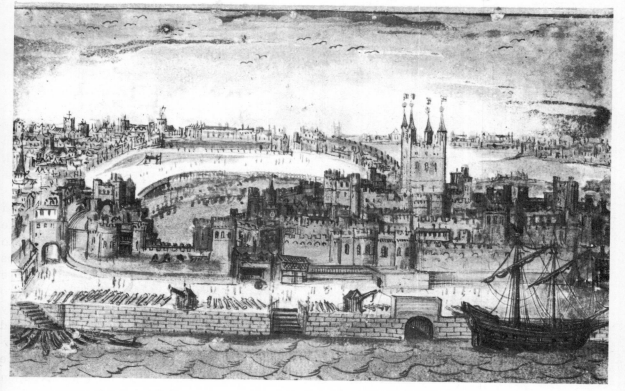

return for turning Queen's evidence. 'If she will spare my life and use me in her service by sea with those she can trust, either to clear the coast of other wicked pirates, or otherwise', he pleaded. For 'I know their haunts, roads, creeks and maintainers so well, I can do more therein than if she sent ships abroad and spent £20,000.' It was probably true. While the Council pondered whether to let the law take its course, the Regent Morton of Scotland intervened on Callice's behalf, while friends offered £500 for his release. As a result Callice was unconditionally pardoned in July 1578 and though he did inform against a few receivers of plundered cargoes in South Wales to settle personal scores, he never kept his side of the bargain, but returned to the seas and his old ways.

For a time after his release Callice served as lieutenant on the *Galleon Fenner* of Chichester, a well-armed craft of 100 tons and a large complement, but before very long he was in business again on his own account. When he captured the *Falcon* of Prestonpans in 1582 – an incident scarcely pleasing to the new Regent of Scotland – he transferred his flag to her and aping what Drake had done for the *Pelican*, he changed the *Falcon*'s name to the *Golden Challice*, a pun on his own. The cargo of this Scottish vessel had included two parcels of religious books for the young James VI. Callice saw to it that news of this literary haul reached appropriate quarters and in consequence the Huguenot printer Vautrollier rode down to Studland Bay to buy all the books from him for £40. Soon even the Welsh harbours were proving too risky to use as bases as the government's net tightened, for Callice's activities had brought a remote area of the kingdom under scrutiny. He knew he could not expect to cheat the gallows a second time and after a run of successes off Ireland and then in the Orkneys he abandoned northern waters for the Mediterranean, where he would have many English and Welsh successors in the early years of the seventeenth century. The most famous of English rovers of Elizabethan days was killed in action off the Barbary coast.

Two Cornish pirates stand out above the rest, Robert Hickes of Saltash and John Piers of Padstow. Hickes had a long run of independent captures and he sometimes operated with Callice. Towards the end of 1576, however, he entered a partnership with the Dutchman Courte Higgenberte, and this proved his undoing, for their plans became too ambitious and they quarrelled over the spoils of one venture and the tactics for the next. After fifteen months with his new associate Hickes was in custody and before he was hanged at Wapping it came out that he had succeeded in swindling Callice out of a very large sum of money. John Piers graduated from local marauding between Lundy and Padstow to more extensive ventures. He became recognized as a daring fellow by the men of Studland Bay, the seal of approval which many rovers coveted, and he had dealings as far north as Chester, where he intercepted supplies intended for the army in Ireland. On one voyage in the Narrow Seas he blockaded the harbour at Rye, so 'none can go forth or come in'. Piers always returned to his native Padstow where his mother would be waiting for him at the waterside, and since she had the reputation of being a witch few dared go near her after dark, so Mrs Piers proved a useful receiver of plunder. Sir Richard Grenville, sent to Padstow to discover all he might, could find little damning evidence, for too many local people had cause to be grateful to John Piers. As we have noticed, he was caught red-handed not in Cornwall, but at Studland.

By the end of the reign although aiders and abettors were still to be found in almost every port, there were very few havens on the mainland which could properly be termed 'pirate bases', where ships could be given a thorough overhaul, without interference. The growing control of the government made it risky for pirates to tarry as they had been wont for weeks on end in harbour, waiting on wind and weather or undergoing repairs. Except in a few well-chosen havens goods were laden and victuals taken aboard only at night. Even in parts of Dorset and Cornwall refitting and careening were becoming too dangerous and vessels stopped merely for the most essential repairs. Instead the pirates turned to the harbours of south-west Ireland. So bold a captain as Purser thought it advisable to spend the worst of the winters at Limerick in the 1580s and others soon followed his example. Baltimore, the most southerly of these havens, gradually became the favourite place for 'graving, careening and trimming of masts'. The foundations of the extraordinary development of Irish bases in the seventeenth century were thus laid.

Open war with Spain had at last opened the gates to legitimate privateering and piracy as such dwindled. Thanks to the Lord Admiral's licences peacetime crime was transformed into wartime heroism. In the stress of the long naval war, when England was straining every nerve, no one doubted the wisdom of this policy, yet it cleared the coasts of English 'pirates' only so long as the war lasted. The future lay not with the plunderers of coastal trade nor with the rovers of the Narrow Seas, but with those who at first secretively and then with full government blessing attacked Spanish shipping in the New World; and when peace eventually came it could never extend beyond the line.

7 THE CHALLENGE TO SPAIN

PLANS FOR A SPANISH ENTERPRISE against England went forward. The Spanish admiral, the Marquis of Santa Cruz, had a few years previously proposed that a combined naval and military expedition should be mounted against heretic England, but Philip II had at first considered it too costly an undertaking; but now that England had openly intervened in the Netherlands to support his rebellious subjects, he decided that he could no longer postpone an attack on Elizabeth's realm and would draft from the campaign in the Netherlands as many troops as could be spared to cross the Channel under Parma while a great fleet controlled the Narrow Seas. All the reports which Philip meticulously conned in his study in the Escorial left him in no doubt that it was his plain Christian duty to invade England, depose Elizabeth and restore the Catholic faith. 'God is my witness', he wrote to the Cortes, 'that it is not the desire to gain new kingdoms that guided me, but the zeal for his service and the hope of glorifying the Holy faith. For this I have risked everything.' Pope Sixtus V blessed the enterprise as a Crusade of the Church. First reports of the Spanish preparations reached London in December 1585, but it was not until the very eve of Drake's return from the West Indies that the Queen began to take the threat at all seriously, by ordering the lord-lieutenants in the shires to muster the militia and arrange for a system of beacons to signal the approach of a hostile fleet.

The Queen's navy had been completely reorganized, first by Benjamin Gonson and William Wynter and, since 1578, by Sir John Hawkins. He created an entirely new arm in evolving a small, streamlined vessel that was much more seaworthy, easier to handle and able to stay at sea for longer periods than the traditional man-of-war; he also constructed a splendid force of larger vessels with long-range guns, of the type of Grenville's *Revenge*, and modified many of the older ships. By wholesale reform of the dockyards and the system of construction, Hawkins, as Treasurer of the Navy, made the fleet a powerful instrument of war, able to fulfil its traditional role of defending the coast and yet fully capable of undertaking expeditions to harry the Spaniards in their own waters or to intercept the plate fleet. What particularly appealed to Elizabeth was that he achieved all this

After the battle of Gravelines, Elizabeth rode in procession to Tilbury to address her troops. At the top of this contemporary painted wooden panel, the Queen is shown giving thanks to God for the victory. It was not known until five days after the battle that Parma would be unable to invade England.

The Pope Consulting with his Cardinalls & Contributing a Million of Gold towards the Charge of the Armada —

The Ld. Admirall Howard Knighting Thomas Howard, the Lord Sheffeild, Robt Townsent, Iohn Hawkins, and Martir Forbisher for their good service

Arthur Ld Grey, Sr Francis Knolles, Sr Iohn Norris, Sr Richard Bingham, Sr Rog. Williams & others in a Councell of War, consulting how ye land service should be Ordered

The Army of 1000 horse, and 22000 Foot, which ye Earle of Leicester comanded when hee Pitched his Tents att Tilbury

Queene Eliz: wth Nobles and Gentry and a great number of people giving God humble thanks in St Pauls Church. and having set upp ye Ensignes taken from the Spaniards.

Queene Eliz Riding in Triumph through London in a Chariot drawn by two Horses and all ye Companies attending her wth their Baners

Seventeenth-century playing cards depicting the events of the Armada year.

and still saved her money. It had been a proud moment for her to show the fleet of new warships at anchor in the Thames to Alençon. Compared with the forest of masts of the galleons at Cadiz and Lisbon, hers was a small fleet – no more than twenty-five major vessels in 1587 – but all were in first-rate condition. Her potential naval reserve was considerable – merchantmen, fishermen and other craft whose owners were eager to join in a syndicate to plunder beyond the line, to go after pirates, and even in a crisis to defend the realm. Elizabeth's naval expenses in 1570 averaged less than £10,000 a year; by 1586 the figure had increased to £32,000, the next year to £43,000 and in 1588 leapt to £153,000 – a year in which her revenues, augmented by exceptional measures like forced loans, reached £392,000, and yet £120,000 of this was needed for the army in the Netherlands. Philip II had his American gold and silver, which in time devalued all Europe's currencies, but Elizabeth had to be cheese-paring or she would have gone under.

168

The English sea dogs were confident that they could rout the Spanish if only the Queen would let them put to sea. 'There is now a very great gap opened, very little to the liking of the King of Spain. God work it all to His Glory', wrote Drake, itching to be afloat. He had in mind to make another raid on the Spanish Main, but the government wanted him near at hand. Another plan was for a squadron to sail to the Peninsula in part to reconnoitre, but also to make an impressive display of English sea power; but this was abandoned for fear that the Armada might slip into the Channel when the fleet was at half-strength. By Christmas 1586 it was decided that the immediate danger was over but preparations were made to have the entire fleet mobilized in three months' time 'to impeach the provisions of Spain'. The plans were kept secret and not until the beginning of March did it become known that Drake was to take command.

His fleet of twenty-three sail, with 2200 men aboard, was the strongest force Elizabeth had yet sent to sea. There were four of the Queen's men-of-war headed by the *Elizabeth Bonaventure* in which Drake again flew his flag. The vice-admiral, who commanded the *Golden Lion*, was William Borough, Clerk of the Queen's Ships, a man relatively inexperienced afloat. Lord Admiral Howard provided a war ship and a pinnace and the Levant Company furnished seven large vessels under Rear-Admiral Robert Flick. Drake himself subscribed four ships, the largest being the *Thomas*, a

Alvaro de Bazan, Marquis of Santa Cruz (left), and Alexander Farnese, Duke of Parma, were appointed to command the combined naval and military expedition against England. Santa Cruz died in February 1588 and the Duke of Medina Sidonia replaced him.

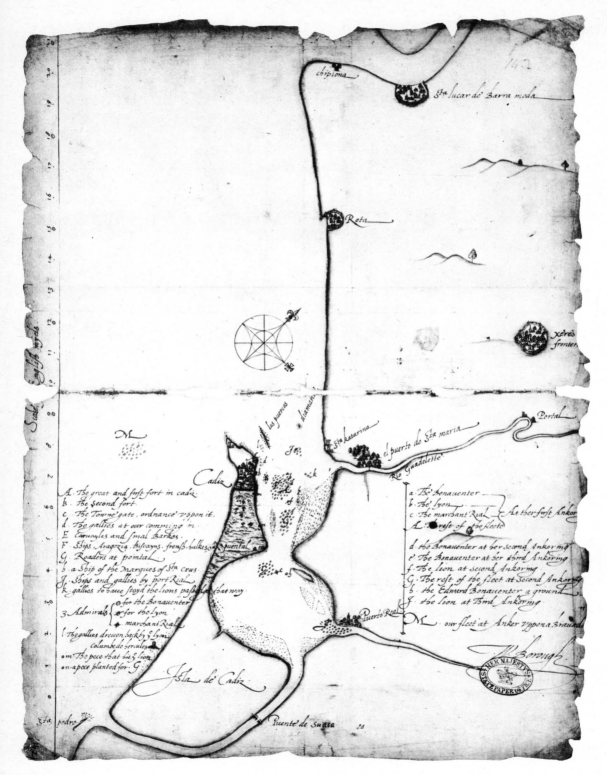

chipiona

Sta lucar de Barra meda

Rota

xéres fronter

las puertas   de la mar...

Cadiz

Sta katarina

el puerto de Sta maria

Portal

Rio Guadelette

A. The great and first fort in cadiz.
b. The second fort
c. The Towne gate, ordnance vppon it.
d. The gallies at our comming in
E. Caruoyles and smal Barkes.
F. Ships Arageza, biscayns, frensh, hulkes, & puental
G. Roaders at pointal
b. a Ship of the marques of Sta crus
J. Ships and gallies by port Rial
k. gallies to haue stoyd the lions passage that way

3. Admirals { ○ for the Bonauenter
              ○ for the Lyon
              ● marchant Rial

l. The gallies dreuen back by ȳ Lyon
   columbe de hercules
○m. The pece that sank lion
n. a pece planted for G

a. The Bonauenter
b. The lyon
c. The marchant Rial   At ther first Ankor
A. The rest of the fleete

d. the Bonauenter at her second Ankoring
e. The Bonauenter at her third Ankoring
f. The lion at second Ankoring
G. The rest of the fleet at Second Ankoring
h. the Edward Bonauenter a ground
J. the lion at Third Ankoring

M. our fleet at Anker vppon a brauada

Puerto Real

Borough

Isla de Cadiz

Sta. pedro

Puente de Suaca

170

privateer of 200 tons. To finance the operations, a special syndicate was formed and each shareholder expected to receive a rich return on his money. The object of the expedition was 'to prevent or withstand such enterprises as might be attempted against Her Highness' realm or dominions', especially by hampering Philip's admirals from concentrating in one port the squadrons being made ready in different harbours for the enterprise against England. If the Armada was already on its way to northern waters, Drake was to go into the attack and then cut off its supplies. He was also under orders to capture the trading fleets returning from both the West and the East Indies. As requested, he was specifically empowered 'to distress the ships within the havens'. Then, as so often, the Queen had second thoughts. Perhaps, if Philip II were not provoked too far, he might still be prepared to negotiate and so she decided to curb Drake's freedom of action. A messenger was to ride to Plymouth with revised orders, emphasizing that he was not to enter any Spanish harbour, nor to undertake warlike acts inside Spanish territorial waters. Sir Francis knew his sovereign; she was liable to change her mind and, since his original instructions were all that he had wished, he left on 2 April, to take advantage of fair weather. As he sailed he sent Walsingham a letter: 'The winds command me away. Our ship is under sail. God grant we may live in His fear as the enemy may have cause to say that God doth fight for Her Majesty as well abroad as at home' – a reference to the execution of Mary, Queen of Scots, and the rounding up of Jesuit priests. 'Pray unto God for us that He will direct us in the right way; then we shall not doubt our enemies, for they are the sons of men.' Drake was only just in time for the next day the Queen's messenger arrived in Plymouth. A natural son of John Hawkins was sent out with the despatch in a fast pinnace but by a happy device he failed to deliver it to Drake, making the excuse that a sudden gale had made it impossible for him to reach the *Elizabeth Bonaventure*. When the news of Drake's subsequent triumphs came to the Queen's ears, she must have been supremely thankful that her countermanding orders had been sent too late.

Off Cape Finisterre a gale scattered the fleet which could not resume company until 16 April off Lisbon, where Santa Cruz was assembling his Armada. Rather than attack Lisbon, Drake decided to sail on with his fastest ships to Cadiz where, he understood, there were many other galleons. Three days later, he was ready to attack the port. He called Vice-Admiral Borough and the other captains to the *Elizabeth Bonaventure* to give them their instructions, but deliberately refused to let them discuss his plans at a formal council of war, as was customary. Borough, a stickler for tradition, protested, saying it was the height of rashness for Drake to sail into Cadiz harbour, since no one knew the exact state of the port's defences. At least, he added, wait until after dark and even then follow the usual conventions of naval warfare by sending a proper challenge to the enemy. Sir Francis cared nothing for such out-dated practices and despised his vice-admiral's timidity. That afternoon the fleet entered Cadiz to take the Spaniards by

OPPOSITE A plan of the attack on Cadiz signed by William Borough, Drake's vice-admiral, who tried to dissuade Drake from making the daylight raid on the port.

surprise. Two galleys from the far side of the outer harbour came out to investigate, but Drake crippled both of them. He saw some sixty vessels, many of them without crews, most of them without a sail hoisted. Those ships that could possibly move to the safety of the inner harbour or across to Port St Mary cut their cables; the rest fell victims to the English onslaught to be sunk, burned or taken as prizes. Resistance was negligible. Drake anchored for the night out of range of the town guns, but instead of quitting Cadiz at first light, as Borough hoped, laid his plans for devastating the inner harbour, for here he had espied the galleon belonging to the Marquis of Santa Cruz himself.

At dawn, on the flood tide, Drake led a flotilla of pinnaces into the inner harbour to complete his work. He gutted the admiral's great ship, pounded a number of other vessels and then withdrew to the relative safety of the outer harbour, where the main fleet had meanwhile been revictualling. By midday he was ready to sail, but the wind dropped completely. After so great a *coup*, in which he had captured six vessels laden with provisions and destroyed thirty-one others together with a vast amount of stores, worth little less than a million pounds, it was no time to lose his head. The Spaniards moved guns down to the sand hills, sent in two galleys to attack and launched a number of fire ships which were carried by the tide towards the English anchorage, yet the fleet proved impregnable and was able to warp its way to safety. When he saw the fire ships Drake remarked in high spirits, 'The Spaniards are doing our work for us by burning their own ships'. Then at 2 am the long-awaited wind came from the land and Drake was able to lead his fleet safely past the galleys and the harbour guns. 'We came out of the Road of Cadiz on the Friday morning with very little loss – not worth mentioning.' They anchored in safe water, in full view of the town they had laid waste, challenging the Spaniards to come out and fight and then Drake opened negotiations for the release of prisoners taken in past actions.

In a calm off St Vincent Drake called his officers to his ship to announce they were going ashore to seize Sagres Castle on the Algarve, which would give the English fleet a foothold on the cape, both as a base for watering and repairs and to command the busy shipping route. Borough was nonplussed and, unable to convince his admiral that it was a foolish plan, he next day protested in writing at his lack of judgement no less than his lack of respect for naval councils of war and making much of the fact that such operations were not envisaged in the sailing orders. Borough concluded: 'I pray you take this in good part, as I mean it: for I protest before God I do it to no other end but in discharge of my duty towards Her Majesty and the service.' Drake was in no mood to overlook this attempt at undermining his authority and the questioning of his professional competence and so he promptly placed the vice-admiral under arrest in his own ship, the *Golden Lion*. He was convinced that Borough's example might otherwise have endangered the entire operation. Subsequently the crew of the *Golden Lion* mutinied to reinstate Borough in his command and the latter deserted the fleet to make for home. Drake had no alternative but to court-martial him in his absence and he was sentenced to death for mutiny and desertion; he was to go free.

Sagres Castle surrendered and the fortified monastery of St Vincent was then taken without any show of defence and those guns that were too heavy to be carried aboard the fleet were thrown into the sea. While Drake was ashore, the rest of the fleet cleared the sea of neutral vessels, including about fifty small caravels carrying staves for water-casks, which were fired. As a result Philip's Armada was to be desperately short of seasoned wood for keeping drinking water. Drake wrote to Walsingham, imploring him to see that at least six more of the Queen's second-rate vessels were sent to join his fleet, for then he would be able to 'bring this great monarchy to those conditions which are meet. . . . God make us all thankful again and again that we have, although it is but little, made a beginning upon the coast of Spain'.

The next target was to have been Lisbon, but he decided it was far too well fortified and in any case his fleet was becalmed. He saw seven galleys with their oars mounted, yet not one of them ventured out of harbour to attack him. Eager for action he sent a challenge to Admiral Santa Cruz, which a merchantman from Hamburg took into port, yet still the enemy would not come out and fight. Returning to St Vincent for water he heard that a great carrack from the East Indies was expected and so he set course for the Azores, ready to pounce. His fleet was battered by a gale and his own ship came near to foundering, while the Levant Company's ships were eager to be home. The admiral, however, would not give up the chance of a rich prize and sixteen days out from Cape St Vincent he came in sight of St Michael's in the Azores; as he approached more closely, he saw the outlines of a very large vessel. At dawn next day she was identified as the Portuguese carrack for which he was hunting, now sheltering in the lee of the islands. This was none other than the *San Felipe*, the property of Philip II himself and widely acknowledged as 'the greatest ship in all Portugal, and richly laden'. The English hailed her with cannon-balls and made short work of her. Drake put a crew aboard her and decided they would all return to Plymouth, rather than prolong the expedition. The capture of the *San Felipe* staggered Englishmen, when the great ship's cargo of silks, jewels and spices worth £114,000 was listed. 'It taught others', wrote Hakluyt, 'that carracks were no such bugs, but that they might be taken.' The remarkable wares she carried made known the extensive riches of the East Indies.

Drake's reputation was at its peak. 'The truth is', wrote a foreigner, 'he has done so much damage on these coasts of Spain alone, that although the King were to obtain a most signal victory against him, he would not recover one half the loss he has suffered.' Quite apart from singeing King Philip's beard at Cadiz and Sagres, he had stolen from him his personal carrack in the Azores. Queen Elizabeth was delighted with her own share of £40,000 of the prize money no less than with Drake's assurances that no Armada could sail for England that year.

Next year, however, would be different, for seers had long ago selected

1588 as a year of disaster and the portents were uncomfortably similar whether one turned to biblical numerology or to the stars. Some English mariners regarded the sudden death of the Marquis of Santa Cruz, whom Philip II had chosen as admiral to command the Armada, as a portent of doom. The Duke of Medina Sidonia, a thirty-eight-year-old grandee from Old Castile, was appointed in his place, although largely ignorant of naval warfare and a martyr to sea-sickness. He found the extensive preparations entirely inadequate, even allowing for the destruction which Drake had wrought at Cadiz. All that Drake heard of developments in Spain increased his anxiety for action. He was eager to be afloat again and told a Spaniard in London during December that the next Christmas he would celebrate

ABOVE The Duke of Medina Sidonia reluctantly accepted the command of the Armada on the death of Santa Cruz.

RIGHT Lord Admiral Howard of Effingham, who commanded the English fleet against the Armada.

victoriously in Portugal. As England's preparations for victualling the fleet and overhauling ships moved forward slowly, Drake and Hawkins were alarmed that Queen Elizabeth was taking at its face value Parma's concern to negotiate for peace. 'Our profit and best course is to seek our peace by a determined and resolute war,' they wrote. Parma, busily digging canals near the coast of Flanders and collecting flat-bottomed boats for the invasion of England once the Spanish grand fleet had gained command of the Narrow Seas, was in fact no less worried about the strength of his army than Lord Admiral Howard of Effingham about the state of the English fleet. Howard had been appointed by the Queen to command the fleet, with his squadron based on Queenborough to defend the Thames Estuary, while Drake in the *Revenge* was to see to the western approaches to the Channel and Lord Henry Seymour to patrol the Straits of Dover. The sea dogs urged that they should again descend on the Spanish coast, but Howard was cautious, fearing the Channel ports would be defenceless. Drake reported that his

An entry in the Privy Council register of April 1588 for the supply of 'provisions' to Sir Francis Drake, among them: 200 muskets, 1000 arrows for the muskets with tamkins (wads), 500 long pikes and 300 short pikes.

The *Ark Royal*, the flagship of the English fleet; a sixteenth-century engraving.

crews were in great spirits but their morale might suffer if they were confined to harbour, when they wanted to weigh anchor and see to 'the finishing of this great piece of work'. He went to London to explain to the Council the tactical advantage of putting to sea and the Queen gave way, authorizing further provisions.

At last Howard, flying his flag in the *Ark*, brought his fleet from Queenborough to join Drake's in Plymouth Sound, foreshadowing a marauding expedition, but the weather was unkind. By now Howard was convinced that Drake, whom he had appointed vice-admiral, was absolutely right in wanting to ravage the ports of Spain and Portugal and he told Secretary Walsingham 'how lovingly and kindly Sir Francis Drake beareth himself'. Howard had feared that the unruly sea dog might find it hard to play second fiddle, yet he was behaving most dutifully. When news arrived early in July that the Armada was at Corunna Drake wrote a memorandum, fully endorsed by Howard, giving instructions to leave harbour as soon as the stores were

176

aboard: 'My opinion is altogether that we shall fight with them much better cheap upon their own coast than here'. Ninety ships left the Sound on 7 July racing towards the Bay of Biscay on a fresh north-east wind to seek out the enemy. As they reached the north coast of Spain, the wind without warning shifted to the south and they had perforce to return home, arriving at Plymouth on 12 July, the same day on which Medina Sidonia left Corunna. It was a disappointment to be cheated of a certain victory by the fickleness of the wind, yet the expedition had been wonderful for morale. This swoop towards the enemy's coast at the eleventh hour has been justly described by Sir Julian Corbett as the most brilliant and daring expedition ever made by a naval commander. Back in port, they took on fresh water and stores, for the southerly wind that had forced them home was bringing the enemy daily nearer England. On 19 July the skipper of an English scout-boat sent news that some Spanish vessels were off the Scillies with their sails struck, waiting for stragglers. That night Howard and Drake brought their ships out of the Sound on the ebb tide, making use of warps, to anchor them in deep water and be ready for action.

At dawn on Saturday the twentieth, Howard brought fifty-four ships to leeward of the Eddystone Rocks and sailed to the south, to enable him, by working to windward, to double back on the enemy. Drake in the *Revenge* was positioning his eight ships to be ready to pounce on the Spanish rear. Late in the evening, he saw the enemy fleet which Medina Sidonia had formed into an enormous crescent, with the largest galleons at the points and flanks, the weakest in the middle. It was an imposing sight – this defensive formation of gigantic vessels 'with lofty towers, castle-like, in front like a crescent moon'. Majestically, this great armada of 132 vessels, thirty-two of them galleons and other first-line ships, moved up the Channel. Though the English had from the first won the weather gauge, they desperately needed to get into a position in which they could use their cannon effectively.

With Frobisher and Hawkins in company, Drake prepared to attack, selecting for their first victim the *San Juan de Portugal*, flying the flag of Vice-Admiral Juan Martinez de Recalde. The English gunfire threw his ship off course so that she forced the neighbouring *Nuestra Señora del Rosario* to foul the rigging of a third galleon. The *Rosario*, crippled by the loss of her foremast and bowsprit, fell astern. That night Drake swore that he would seize the laggard as his prize. After the Armada had been defeated, Drake faced criticisms for leaving his station to pursue the Spaniard; Frobisher especially was severe on him, calling it a traitorous act. At any rate, Howard was entirely satisfied with Drake's explanation and the Admiralty Court duly awarded Drake and his crew their prize money. (At a later stage of the action, Howard also left the line of battle to go after a prize.) To stop the rest of the fleet from following him, Drake had put out his poop lantern. On that dark night, the vessel which he thought was the *Rosario* proved to be a merchantman. Later he found his prey and though she was much more heavily armed than the *Revenge*, the Spanish commander

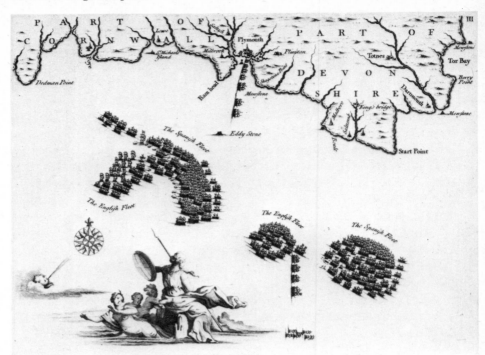

An Armada chart
showing the
Spanish and English
fleets off Eddystone Rock.

surrendered once he learned the identity of his opponent. He put some of his
men aboard the *Rosario* to take her into Tor Bay, while the commander and
several of his officers were transferred to the *Revenge* as prisoners of war.

There was a brisk action off Portland Bill early on 23 July and a much
greater battle, which lasted for many hours, south east of the Isle of Wight
on the following day, 'with great expense of powder and bullet' on both
sides. Despite overall superiority of fire power, the English could not succeed in sinking galleons. Medina Sidonia's crescent formation had proved
its value. Drake almost claimed another victim, but the wind dropped at the
vital moment and the *Gran Grifon* was safely towed off by a galleon to the
centre of the crescent. The running fight continued up the Channel for
another three days; both sides were getting short of shot, but Howard and
Drake could not break the enemy's defensive formation. The Spaniards came
to anchor in Calais Roads on Saturday 27 July to keep their rendezvous with
Parma. So far it was stalemate, but the English hoped that in confined
waters they would be able to command the initiative.

Medina Sidonia was dismayed that the Prince of Parma had insufficient
flat-bottomed craft to bring his soldiers, camped between Dunkirk and
Nieuwport, to the anchorage; and yet Admiral Howard could not bring his
ships safely within gunshot range of the enemy. At a council of war on the
Ark, it was decided to send in fire ships to wreak havoc in the Spanish
anchorage. Drake was the first to volunteer an armed merchantman that he
owned – the *Thomas*, a Plymouth ship of two hundred tons. Hawkins

The battle off the Isle of Wight on 24 July 1588.

followed by offering one of his vessels, and soon eight ships were speedily being filled with pitch, tar, dry timber and anything that would easily burn. The guns were left aboard but were double-shotted so that they would explode from the intense heat. Before midnight on the Sunday, these fire ships, lashed together, were carried by the wind and a strong tide on their mile-and-a-half voyage – pilotless phantom ships. The Spaniards had feared that the English would use such a weapon as the dreaded 'devil ships'. In utter confusion, the Spaniards cut their cables as the ships penetrated the cordon of fly-boats and pinnaces which protected the galleons. No galleon caught fire, but Medina Sidonia was forced out of his anchorage into the open sea, placing his fleet at the mercy of the English.

Soon after dawn, a battle began in earnest off Gravelines. Drake's squadron opened the attack by pounding the flagship, the *San Martin*, though she proved impregnable. For seven hours there was fighting at close quarters during which the English showed their superiority over their opponents in handling their ships in difficult water. Then, at 4 pm, the wind changed to the north-west and there was a blinding squall. Howard called off the attack and stood his fleet out to sea for the galleons which had survived the battle seemed certain of being driven on to the perilous lee shore of the Dutch sands. That evening Sir Francis wrote in high spirits to Walsingham: 'God hath given us so good a day in forcing the enemy so far to leeward as I hope in God the Prince of Parma and the Duke of Sidonia shall not shake hands these few days; and whensoever they shall meet, I believe neither of them will greatly rejoice at this day's service.' The general verdict on the battle was that of the Venetian ambassador in Paris, who reported, 'The English have shown that they are in fact the skilled mariners which rumour reported them to be, for while they have always been on the enemy's flank, they have not lost a single ship'.

The Spanish admiral was saved from disaster early the next day by the wind's backing to west-south-west, so he could move his fleet into the deeper water of the North Sea. He decided that if the wind changed again, he would fight his way back through the Straits of Dover and attempt to take an English harbour, to hold it for Parma; if, on the other hand, the wind stayed in the south west, he would have no alternative but to lead the remnant of the Armada home as best he could, sailing north through the North Sea and westward around the Orkneys and Shetlands and the west of Ireland. In the event, the south-westerly wind held and so he began the long hazardous voyage back to Spain (which he reached with sixty-seven vessels by 10 September). Howard and Drake gave chase with their squadron, but Seymour to his dismay was ordered to patrol off Dover. Howard and Drake still hoped to give battle as they followed in the wake of the great ships, but when the Armada had passed beyond the Firth of Forth, perhaps sixty miles from shore, they decided to give up the chase and return to the Downs. It was clear to the sea dogs that the threat from Parma was over for the present; at Tilbury Camp, however, where the main army for the defence of the realm waited with Leicester, uncertainty remained about the outcome of the naval

The Armada crescent off Calais; a contemporary engraving with portraits of the English captains.

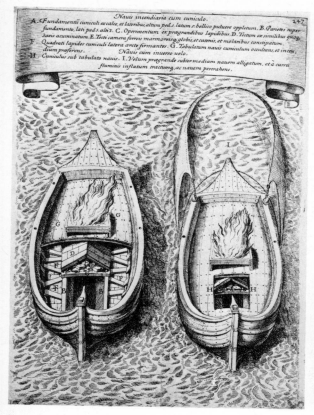

ABOVE Fire ships, filled
with pitch and dry
timber, forced the
Spanish to abandon the
safety of their anchorage
at Calais Roads; an
engraving from a
contemporary ship-
building manual.

RIGHT The resolution
signed by the English
commanders 'to followe
and pursue the Spanishe
Fleete untill we haue
cleared oure owne
coaste' and dated 1
August 1588.

battle and its effects on Philip of Spain's grand strategy.

The Prince of Parma, Drake wrote, was like 'a bear robbed of her whelps'
and to make him banish from his mind all thoughts of invading the realm, he
suggested a naval demonstration off Dunkirk, yet the Queen did not want
the emergency to last a day longer. It was only now she fully grasped that
the battle of Gravelines had been an overwhelming defeat for the Armada
and consequently became tetchy about the lack of plunder. She had already
sent an equerry to enquire among the fleet how much treasure had been
taken in the actions and why no Spanish ships had been boarded. Now she
summoned Howard to Whitehall, to order him to pay off the armed merchantmen. With the fighting over, the bickering in the fleet began. Frobisher had
been heard attacking Drake's reputation in the presence of John Hawkins
and others. In the fight, said Frobisher, the vice-admiral had behaved 'like
a cowardly knave' and now was saying that 'no man hath done as good
service but he'. What rankled with the Yorkshireman was Drake's prize, but
others were jealous of his rank as second-in-command – a second-in-
command, indeed, on whom the admiral relied so heavily that he had
'practically surrendered to him the command of the fleet'. Lord Seymour,
who always signed himself in his despatches 'Your Majesty's most bounden
and faithful fisherman', nursed a grudge. After the battle of Gravelines, he

had been ordered back to Dover when he felt that he should have been chasing the Spaniards in the North Sea.

Richard Hakluyt returned to England from Paris in the *annus mirabilis* 1588 to see through the press his topical account of the achievements of English navigators. While still a schoolboy he had come under the spell of his elder cousin, another Richard, who though a lawyer by profession had a scholar's interests in geography and the map of the expanding world. He showed his nephew 'certain books of cosmography, or universal maps' and much besides. After taking his degree at Oxford the younger Richard Hakluyt absorbed himself in all the printed account; of voyages and discoveries in many languages and began collecting globes, maps and nautical instruments. He may even have delivered the first series of public lectures in geography at Oxford. As we have seen, Humphrey Gilbert enlisted his aid to promote the English colonization of America and his first publication, *Discoverie of America* (1582), brought him to the attention of Lord Howard of Effingham. The following year Howard's brother-in-law, Sir Edward Stafford, took him as his chaplain when he began his embassy in Paris. Already Hakluyt was noted as being well acquainted with 'the chiefest captains at sea, the greatest merchants and the best mariners of our nation'. Secretary Walsingham gave him a special brief to seek out intelligence about French and Spanish achievements and future plans for colonial development – a congenial task – and in 1584 he completed *A Particular Discourse Concerning Western Discoveries*, which advocated English settlements in the New World. He presented a copy to the Queen together with a Latin exercise on Aristotle's *Politics* for intellectual stiffening, which secured for him the next vacant prebend in Bristol Cathedral. He edited Peter Martyr's *Decades*, adding much fresh material, and then translated into English the recently published journal of Laudonnière dealing with the French settlements in Florida. But it was the remarkable achievements of English mariners that he wanted to celebrate. While in Paris he had 'both heard in speech and read in books other nations miraculously extolled for their discoveries and notable enterprises by sea, but the English of all other for their sluggish security and continual neglect of the like attempts ... either ignominiously reported or exceedingly condemned'. He would be the chronicler of the sea dogs.

The Principall Navigations, Voiages and Discoveries of the English Nation appeared in 1589, dedicated to Walsingham, the constant supporter of English maritime endeavour in the Council, now nearing the end of his busy life. This roll-call of heroes was also a tract for the times, and, with its clarion call for greater endeavour, became a bestseller, like Foxe's *Book of Martyrs*, and has remained an epic work of English prose. The word 'nation' in the title, which recurs in the greatly enlarged edition of 1598–1600, speaks volumes. Thanks to the sea dogs, out of the crucible of the struggle with Spain the people of England were being forged into a nation and Hakluyt's book was a paean to nationalism. At the outset Hakluyt states the thrilling message that the subjects of the Queen 'in searching the most opposite corners and quarters of the world, and, to speak plainly, in compassing the vast globe of the earth more than once, have excelled all the nations and peoples of the earth'. He had hunted down the first-hand accounts of men such as Drake's chaplain, Francis Fletcher, and Francis Pretty, who accompanied Cavendish, turned up the journals and manuscript narratives of the less well-known voyages and talked to the survivors of expeditions, so that his anthology remains the prime source for the history of the sea dogs. Hakluyt made the average Englishman proud of this honourable record from which so much was to stem.

For which of the kings of this land before Her Majesty had their banners ever seen in the Caspian Sea? Which of them hath ever dealt with the Emperor of Persia, as her Majesty hath done, and obtained for her merchants large and loving privileges? Who ever saw before this regimen an English lieger in the stately porch of the Grand Signior at Constantinople? Who ever found English consuls and agents at Tripolis in Syria, at Aleppo, at Babylon, at Basra and, which is more, who ever heard of Englishmen at Goa before now? What English ships did heretofore ever anchor in the mighty river of Plate; pass and repass the unpassable (in former opinion) straight of Magellan, range along the coast of Chile, Peru and all the backside of Nova Hispania, further than any Christian ever passed, traverse the mighty breadth of the South Sea, land upon the Luçones [Philippines] in despite of the enemy, enter into alliance, amity and traffic with the princes of the Moluccas and the Isle of Java, double the famous Cape of Bona Speranza, arrive at the Isle of St Helena, and last of all return home most richly laden with the commodities of China, as the subjects of this now flourishing monarchy have done?

The same day that Medina Sidonia brought the remnant of his fleet back to Spain there returned to Plymouth a Suffolk gentleman of thirty-three, Thomas Cavendish, who had completed the circumnavigation of the globe. He had sailed with Grenville to Virginia and on his return began to prepare for his own expedition which he modelled on Drake's voyage round the world. Three ships left England in July 1586, the *Desire* of 140 tons, commanded by Cavendish, the *Content* and a bark, the *Hugh Gallant*. They sailed by the Barbary Coast and the Canaries to Sierra Leone, which they reached in a month. Here Cavendish burnt a native town and after a short stay in the Cape Verde Islands he set out for South America, reaching Brazil on the last day of October, to anchor at the island of San Sebastian where he provisioned, overhauled his ships and built a pinnace. From here he shaped his course towards the Strait of Magellan and on the way discovered a fine harbour in Patagonia almost as large as Plymouth Sound, he reckoned, which he named Port Desire after his flagship. As 1587 opened he was negotiating the entrance to the Strait. Each night he anchored close to the shore and was in constant danger of dragging his moorings. A Spaniard he rescued from starvation pointed out the hull of a small bark which they took to be the *John Thomas* abandoned by Drake nine years earlier.

EXTREMOS PVDEAT
REDIISSE

Cavendish took nearly seven weeks to pass through the Strait of Magellan, for the going remained tough. For many days they fed off 'musells and limpets and birds, or such as we could get on shore, seeking for them every day as the fowls of the air do'. Then on 24 February they entered the Pacific Ocean and followed the coast of Chile. Near Valparaiso the Spaniard, Hernado, was put ashore to talk with settlers but he rode off into the city and gave the alarm that another Drake was on the coast. A few days later while they were watering they were attacked by a large body of horsemen and lost twelve men. At Arica Cavendish burnt shipping and then intercepted several vessels making for Lima, one of which carried warnings to the viceroy about Cavendish's marauding. More profitable captures followed before they found a suitable beach at Puma Island in the Gulf of Guayaquil where the vessels were thoroughly overhauled. Francis Pretty described in his account of the voyage the splendid house of the governor of the island, with its old-world hangings of 'Cordova leather, gilded all over and painted very rare and rich'. Soon Cavendish decided he had insufficient men to handle the bark *Hugh Gallant*, so she was sunk near the equator. As he ventured north in the region of Guatemala, the pilot of a prize told him of the likely arrival in the near future of a great ship from the Philippines. He overshot Acapulco, the port in Mexico which would undoubtedly have been the destination of the galleon, and as there was no sign of her, he plundered various small towns and patrolled the coast.

At last on the morning of 14 November the look-out in the maintop of the *Desire* cried 'a sail'. This proved to be the *Great Saint Anna*, belonging to King Philip himself, which was commanded by the admiral of the South Sea. She was 'one of the richest vessels that ever sailed on the seas'. After a six-hour fight off Cape St Lucas in southern California the galleon surrendered to them and was taken into the harbour of Aquada Seguna for the sharing-out of spoils. The crew of the *Content* was near to mutiny since they felt they were being cheated of their due, but there was plenty of loot for each man, for the galleon carried 22,000 gold pesos and 600 tons of rich merchandise which was nearly ten times as much as the two English ships could carry. The Spanish crew was put ashore and the great vessel and the residue of her cargo burnt, though it hurt them all to see so much wasted, especially the dissatisfied men on the mis-named *Content*. Cavendish took as prisoners a Portuguese named Rodrigo who had lived in Canton and had with him a detailed map of China, a Spanish pilot who knew the Philippines, and five boys, two of them born in Japan, the others from Manila. In due course one of the latter was found a place in the household of the Countess of Essex.

Cavendish now decided to cross the Pacific and slowly make for England, but the men in the *Content* would not accompany him so he left them at anchor and they were not heard of again. The lone *Desire* touched at one of the Ladrones group of islands where the natives appeared no less fierce than when Magellan had paid his visit, and then began the difficult task of negotiating passages through the Philippines and the Moluccas. Thomas de

Ersola, the Spanish pilot, had written a letter intended for the governor of Manila betraying Cavendish, but when his treachery was discovered the man was hanged. By the beginning of March Cavendish was sailing along the coast of Java into the Indian Ocean and on the nineteenth sighted the Cape of Good Hope. He did not hug the African coast, for his next port of call was the island of St Helena, which provided much needed provisions. There is no reason to doubt that Cavendish was the first Englishman to land in St Helena. At last after a welcome respite, they began the long haul home and eleven weeks later were off the Lizard when a Flemish vessel hailed them to give news of the defeat of the Spanish Armada. In the final few days they experienced a terrific storm, which made some of the feeble-hearted think that the *Desire* would never reach port, but on 10 September 'like wearied men, through the favour of the Almighty, we got into Plymouth'.

For their entry to port, the *Desire* was dressed to display the extent of the booty, for she had damask sails, the top mast was covered with cloth of gold and every man was rigged out in silks. They had been away from Plymouth 780 days, 230 days less than Drake on his voyage round the world. Cavendish at once wrote a report of his adventures which he sent to Lord Hunsdon, the Lord Chamberlain, for conveying to the Queen, who was 'the most famous and victorious prince that liveth in the world'. In turn, after Drake's precedent, he brought his ship round to the Thames for Her Majesty to inspect, and she was anchored off Greenwich, though unlike the *Golden Hind* the *Desire* was not laid up for public exhibition but was refitted for a new voyage which Cavendish intended to make the following year. There were ballads and broadsides welcoming his return, but the celebrations were in a much lower key compared with the way Drake had been fêted. After all, to be England's *second* navigator to encompass the globe was of much less significance than being the first, and quite apart from Cavendish not having Drake's ebullient personality, by September 1588 England had something else to celebrate.

Lane, Hariot and White, who had returned from Roanoke with Drake in 1586, remained most enthusiastic about furthering English settlement in Virginia, this time in Chesapeake Bay. Raleigh now agreed with them that the shareholders in this 'third' colony should be principally those who were themselves prepared to settle. Privateering had become so profitable that it could no longer be expected that financiers would put up money for colonial developments which would at the best be a long-term investment, at the worst a swift disaster. Colonization itself was to be no longer the hand maiden of piracy in Raleigh's view. The new scheme proposed that each individual prepared to settle in Virginia should be assigned 500 acres as minimum holding and those who subscribed to the expenses of the expedition would receive additional land in the New World according to the level of their investment. The colony was to be reorganized as a company, which would have officials in London charged with ensuring that regular supplies were sent out. By Raleigh's charter of January 1587 the settlers were incor-

porated as 'the Governor and Assistants of the City of Raleigh in Virginia' and he appointed John White as governor; among the twelve assistants was Simon Fernandez.

In May three ships sailed, with White in the *Lion*, carrying 150 men, women and children prepared to seek a permanent home in Virginia. In the West Indies they traded for fresh provisions, cattle and plant cuttings, but Fernandez proved a liability to this peaceful commerce with the Spaniards for he was bent on hunting prizes. White and his Portuguese pilot were uneasy bedfellows and each day it became more painfully clear that Fernandez had enjoyed too long a record of privateering to change his spots. White felt that any naval engagements would terrify the women and children aboard and his quarrels with Fernandez took on a sharper edge when the latter nearly wrecked all three ships on Cape Fear through careless navigation. Now it was obvious that Fernandez did not contemplate becoming a settler himself after all his protestations to the contrary. They reached Port

On the return voyage Cavendish called at St Helena. He was the first Englishman to land there.

187

Fernandino on 22 July, hopefully to collect the fifteen men left behind from Grenville's party before sailing to Chesapeake Bay. The pilot argued that it was too late in the year to make for the Chesapeake and White, meekly giving way, agreed that they should re-establish themselves for the winter in Roanoke, which had its compensations, though they were rudely shaken to discover the skeletons of their old compatriots and to find the houses destroyed and the stores rifled. Then Indians killed one of the party who had gone out searching for crabs.

They were in better spirits by mid-August when White's daughter Eleanor, who had married Ananias Dare (one of the twelve assistants) gave birth to a daughter who was christened Virginia, 'because this child was the first Christian born in Virginia'. But the uncertainty of the future, particularly the attitude of the natives and the problem of supplies during the coming winter, cast a shadow. The settlers felt it fundamental that one of their number should return to England in the fly-boat, to organize fresh provisions, for not a man now trusted Fernandez to be mindful of their interests. The assistants chose John White himself for this task, largely because the presence of his daughter and granddaughter in Virginia would give them some hold over him. He was most reluctant to go, for he feared that for the governor of the settlement to desert them in their tribulations would be interpreted at home as an admission of failure. Only when the assistants had signed a document, dated 25 August, showing that he was their universal choice, would he agree to go. White left behind him a hundred and fourteen English settlers, seventeen of them women and eleven children.

White reached Southampton after a miserable passage and reported the

OPPOSITE Sir Walter Raleigh.

In 1587 John White arrived at Roanoke with 150 settlers; a contemporary engraving.

state of affairs to Sir Walter Raleigh, who undertook to send out a pinnace with supplies immediately and 'a goodly supply of shipping and men' would follow under Grenville the next summer. Alas, Raleigh's pinnace was prevented from sailing in the winter of 1587–8 by the general orders forbidding ships to leave harbour during the political crisis when invasion seemed imminent; and when Grenville was ready to leave Bideford in the spring there came an order from the Privy Council commanding him on his allegiance 'to forbear to go his intended voyage' and instead to be ready to serve the Queen against the Spaniards. He was, however, allowed to send supplies in any ships that Drake might not need in the defence of the west and White wheedled out of Sir Francis two tiny pinnaces which left late in April with fifteen new settlers and 'certain relief for those that wintered in the country'. White sailed in the *Rose* whose captain, Arthur Facy, was too ingrained a privateer to give up the chance of prizes, but a bark from La Rochelle got the better of him and he could only limp back to Bideford. White was at his wit's end: 'By this occasion, God justly punishing our former thievery of our evil-disposed mariners, we were of force constrained to break off our voyage'. Soon the other pinnace, the *Brave*, also abandoned the Atlantic crossing and John White could do nothing until the Armada emergency was over.

Early in 1589, through the energies of White and Hakluyt, the Virginian Company was reorganized, bringing in such people as William Sanderson and Thomas Smythe, chief customs officer at London, who were both to be prominent in the founding of the East India Company. A series of embargoes on the sailing of merchantmen prevented help from being sent to Roanoke until the middle of 1590, when the *Hopewell* and the *Moonlight* received permission to sail. They reached Port Ferdinando on 15 August, when White found Roanoke deserted, his books and maps spoilt and other goods looted. He still hoped to find the English party he had left behind and felt sure they had moved to Croatoan, fifty miles away, but heavy storms prevented the ships from attempting to reach the district. They would winter in the West Indies and have a further search in the spring, but again gales altered their plans. Soon hope evaporated and the young community which had produced Virginia Dare was being talked of as 'the lost colony'. White could not bear the thought of returning and, as he told Richard Hakluyt, 'wanting my wishes, I leave off from prosecuting that whereunto I would to God my wealth were unanswerable to my will'. Raleigh himself, thrown from favour, was in no position to try again. Whether the 'third colony' would have survived if the provisions *had* arrived in 1588 is conjectural, but it is clear that the coming of the Spanish Armada, and the fear of its return, killed off England's first colony in the New World.

The young Robert Devereux, Earl of Essex, now carried all before him at court. At eighteen he had been taken by his stepfather, Leicester, to the Netherlands and at Zutphen, where Sidney was mortally wounded, earned

Robert Devereux, Earl of
Essex.

191

his spurs and acquired a taste for martial glory. He could not abide Raleigh and when the Queen took the elder favourite's part in a quarrel he petulantly reminded her of what Sir Walter 'had been and what he was'. He ran away to the coast in his misery to find a boat to take him to Holland and a hero's grave, but Elizabeth had him escorted back to court and at Christmas 1587 appointed him Master of the Horse. Next summer he equipped a private company of *harquebusiers* and light horsemen in the Devereux livery to serve by the Queen's side at Tilbury Camp. He stayed in the limelight by staging the grand review of soldiers and sailors in the Whitehall tiltyard as a victory celebration. On Leicester's death Essex succeeded to his coveted position as the prime favourite and assumed it was his ordained right to be architect of England's great triumphs by land and sea. Had he not inherited Sir Philip Sidney's sword? With no maritime experience, his greatest assets for a command at sea were his courage and his magnetic personality, which made him a natural leader. But as with Raleigh, the opportunity of service afloat depended on whether the Queen would be prepared to let him go.

Since September 1588 the Queen had been under pressure from her sea captains to carry the war into the enemy's territory. The chance of destroying the galleons which had succeeded in limping back to Santander, San Sebastian and other ports for refitting was an opportunity, Drake and Hawkins agreed, that should not be missed. A single mighty swoop on the Spanish harbours would eliminate all future danger from Philip II, forcing him to seek peace. Elizabeth saw the force of her captains' argument but she was not able to bear the total cost of such an expedition. She much preferred the rival plan of sending out a small squadron to intercept the Spanish treasure-ships in the Azores for, if successful, this would at a stroke provide a rich return for her investment. Drake weaned her from this plan and instead persuaded her that the main financing of a voyage to the Peninsula could be delegated to a joint stock company. The Queen would, of course, be a major shareholder and would retain the prerogative of issuing the commanders with their instructions, but the bulk of the money would be subscribed by others. As a result of her enthusiasm for this plan the Portugal expedition was prepared and as early as 19 October, Drake and Sir John Norris were named as joint commanders. This put Lord Howard of Effingham's nose out of joint at being supplanted from the command of the fleet.

Sir Francis aimed at a complete annihilation of Spanish maritime power, as the climax of a lifetime's personal endeavour. His own company subscribed £5000, while the Queen advanced £20,000 and lent six of her 'second sort of ships'. In this combined operation by sea and land, England's Dutch allies were to provide transports for the soldiers. London merchants whom Drake had persuaded to put up money looked for considerable dividends from the plunder to be captured. Never had it been so easy to recruit soldiers and sailors so that in the end perhaps twice as many sailed in the fleet as had been originally intended, upsetting the victualling arrangements. Sir John Norris, commander of the land forces, was not just a favoured son of a warm

An · dñi · 1571 ·
Ætatis · svæ ·
· 29 ·

Sir Richard Granville, killed
in a sea-fight near the Azores.
1591

friend of the Queen, Lady Norris of Rycote, but a professional soldier of the first rank whom Drake had known in Ireland in years gone by. More recently 'Black John Norris' had served as colonel of the English volunteers who had come to the aid of the Dutch to fight alongside William the Silent, and of late he had won golden opinions for his leadership in the Netherlands campaign against Parma. He, like the admiral, was an innovator, and in the Portugal expedition, for the first time, an English army was organized on the regimental system.

The Queen tied the commanders to detailed instructions. They were first to destroy Spanish shipping in the Biscayan ports and then the fleet was to deal with the shipping in the River Tagus. If conditions in Portugal were favourable, they were to reinstate Don Antonio, the ex-King, who had been in exile in England for the past eight years, but if there was no hope of his restoration, the fleet was to proceed to the Azores and occupy the islands as a base for operations against the Spanish plate fleet. Men-of-war, armed merchantmen and transports numbered as many as 150 vessels in which perhaps over 23,000 men embarked. Drake again flew his flag in the *Revenge*.

The grand fleet forming England's armada was to have left on 1 April. The delays in sailing were, indeed, largely due to wranglings with the Dutch, whose aid in providing transports for the soldiers were so badly needed. In the end she had perforce to increase her share of the costs to £50,000. Essex desperately wanted to take part and so, disobeying the Queen's instructions, he had joined the expedition. Knowing she would refuse his special pleading he had slipped away from court and taken passage in the *Swiftsure* at Falmouth. First she sent Sir Francis Knollys to look for him at Plymouth, then Huntingdon was ordered to secure his return. It was too late, and the peremptory summons for 'immediate repair unto us' took two months to deliver:

Essex, your sudden and undutiful departure from our presence and your place of attendance [as Master of the Horse] you may easily conceive how offensive it is, and ought to be, unto us. Our great favours bestowed on you without deserts hath drawn you thus to neglect and forget your duty; for other constructions we cannot make of those your strange actions.

By the time he read this he had achieved his ambition to be in the thick of the fighting. The generals in Portugal, however, received another royal command for the young earl to be shipped home forthwith – 'if you do not, ye shall look to answer for some of your smart, for these be no childish actions'. Essex preceded the rest of the fleet to England and was forgiven as soon as he was back at court. The next large-scale expedition to the Peninsula would be under his command in 1596.

Against instructions, which had required him first to sack the ports in the Bay of Biscay, Drake began by attacking Corunna. Here he burned several ships and plundered the lower town, but the army failed to capture the more strongly fortified upper town. A store of wine on which the men had laid

OPPOSITE Sir Richard Grenville, killed in the Azores in 1591.

The port of Lisbon, 1592; an engraving by Hans Staden.

their hands proved to be their undoing. Having re-embarked his men, Norris was taken down the coast to land at Peniche, forty miles north west of Lisbon. It would have been more effective to have forced the entrance to the Tagus, but conditions were unfavourable. Yet all element of surprise had gone in Norris's march towards the Portuguese capital and it was a gruelling experience for the soldiers in intense heat. There was not the slightest show of support for Don Antonio's cause and the Cardinal Archduke, iron-handed governor of Lisbon, harried the inhabitants into defending the city. Drake had meanwhile bombarded Cascaes on the Tagus and here Norris embarked such of his troops as had survived sickness on the march. The only redeeming feature of the fighting was Drake's seizure of sixty small trading vessels from Hamburg.

Drake burned Vigo on the way home and despite sickness in the fleet was prepared to undertake further ravaging, but gales scattered the fleet and even the *Revenge* sprang a serious leak. It may be that as few as six thousand of the 23,000 men returned alive from the Portugal expedition, and the plunder and prizes were valued at a mere £30,000. The Queen was bitterly disappointed. The descent on Lisbon was an inglorious episode compared with the dogged fight of Gravelines and though Drake had done his best to follow his rigid instructions, once home he was accused of blunders and lack of judgement. Howard who had relied on him so heavily in the Armada campaign had been saved by not having the command at Lisbon and he did nothing to hide his private satisfaction that England's hero had fallen from his pedestal.

When she heard of the raid on Corunna, the Queen reminded Drake and Norris of their solemn promises that their 'principal action should be to take and distress the King of Spain's navy and ships in ports where they lay; which if ye did not, ye affirmed that ye were counted to be reputed traitors'. The opportunity of preventing a resurgence of Spanish sea power had been lost, prize money was negligible and English casualties were extremely heavy. Raleigh characteristically championed the commanders and said that if only the Queen had given them a free hand, Philip of Spain would have been reduced to 'a King of figs and oranges'; sometimes her instructions had shown the worst limitations of an armchair strategist, but for the mishaps of the 1589 expedition one must fairly blame the men of action. On their return, Elizabeth put on a brave face and publicly thanked Drake and Norris for their services: 'We cannot but acknowledge ourselves infinitely bound unto Almighty God in that it hath pleased him in his great goodness and mercy to bless your attempt' and she acknowledged that they had accomplished 'as much as true valour and good conduct could achieve'. The Queen had always been fond of the Norris family and so Sir John soon had fresh employment, but Drake, the scapegoat for the road that had fallen so flat, remained ashore for five years.

After the failure of the Portugal expedition Elizabeth would not countenance another expedition to the Peninsula and instead the sea dogs looked westwards. The Azores were to be the scene of several notable actions, some English successes and many disappointments, for they were on the route between the Caribbean and Spain that the plate fleets regularly took and they were also a staging post for ships bound for Lisbon from the East Indies. Hawkins was foremost among strategists in recommending that the English fleet should patrol the seas between the Peninsula and the Azores. In every sea dog's most optimistic moments he had only to hover with a squadron near the Azores to be assured of a rich prey. Englishmen underestimated the revival of Spanish sea power which the reverses of 1586–8 had stimulated. Philip II had launched a massive ship-building programme, so that his fleet was stronger than ever. Improved artillery and better training gave his seamen fresh confidence after the failure of the Armada campaign.

Some even said that they could be more daring and take greater chances against the English since they knew that Drake was kept ashore. In the months following the return of his battered armada, Philip II ordered twelve new galleons to be laid down in an 'Apostles' class and another nine ships of the second line were being built in Lisbon. At the same time, Pedro Menendez Marques, son of the admiral, designed at Havana a new, fast vessel, the *gallizabra*, which could carry bullion from the Caribbean to Spain without need of a string of escorts. The days of the slow plate fleet convoys were passing and with them the chances of easy prey. Just as Drake was improving the fortifications at Plymouth Sound, so every Spanish governor in the Americas was making sustained efforts to strengthen the coastal defences.

In March 1591 Lord Thomas Howard was ordered to sea with a squadron and Grenville was appointed his vice-admiral. At first it had been intended that Raleigh should be joint-commander with Howard, but it was doubted whether he and Lord Thomas could really co-operate. Howard flew his flag in the *Defiance*, while Sir Richard commanded the *Revenge*, which had been Drake's flagship in the 1588 campaign. Among the other first rates was the *Bonaventure* and the squadron was later reinforced by the *Golden Lion* of 500 tons and the smaller *Foresight*; the Earl of Cumberland was to command a squadron off the Spanish coast. There was 'the extremest fury of the weather' after they left Plymouth, which forced Lord Thomas to shelter in Falmouth though Grenville rode out the gale. The *Revenge* as a fast ship went ahead of the fleet, for no time was to be lost. Her first prize was a great hulk from Lubeck with masts and other naval stores bound for Spain, which was taken off the Burlings. For three months Howard and Grenville cruised in the region of the Azores and they prayed 'every day heartily for the Spanish fleet's coming'. Then reinforcements and provisions arrived from London with news that the flotilla would be protected by over twenty men-of-war, as well as the fleet coming out from Spain to meet it. Severe infection had broken out in the English fleet which meant sending home the *Nonpareil* with the worst cases, while others were put ashore in Flores and Corvo to recuperate. The remaining six men-of-war were 'rummaged', with the ballast cleared out and the entire vessels scrubbed out and disinfected. Howard planned to complete this very necessary operation before the enemy appeared on the western horizon.

The fleet from Spain under Don Alonso de Bazan arrived at Terceira in the Azores on 30 August to await the coming of the Mexican plate fleet and learnt that the English were at Flores and Corvo, lying to the extreme north west of the group of islands. A week later, taking advantage of a good easterly wind Don Alonso set his course for Flores, hoping to surprise the English. He was largely successful in this, because Grenville and Howard had been expecting the plate fleet from the west, not a strong squadron of warships from the opposite quarter. They scarcely had time to weigh anchor and Grenville was the last, for he insisted on picking up the ninety sick members of the crew of the *Revenge* who were on land. Howard tacked against the wind to get to windward of the approaching Spaniards (as the Lord Admiral and Drake had at the opening of the Armada campaign), but Grenville, being last in the line, would have been hard put to complete the manoeuvre and steer away from the enemy in time. Instead he decided to fight his way to safety through the two Spanish squadrons – a desperate chance, but one he felt he must take. His sailing master wanted him to turn from the enemy, but Grenville said such would be dishonourable to himself and his country. The *Revenge* passed the leading Spanish galleons, but then the *San Felipe*, the largest of the 'Apostles', came level and tried to board her. Caught under the lee of this monster of 1500 tons, the *Revenge* was becalmed, her empty sails flapped, the helmsman could not alter course and she became a sitting target. The enemy put a rope on her stern, but it parted after they had sent nine Spaniards aboard. The *San Barnabe* took over from the port side, another towering galleon, commanded by General Bertendona who had a personal score to settle with the *Revenge*, for Drake had forced him to fire his own ship at Corunna two years before. His grappling-irons held, and then another galleon was right on the *Revenge*'s poop. There was tremendous cross-fire at point-blank range with cannon, muskets and hand grenades well into the night. The Spaniards made many attempts to put their soldiers across in numbers, but they were repulsed again and again. The English men-of-war could do nothing to assist their isolated comrade and after dark it would have been foolhardy to have entered the fray.

'The Loss of the *Revenge*'; a nineteenth-century oil painting by O. W. Brierly.

The Spaniards could not believe the *Revenge* could survive that night of carnage, yet at dawn she was still unbeaten and had to her credit two Spanish ships sunk. Sir Richard had stayed on deck until 11 pm when he was injured by a musket shot and as his wound was being dressed the surgeon was killed beside him and the admiral received a serious head wound. He had begun battle with only a hundred able men, for the sick were lying in the hold, but there were soon heavy casualties which made the decks like a charnel-house – 'marvellous unsavory, filled with blood and bodies of dead and wounded men'. There were holes in the hull and by dawn six feet of water in the hold; most of the shot had been spent. Yet Grenville would not surrender. He ordered the master gunner to split and sink the ship 'that thereby nothing might remain of glory or victory to the Spaniards', and persuaded the residue of his crew that 'as they had like valiant resolute men repulsed so many enemies, they should not now shorten the honour of their nation by prolonging their own lives for a few hours'. (Those words are from the account which Raleigh pieced together by interviewing the survivors.) The other senior officers – the captain and the sailing master – disagreed with their admiral, knowing that the *Revenge* was so badly damaged that she could not long stay afloat, and so they arranged an honourable surrender. By then Grenville was unconscious from lack of blood or he would have had his way. All but the dead were conveyed to the Spanish galleons to be treated with great humanity, and Grenville died two or three days later from his wounds.

The *Revenge* did not long remain in enemy hands. The Spaniards had hoped as a matter of pride to sail her home to Cadiz, after essential repairs had been completed in the Azores, but a few days after Grenville's death there was a gale of cyclonic proportions while the Spanish were making for Terceira and she foundered, together with many of Bazan's fleet. 'So it pleased them to honour the burial of that renowned ship the *Revenge*', wrote Raleigh, 'not suffering her to perish alone for the great honour she achieved in her lifetime.' When it became known at home, Grenville's heroism, like Philip Sidney's before him, profoundly affected the nation. With the spirit exemplified at the fight off Flores in the Azores England would continue to meet the challenge from Spain. Grenville was essentially a sea dog's hero, but everyone who read Raleigh's narrative or heard the stirring tale of the last hours of the *Revenge* recognized that here was an unusual man. Only the Queen denigrated his gallantry, which she thought a crass waste of life.

8
PRIVATEERS
AND GENERALS
AT SEA

SPAIN HAD BEEN HUMBLED AT SEA and could, it was thought, be brought to her knees to sue for peace by relentless pressure from the sea dogs, whether commanding squadrons of the Queen's ships or fighting as lone privateers. Never had there been such intense, if at times dispersed, maritime efforts as in the years following Sir Richard Grenville's death. The greatest single prize of the century, the Portuguese carrack, the *Madre de Dios*, captured off the Azores in 1592, lured men on to take greater risks at sea, promoters to look for easy profits and hypnotized amateur seamen into thinking a privateering voyage was the surest way to a fortune. Raleigh was appalled at the ease with which letters of marque to go a-roving could be obtained: 'It is more than time that there be restraint of all shipping bound out to the seas; for there are multitudes going for the Indies. If any man be taken (as some every year are), the Queen's purpose will be frustrated.' Besides the new wave of privateering in the narrow seas and further afield, there was increasing optimism that with Philip II restrained the plate fleet would be an easy prey and that west of the line the Spanish colonial empire lay undefended and ripe for wholesale attack.

Raleigh had raced into print with his *Report of the Truth of the Fight about the Isles of Azores*, to glorify the name of his kinsman Grenville and declare his own undying hostility to Spain, the aggressor in Europe and disturber of the oceans. He was anxious to prepare for a further voyage himself to avenge Sir Richard's death and this time he fervently hoped to be allowed to sail. The Queen put up £3000 and two of her ships, including the *Bark Raleigh*, which she had bought from her favourite. There was backing from city merchants and the Earl of Cumberland had a greater stake than he could afford. Raleigh himself provided the *Roebuck* and as much ready money as he could muster. The original intention was to attack the Isthmus of Panama and intercept the plate fleet, but first the men-of-war were to sail down the Spanish coast to deal with any fresh armada that Philip might be launching. Raleigh was appointed commander, with Sir John Burgh as vice-admiral. With some difficulty he persuaded Elizabeth to let him sail, but she said he could only accompany the fleet as far as the Spanish coast, then he must return. They sailed from Plymouth on 6 May 1592, but the following day the Queen sent Frobisher ordering him to take over the command and to instruct Raleigh to return forthwith. He had no intentions of obeying, for he feared the Queen had now discovered his secret marriage with Bess Throckmorton, a maid of honour; there had been rumours enough before he sailed and if he could make some great *coup* at sea, the Queen's anger might be tempered. Raleigh ordered Frobisher to guard the Peninsula and Burgh to make for the Azores to await the treasure ships. Reluctantly Raleigh returned to England after a fortnight's absence, but though Elizabeth was indignant that he had not unquestioningly obeyed her command to return, it was not until the end of July that she was assured of his matrimonial folly and sent both husband and wife to the Tower.

Burgh's fleet, meanwhile, had been reinforced by six of Cumberland's

OPPOSITE George Clifford, Earl of Cumberland; a miniature by Nicholas Hilliard dated 1589.

privateers and although they found no sign of the *flota*, they met with two Portuguese carracks returning from the Indies. The *Santa Cruz* provided little loot after she had been driven ashore in the islands and set on fire, but the other vessel was the *Madre de Dios* which proved to be a fabulous haul. Gradually the English craft like Lilliputians made themselves master of this Gulliver, for she was a 1600-ton vessel and her seamen put up a very stiff fight. Once the English had boarded her, gone below and inspected the chests, coffers and bales it was as if they had been transported to Aladdin's cave. There were diamonds, chains encrusted with jewels and gold objects of rare workmanship; they feasted their eyes on crystal-ware garnished with gold and pearls, gold cutlery set with precious stones, elaborate collars, 'strings of pearls orient', gold buttons, rings and bracelets. Then there were considerable quantities of pepper, cloves, nutmeg, ginger and less common spices, drugs like camphor, benjamin and frankincense, musk and other perfumes, Chinese silks, damasks and taffetas, curled Cyprus cloth, Indian calicoes and lawns of many varieties, carpets, quilts and hangings of rare design and luxuriant texture. The inventory of what was still aboard the *Madre de Dios* when she was brought into Dartmouth, worth £150,000 in the currency of the day, continues with entries for 'elephants' teeth, porcelain, vessels of China, coconuts, hides, ebony wood as black as jet, bedsteads of the same, cloth of the rind of trees, very strange for the matter and artificial

The title page and an illustration from *The Mariner's Mirror*, the principal nautical manual of the period; it was first published in English in 1588 and dedicated to Sir Christopher Hatton.

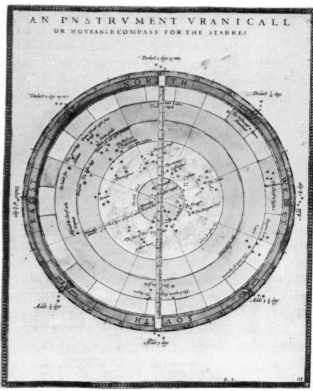

in workmanship'. Here were the riches of the east in abundance, yet from the moment she came into English hands considerable pilfering had been taking place and as the great ship neared the Devonshire coast some of the ships escorting her made a dash for port with assured pickings. Once in harbour droves of middlemen came to the quay to trick seamen out of their loot by offering ready coins of the realm and soon agents of London goldsmiths, jewellers and tailors were doing brisk business in the taverns.

As soon as the Queen heard of these 'privy dealings' she appointed commissioners to prevent further looting and to make strict enquiries for recovering as much as possible of the goods that had gone astray. Drake was the first commissioner to arrive at Dartmouth, but he could get no cooperation from the seamen, who thought that in looking to their own interests after so successful a capture they were merely treading in his own footsteps. Robert Cecil, another commissioner, hastened down from London, passing many packhorses smelling of cloves: 'Everyone I met within seven miles of Exeter that either had anything in a cloak, bag or malle which did but smell of the prizes at Dartmouth or Plymouth (for I could well smell them also, such had been the spoils of ambergris and musk among them) I did retain him with me to the town.' Drake persuaded Cecil and Richard Hawkins to report to Elizabeth that they could not fully carry out the terms of their instructions since it was 'an offence to God to put the seamen on their oath'. They succeeded in tracing some of the pepper, but sundry rich items of jewellery had been broken into small lots and passed into the hands of dealers long before they arrived in port. Elizabeth had already released Raleigh from prison to travel to Devon in the charge of a keeper to look to her interests as a principal share-holder in the voyage. The mariners cheered to see him again and congratulated him on his liberty. 'No, I am still the Queen of England's poor captive,' he told them and his detailed inventories, accounts and methodical calculations persuaded her to accept not less than £60,000, when the residue of the goods was sold, in return for the service of her two vessels that had been in the expedition. Cumberland did handsomely, being awarded £36,000, but Raleigh and John Hawkins fared pitifully, barely recovering their outlay. For once, perhaps, it was the ordinary rank and file seamen who made the capture that lined their pockets, though some were foolish enough in Devon to sell off porcelain dishes and the like for the price of a drink.

Cavendish planned to repeat his circumnavigation in 1591, largely to recoup his finances for his sudden wealth had been squandered 'in gallantry and following the court'. He intended to pass into the Pacific, sail to the Philippines and on to China. John Davys came with him as second-in-command, taking over the *Desire* that had been round the world, while Cavendish flew his flag in the *Leicester Galleon*. Davys wrote that he was 'only induced to go with Mr Cavendish upon his constant promise that when we came back to California I should have his pinnace (the *Desire*) with my own bark which went with me to my great charges, to search that north-west discovery upon the back parts of America'. The thought of the passage to Cathay still haunted him. They left Plymouth at the end of August and were off the coast of Brazil three months later. During the gales the ships became separated and it was not until the middle of March 1592 that they met at Port Desire – Cavendish's notable discovery – and prepared to negotiate the Strait of Magellan. But Cavendish was going to pieces; he had lost his power of commanding men and wished he had never set out. He feared the responsibility of taking his ship through the Strait and lamented that he were not

Port Desire discovered by Cavendish in 1586 and revisited by him in 1592; an engraving by de Bry, 1603.

in his old vessel, the *Desire*, with Davys making the decisions. This time the storms were much worse than anything he had experienced. After a gruelling month, when about half-way through the Strait, they anchored in a reasonably sheltered cove for many days, while Cavendish lived on board the *Desire* with Davys. He began to be melancholy and when his spirits improved proposed to make for the Cape of Good Hope, but Davys advised against this, saying he had 'so feeble a crew'. He then decided to return through the Strait and his companion reluctantly came with him, but the vessels lost contact one night. Cavendish persisted, with the *Roebuck* in company, and reached Brazil, but his health was failing as well as his mind. He died at sea, perhaps near Ascension Island.

Davys had returned to Port Desire to look for the *Leicester Galleon* and refit his vessel. Subsequently he made three further attempts at sailing through the Strait yet 'furious weather forced me back'. He was despondent at being cheated of the chance of searching for the passage. Much later he would learn of Cavendish's deathbed accusation that he had deserted him and such a charge shows how embittered and self-centred the circumnavigator had become. But Davys kept his head and was determined to stay fit in the face of a sick crew and the threat of starvation. Some of his crew deserted at Port Desire and could not long have survived. The captain provisioned his ship with 14,000 dried penguins to keep them going and the party he put ashore in Brazil to find food and water was massacred by the Portuguese. It was a desperate situation; as one of the crew recalled it, 'divers grew raging mad and some died in most loathsome and furious pain. It were incredible to write our misery as it was. There was no man in perfect health but the captain and one boy.' Only sixteen of the crew of seventy-six which had left England in the *Desire* returned alive and of these only five were able to move themselves in the last stages of the voyage. Somehow Davys brought the ship into Beerhaven in Ireland and after sleep and food sought passage in a fishing craft to Padstow. In time he heard of Cavendish's death at sea and was reluctant to go to law to recover the £1100 he had lost. No less of a blow to Davys was the behaviour of his wife Faith, for in his absence she had taken a lover. John Davys did not brood on his misfortunes. He had a dozen years of active life and (as we shall see) was to be one of the English pioneers in the East Indies, where he was hacked to pieces by Japanese pirates.

For George Clifford, third Earl of Cumberland, to be afloat provided a thrilling relief from gambling at court and from this experience he was able to embark on a successful career as a privateer, happily combining both these vocations. He had succeeded his father in 1570 when twelve and on coming of age wasted his inheritance. As a symbol of chivalry he always wore in his hat a glove which the Queen had once dropped, having emblazoned it with diamonds. (The portrait that Hilliard painted of him shows Cumberland wearing fancy dress over full armour, ready for the tilt, but the glove is there.) His daughter Lady Anne Clifford was to write of him 'applying himself to the sea and to navigation, especially towards the West Indies and those new found lands, wherein he became the most knowing and eminent man of a lord in his time'. His first expedition, 1586–7, had taken him through the Strait of Magellan, but the plunder had been negligible – a Portuguese craft with Negro women, friars and Catholic devotional wares, and then a little sugar taken from the coast of Brazil.

Two months after the Armada campaign Cumberland set out in the *Golden Lion*, lent by the Queen but fitted out at his own expense. The loss of his mainmast in a gale prevented him from exploiting his captures, but he was eager to try again the next year with a larger expedition in the *Victory*;

209

William Monson came as his vice-admiral and his crew mustered 400. After ten days at sea they met with some of the scattered English fleet returning from the Portugal expedition who were desperately short of provisions so Cumberland relieved them and then made for the coast of Spain to seize no fewer than sixty-three small Hanseatic craft carrying spices. Then he stood over towards the Azores and at St Michael's captured vessels by a bold ruse; at night he went out in the ship's boat to cut the cables of each in turn, and tow them away. Later on luck turned against him, for though a richly laden ship from the West Indies was taken and placed under Captain Lister with an English crew she foundered near to home, in Mount's Bay, Cornwall, and all aboard her were drowned. Before then Cumberland had the worse of an engagement with a Spanish vessel anchored under the castle at St Mary's in the Azores, when he again went out in boats to drag it away. Most of his men were killed, the rest wounded including Cumberland himself who had a shot in his left side, his head badly cut and his legs scorched by grenades. The survivors reached their ships but it was touch and go whether they would make an English harbour for they ran out of fresh water. Cumberland rationed each man to a few spoonfuls of vinegar mixed with rain water and did his best to stop the foolhardy drinking salt water.

These experiences did not cure Cumberland of the life afloat. In 1591 he was again in a privateering foray in Spanish waters, for which the Queen had lent the *Garland*. Fond of his bizarre ways she wrote him a cheeky note, mocking the formal phrases of her letters patent: 'Right trusty and well-beloved cousin, we greet you well. It may seem strange to you that we should once vouchsafe to trouble our thoughts with any person of roguish condition ... but such is our pleasure at this time as we are well content to take occasion by our letters to express our great desire to learn of your well-being ... hoping well of good success in the action now you have in hand'. (Naturally! Elizabeth was a prominent shareholder.) She asked him playfully not to let the Knight Marshal of the royal household know of her solicitations or he would think she favoured men whose misdemeanours ought to be firmly corrected. This was something of a private joke, because the Knight Marshal was not only the disciplinary officer at court but also the individual who recorded wagers and would know exactly what sums the gambling earl owed to different courtiers. Elizabeth assured him of her concern for his safety at the seas and looked forward to his return, 'whereof we shall be right-glad as any friend you have'. That particular trip, however, was an unrewarding one, for Captain Monson was taken prisoner by the Spanish. Next year at the end of a profitable voyage (as we have seen) some of the earl's ships took part in the attack on the *Madre de Dios*. The Queen now regularly took shares in his expeditions, but prohibited him from laying any vessel alongside the enemy for fear of her being fired. In 1593 Cumberland in the *Golden Lion* became separated from the rest of his squadron and met with twelve Spanish hulks off the Peninsula. When they refused his order to lower their flags in respect of the Queen's ensign he took on all twelve, made them submit and

OPPOSITE Hilliard's portrait of the Earl of Cumberland wearing fancy dress over his armour; in his hat he wears the Queen's glove.

secured a great quantity of ammunition from them. The earl was not himself present at the fight in 1594 when two large carracks, bigger, men said, than the *Madre*, were attacked for a whole day by three of Cavendish's ships – 'like three good English mastiffs upon the Spanish wild bull'. They fired the *Five Wounds of Christ*, but her captain refused to surrender and all aboard, including a number of women, jumped into the sea. Nor would the *San Felipe* surrender a fortnight later, as her captain explained: 'I was at the taking and burning of the *Revenge*, the Queen of England's. Let him [the English admiral] do as much for his Queen; I will do as much as I can for my King.' After dark the brave Spaniard succeeded in making off. Reports of the failure to capture the two great carracks persuaded Cumberland to build an enormous man-of-war of his own. At 900 tons it was the largest vessel by far ever built by a subject and the Queen was so delighted that she asked the owner to name her the *Scourge of Malice*.

Cumberland led his last and largest expedition in his new vessel in 1598, but though he laid waste Lancerota in the Canaries and took Puerto Rico, there was little to show for the expenses of the voyage. Its merit lay in preventing the sailing of the treasure ships from the New World. The earl was not a professional mariner of the calibre of a Drake or a Frobisher, yet he was very far from being 'a courtly seaman', that term of abuse that the sea dogs used for rank amateurs. An incident on the last leg of his final voyage shows Cumberland's intuition in making the right decision when there were conflicting views about the ship's position. In the evening he ordered soundings to be taken and from the depth reached on the line, and the sample of the sea's bottom sticking to the tallow on the lead, he reckoned he must be entering the English Channel, but there was an argument whether they were near the French coast or the English. The sailing master was sure on his reckonings that they must be approaching the Scillies, and though the earl disagreed with him he let him continue to steer his course of north-east-by-east for the present, but saw to it that further soundings were taken. Scallop shells sticking to the tallow on the lead could not convince the sailing master they were near the French shore so he held his course. 'His lordship about midnight absolutely commanded otherwise and gave instruction to sail a more northerly course, which the event showed was the saving of us all from utmost danger. For the next morning very early we saw land and quickly it was made [out as] Normandy, so that clear it is that when we began to alter our course we were exceeding near Ushant and the rocks, upon which if we had fallen in the night there had been very little twixt us and death.' The great ship, the *Scourge of Malice*, he had saved from destruction was to be sold before long to the new East India Company. If Humphrey Gilbert was a man 'of no good hap at sea', the Earl of Cumberland was the very opposite. Almost alone of the English sea dogs he died on dry land. Despite his many successes he never balanced his books and, for all his persistent efforts and undiminished optimism, he never found another *Madre de Dios*.

Drake was itching to be afloat again, but he had to live down the ignominy of the Portugal expedition. He was too rich to want to take part in run-of-the-mill privateering himself, but looked for a royal command so he might come to grips with the wider problems of national defence and sea power. In November 1592 he was suddenly called to court 'about some sea service' to discuss grand strategy with Lord Thomas Howard and Martin Frobisher, and 'carrieth it away from them all'. The next New Year's Day he presented the Queen with a personal narrative of his raid on Nombre de Dios twenty years earlier, finely bound. This was not an old man reliving the marvellous adventures of his prime, but a composition intended to spur Her Majesty into employing him again. He was, he wrote, not 'setting a sail for maintaining my reputation in men's judgement, but only as sitting at helm, if occasion shall be, for conducting the like actions hereafter'. The old magic worked. Occasion there would be, and there was talk of a fresh expedition to Nombre de Dios, to lead an army across the Isthmus to capture Panama. Then Elizabeth had second thoughts. If Philip should launch another Armada against England, while Drake and his grand fleet were in distant waters, the island would be defenceless. Moreover the Spaniards with a foothold in Brittany, in their campaign against Henry of Navarre to win the French succession, were striving to attack Brest, and if Brest fell the English command of the Channel would be threatened as never before. Thus the plan for sending a fleet to the Caribbean was shelved. In operations against the Spanish in Brittany the next year Martin Frobisher was killed.

At last, in January 1595, Drake and Hawkins were jointly commissioned to undertake a large-scale raid in the Caribbean to 'offend our capital enemy, the King of Spain'. It was because the Queen could not now implicitly trust Drake that she harnessed him with Hawkins. As Thomas Maynarde, who sailed with them, put it, since Drake had habitually acted 'as a child of fortune, it may be his self-willed and peremptory command was doubted'. John Hawkins, long past his prime and latterly broken by misfortune, now found himself serving with his cousin for the first time since that memorable fight at San Juan de Ulua in 1568. It was not on the face of it a happy partnership; yet the news that Drake was to sail again had an electric effect on Plymouth and beyond. Men came to volunteer their service under him, as seamen or soldiers, in such numbers that the press-gang was unnecessary.

Drake still hankered after his scheme for sacking Panama and holding it as an English stronghold, but Elizabeth could not make up her mind. She feared England would be defenceless. Let them first sail to the Spanish coast to destroy any galleons they met with and to keep a sharp look-out for the plate fleet, before they left for the Indies. Moreover, they must solemnly undertake to be back in Plymouth by May 1596. The commanders had been assembling their forces in the Sound on the understanding that they were to engage in amphibious operations in the West Indies, for which they had been recruiting soldiers and hiring transports; yet now their Queen was altering the entire plan of campaign, with talk of naval battles off the Peninsula and

213

In July 1595 four Spanish galleons entered Mount's Bay in Cornwall and attacked the surrounding villages; an early sixteenth-century chart of the bay.

hunting for the plate fleet. Since Elizabeth was providing six of her best warships, including the *Garland* and the *Defiance*, and was investing £30,000 in the operations, it was imperative to retain her goodwill. While they assured her of their readiness to spend their lives in her service, they told her that she was expecting the impossible, for their fleet was not fitted to execute the revised plan. If at this late stage she wanted to launch an expedition against a mighty enemy fleet and go hunting for prizes, then she must bear the whole cost of it herself and her commanders would do their utmost to reorganize their forces to suit such operations.

The commanders shrewdly sought the support of young Essex, the Queen's favourite, in pleading their case and 'if Her Majesty do alter our first agreement, you stand strongly for us'. Thanks to the earl's intervention, Elizabeth ruled that they need not visit the coast of Spain, but she would not retract over the time-table – they must be back in port by May 1596; and, as if the delays in departure were solely due to them, she chided them for being laggard. When they replied that the date of their return depended on God's blessing, she reprimanded them for calling on the Almighty to cover up 'an uncertain and frivolous answer'. Intelligence reaching Spain that Drake was preparing to leave with a large fleet provoked heavy desertions; there was a general evacuation from Lisbon where the inhabitants feared another raid. '*El Draque*' was the devil incarnate for simple folk in the Peninsula.

The fleet would have sailed at the end of July, but for a sudden panic in the West Country. Four Spanish galleons from Brittany came into Mount's Bay in Cornwall to land six hundred men who proceeded unopposed to lay

214

waste the villages of Mousehole and Newlyn and the town of Penzance, firing houses and churches. Some feared a large-scale invasion, but it was soon obvious that this was no more than a side-show, and when the Spaniards learned that Drake's fleet had not yet sailed, they rapidly returned to their base in Brittany. Even now the voyage was in danger of being cancelled, but Drake and Hawkins suddenly had news that a lone galleon of the Mexican plate fleet, laden with bullion perhaps worth 2,500,000 ducats, had been forced to shelter in Puerto Rico and it would take longer for her to be repaired than for the English to reach her. They sent word to the Queen that the crippled treasure-ship 'lieth in our way and will in no way impede us' and this letter with its promise of booty swung Elizabeth round to grant permission to sail. Drake and Hawkins left Plymouth Sound on 29 August with a crowd cheering from the Hoe and guns signalling 'Godspeed'. Neither would see England again.

This was a far stronger fleet than Drake had taken to the West Indies in 1585, for besides the Queen's six warships there were twenty-one heavily armed merchantmen, manned by fifteen hundred seamen, and a force of a thousand soldiers under Sir Thomas Baskerville, who had won honours in the Brest campaign. Sir Thomas Gorges, who had ridden to Plymouth as the Queen's messenger, reported at court that the two admirals 'do agree very well', but such was wishful thinking. They made an ill-assorted pair and, effectively, Hawkins in the *Garland* and Drake in the *Defiance*, commanded separate fleets. The younger man was impatient and confident of his superiority, the other cautious and ill at ease. Hawkins, wrote Maynarde, was 'old and wary, entering into matters with so leaden a foot that the other's meat would be eaten before his spit could come to the fire'. Drake required all vessels under his command to hold divine service twice daily, to forbid gambling and to keep to their proper stations in company. At a council of officers off Cape St Vincent, the two commanders nearly came to blows. Hawkins wanted to make straight for Puerto Rico, but Drake was determined to attack Las Palmas in the Canaries, to boost morale and obtain extra provisions because, as so often, he had overmanned his fleet. After much argument, Drake had his own way.

They came to anchor at Las Palmas on 26 September to the west of the harbour, not far from the fort, but too heavy a sea was running to put the soldiers ashore that day and thus the element of surprise was lost. For four days, Baskerville tried to take the fort but found it impregnable; here, as also in the West Indies, as Drake would discover, the Spanish defence system had been vigorously strengthened. He now sailed round to the lee side of the island where his ships took on water undisturbed, but a party which penetrated too far inland was captured and betrayed the destination of the fleet. This was a miserable beginning to the enterprise, and the ill luck held. By the end of October all but two of the ships were at Guadaloupe to water, prepare their launches and pinnaces for landing and mount the extra guns. The day after their arrival, however, five Spanish *gallizabras* came into

215

sight. They had been sent out from Spain to bring home the treasure from the damaged vessel that had taken refuge at Puerto Rico. This was an unwelcome sight, for the Spaniards captured one of the laggard armed merchantmen from Drake's flotilla and chased the other one into the anchorage. The enemy could assess the strength of the English expedition lying in harbour and left at once for Puerto Rico to give timely warning of the coming attack. Drake was anxious to give chase, but Hawkins obstinately resisted and by now Drake could see that his cousin was seriously ill.

They left for the Virgin Islands where their ships could lie hidden while they prepared for action. Baskerville exercised the troops ashore while Drake scouted for fresh passages between the islets that could take the fleet to Puerto Rico. Thanks to his careful survey, his ships were able to arrive unheralded, weaving their way through unconventional channels to anchor in a sandy bay to the east of the town. Yet the Spanish had reinforced the defences with many additional cannon, and extra troops had been sent to beat off any attack on the citadel where the treasure lay. As the English fleet anchored, with the guns from the fort blazing, John Hawkins died, having in his last hours begged Captain Troughton to assure the Queen of his continued devotion to her service and of his despair at the ill success attending this, his last venture. To atone for his responsibility in persuading her to send the expedition, he would ask her to accept a legacy of £2000. Troughton said of his friend, dying in the *Garland*, that he had become struck down a fortnight before through grief at the failure of the voyage and in his weak state of health, as he brooded on this, the burden became intolerable for him.

Even if John Hawkins had died, this was no time for lamentation. Already a shot from the shore batteries had crashed through the cabin of the *Defiance* where the officers were at supper and Drake had his seat shot from under him, while two comrades, Sir Nicholas Clifford and Brute Brown were mortally wounded. 'Ah, dear Brute', Drake exclaimed as his friend sank to the deck, 'I could grieve for thee, but now is no time for me to let down my spirits.' In the face of disaster, he remained calm, moving all the fleet out of range of the enemy's guns, and from a pinnace looked for a likely landing-place. That night, Baskerville led in his men but the defences were too strong for them and after an hour of heavy casualties they were forced to withdraw. Drake still did not give up the attempt and moving his ships outside the harbour next day, planned a further attack, keeping up the spirits of his men. The Spanish admiral, as a desperate move, had sunk two frigates to block the entrance and at a council of war Drake reviewed the situation. Some of the younger officers were convinced that Puerto Rico was easily worth a further attempt in view of the treasure it contained, but Drake grandly told them, 'I will bring you to twenty places more wealthy and easier to be gotten'. No man disputed this claim and so they left by night to find an isolated spot for watering and repairing damage. With Hawkins gone, he was at last his own master. He was determined once more to sack Panama and on the way he

OPPOSITE Sir John Hawkins; an early seventeenth-century engraving. For both Hawkins and Drake the 1595 expedition was to be the last. Hawkins died while the fleet unsuccessfully attacked Puerto Rico.

216

IOANNES HAWKINS

Advancement by diligence

would revisit the ports of the Main which he knew better than any man.

He sacked Rio de la Hacha, the scene of the earliest reverse of his career; this settled a personal score and also helped improve the morale of his men. Though the inhabitants had hidden all their valuables, the English were able to discover most of them and while the soldiers under Baskerville roamed the neighbouring villages, Drake raided the headquarters of the pearl fisheries and bargained with the citizens of Rio for a ransom. Since the governor would not treat with him, Drake razed the town to the ground, sparing only two buildings, the church and the house of a lady who had implored mercy. Two days later, he took Santa Maria, though nothing of value was found, for it had· been warned of the English approach, and then Sir Francis decided that Cartagena was too strongly held to be taken.

Two days after Christmas, Nombre de Dios fell to Drake for the second time and Baskerville began leading his men on the perilous march in pouring rain towards Panama. After three days of marching, however, he was forced by a well-armed Spanish force to retreat and returned with less than half his men to the ships. Drake was scarcely able to hide his depression. 'Since our return from Panama,' noted one of his company, 'he never carried mirth nor joy in his face.' Yet he pulled himself together and at a council of war unrolled a chart to point in turn to Truxillo in Honduras and the forts on the Nicaraguan coast. Which should be their objective? 'Both! One after the other,' cried Baskerville, as confident as ever in his admiral, and Drake nodded assent; here indeed was a man after his own heart. They set sail, but contrary winds forced them to come to anchor by the isle of Escudo de Veragna in the Mosquito Gulf, to the west of Porto Bello, and here they tarried, waiting on the wind. It was a pestilential place and men went down like flies from dysentery and fever. This was certainly not the 'delicious and pleasant arbor' of the Indies, as he remembered it, but he would not admit defeat, would never reproach himself that his judgement had been at fault or that it would be impossible even now to retrieve his reputation. 'God hath many things in store for us,' he said, 'and I know many means to do Her Majesty good service and to make us rich, for we must have gold before we see England.' Then Drake himself became stricken with dysentery and had to take to his cabin. The wind still stayed in the west and after a further three days, he gave from his bed the order to weigh anchor and 'to take the wind as God had sent it'. He became delirious. With a tremendous effort, he rose from his bed to dress himself and called for his servant Whitelocke to help him into his armour, for he meant to die like a soldier. That accomplished, he was put to bed again and in the early hours of 28 January 1596 Drake died, at peace with the world. A few hours later, the fleet came to anchor again at Nombre de Dios. Baskerville had his body laid in a leaden coffin, which was carried out from shore for sinking in the bay, with trumpets sounding, the admiral's three drums beating their lament and 'all the cannons in the fleet were discharged according to the custom of all sea funeral obsequies'.

Baskerville did not delay his departure from the Spanish Main. Though he had to fight off the Spanish fleet sent to intercept him south of Cuba, he was still back in Plymouth towards the end of April, thus honouring the promise which Drake and Hawkins had made to the Queen. Although there was rejoicing in the Americas and in Old Spain, with Seville illuminated, when news of Drake's death arrived, before the remnant of the expedition was back in England, Howard and Essex had left with a mighty fleet to attack Cadiz in the tradition which Drake had established. The great hopes for this new expedition in some measure compensated for the disasters of the West Indian voyage, which had lost England her two greatest seamen and the shareholders a large sum of money.

Richard Hawkins, son of Sir John, had been bred to the seas and had commanded the *Swallow* in the hectic summer of 1588. A thorough professional, there was little worth knowing about ships and the men who sailed them that he did not know and he imparted this specialist knowledge in his *Observations*, a wonderfully practical manual, that was published as he was dying in 1622. In this, for example, he discussed the pest of sea worms 'no bigger than a small Spanish needle' that could eat their way into the planking of a hull and eventually destroy a vessel unless his father's patent method of sheathing the hull (which he described) was used. Richard was a man of ingenuity and when in the Pacific he had to repair broken anchors he succeeded in 'making coals', as he put it; at another time, when they ran out of drinking water aboard, 'with an invention I had in my ship, I easily drew out of the water of the sea a sufficient quantity of fresh water to sustain my people, with little expense of fuel. The water so distilled we found to be wholesome and nourishing.' One would be fascinated to learn the details of his method.

In June 1593 Richard Hawkins sailed in the *Dainty* with two vessels in company for the Pacific. One was a victualling ship which was unloaded and abandoned off Brazil, following a gale; the other, the *Fancy*, deserted him in the region of Rio de la Plata. So like Drake in the *Pelican*, Hawkins entered the Strait of Magellan alone. He entered the Pacific on 29 March 1594 and sailed north, taking prizes at Valparaiso, Coquimbo and Arica. The Spanish authorities were much more alert than during Drake's voyage and had improved communications between the various harbours. The viceroy of Peru in Lima ordered six men-of-war to go after him, and Hawkins not only eluded them but cheekily took another prize. At length three of the Spaniards caught up with the *Dainty* in the Bay of Atacama. Hawkins thought it best to stand out to sea, rather than be confined to the bay, so he went to meet the enemy. 'We hailed first with our trumpets, then with our waits and after with our artillery, which they answered . . . two for one; for they had double the ordnance we had and men almost ten for one.' It was certainly an unequal struggle, yet the fight lasted for three days and three nights before the battered *Dainty* was boarded and Hawkins felt he must surrender. There had been many casualties and Hawkins himself received six wounds, becoming very weak from loss of blood. His sailing master persuaded him they must

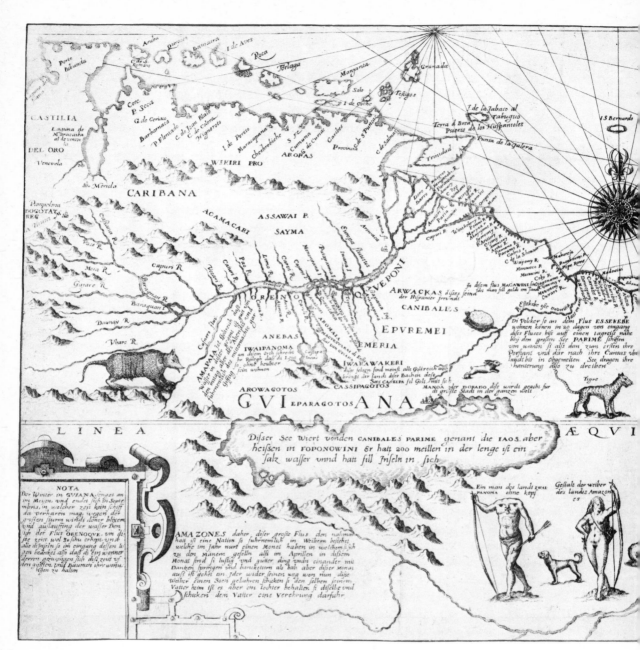

put up a flag of truce and discuss terms of surrender. All lives were to be spared and the captains treated honourably. The admiral, Don Beltram de Castro, gave Hawkins his glove as an earnest that his word would be kept. Sent to Lima as prisoners of war, Hawkins and the others escaped interrogation by the Inquisition. Worried about the admiral's personal assurances the viceroy referred the question of examination by the church authorities to Philip II, who in due course answered that in view of Hawkins' name and

220

standing as a gentleman he and his fellow officers should be treated with respect and justice. From Panama Hawkins was taken to Spain for internment for several years and was only released at the instigation of Don Beltram. Richard Hawkins was the last Elizabethan sea dog to sail in the Pacific and the last of the Hawkins sea-faring dynasty.

Sir Walter Raleigh's expedition to Guiana in 1595 was prompted by his urgent need to win his way back to royal favour, but ever since the failure of the Roanoke colony he had been restlessly considering afresh the New World and had recently concentrated on the northern stretches of the River Amazon and the Orinoco basin. In part this was an explorer's genuine desire to investigate the unknown, yet in the way he promoted his design it was primarily a quest for gold. He explained that it was the King of Spain's 'Indian gold that endangereth and disturbeth all the nations of Europe as it purchaseth intelligence, creepeth into councils and setteth bound loyalty and liberty in the greatest monarchies of Europe'. To subdue Spain, England needed her own source of precious metals and Guiana seemed to offer the surest hope. For two generations there had been sporadic searches by Spanish adventurers for another Inca civilization in that region and strange legends had been woven from Indians' tales about the treasure of a great ruler, El Dorado, 'the gilded one', who powdered himself with gold-dust. His capital had been named as Manoa, a city by the shores of Lake Parma, hidden in the mountainous region of Guiana that travellers had found inaccessible. Raleigh had learnt something from a Spaniard, Don Pedro Sarmiento, who had been brought to England as a prisoner by Captain Whiddon in 1586. The man had considerable knowledge of South America and had once been instructed to found a colony in Patagonia. Though he was guarded in what he told Raleigh about the Orinoco region, the latter never forgot Sarmiento's enthusiasm. A decade later he wrote: 'Many years since, I had knowledge by relation of that mighty rich and beautiful Empire of Guiana and of that great and golden city which the Spaniards call El Dorado, and the naturals Minoa.' Sarmiento told him a little of the endeavours of Don Antonio de Berrio from Trinidad to explore the unknown region and he had continued these explorations.

Now that Raleigh was sure that the only way of recovering his position at court was by a singular adventure, he had become fascinated by the search for the fabled El Dorado of the Incas. Early in 1594 Elizabeth Raleigh was sufficiently alarmed by his conversation to write to Robert Cecil, begging him to change her husband's direction that 'you will rather draw Sir Walter towards the east, than help him forward towards the sunset'. That year he sent out James Whiddon to reconnoitre. Whiddon sailed to Trinidad to meet Berrio who, while outwardly friendly, succeeded in misleading him.

If Raleigh needed any further encouragement for the enterprise it came from Whiddon's highly-coloured reports which enabled him to ensure financial backing – not, of course, from the Queen, but from the Lord Admiral

In 1595 Raleigh's expedition set out to explore the Orinoco river in search of the mythical kingdom of El Dorado; early seventeenth-century map of Guiana.

Howard, who lent him the *Lion's Whelp*, and from Robert Cecil. Four vessels commanded by Whiddon, Laurence Keymis, George Gifford and Cross left England in February 1595, carrying about 350 men, and they were to rendezvous in Trinidad with Captain Popham and Sir Robert Dudley, Leicester's natural son, who were already privateering at sea. Raleigh sailed with them under the Queen's commission, though the document omitted the customary description that he was 'trusty and well-beloved'. At Trinidad, which he reached in seven weeks, Raleigh was determined to put Governor Berrio in his place in retaliation for his maltreatment of a party of Whiddon's men the previous year, so he destroyed the fort, burnt the town of St Joseph and took Berrio prisoner. This endeared him to the Indian population of Trinidad from whom he picked up helpful information about Guiana, whereas the

Raleigh's arrival in Trinidad; a sixteenth-century engraving.

governor did his utmost to dissuade Raleigh from his explorations. Berrio said that the tributaries of the River Orinoco were too shallow for his craft, the current too fast, the climate too sickly and the Indians too fierce. But Raleigh was not to be put off. The governor did not mention that a fresh expedition to explore Guiana was even then being fitted out in Spain under Domingo de Vera.

With a month's provisions Raleigh set out with a hundred men. It was laborious work in gruelling conditions as they rowed upstream in the swollen waters. The boats were their home; 'there was never any prison in England that could be found more unsavoury and loathsome'. Only the thought of gold kept the men going. For fifteen days they negotiated shoals under the burning sun with the inhospitable forest going down to the water's edge. 'If God had not sent us help, we might have continued a whole year in that labyrinth of rivers,' wrote the leader. Help came in the person of an Indian in a canoe whom they captured and used as their pilot, and then at length they came to clearer water and more open country. There was excitement as they discovered in a bush by the bank a set of refiner's tools. There were fresh fruits, including pineapples which Sir Walter called 'the princess of fruits', and there were friendly natives who lent them a knowledgeable pilot. After halts they came to the province of Arromaia and its aged ruler, King Topiawari, walked fourteen miles to greet them, bringing food and the gift of an armadillo. He paid homage to the portrait of Queen Elizabeth the explorers had brought and agreed to accept her sovereignty. Now they began to navigate the River Caroni, a tributary of the Orinoco, but it was already rising too dangerously and the rainy season was approaching. Various parties were sent out to prospect for samples of ore that might contain gold, but with their lack of equipment and so small a force it would have been foolhardy to have attempted to proceed further, to find a way to the mountains where Raleigh was convinced lay El Dorado and its glittering civilization. He began the difficult return journey, taking with him Topiawari's son, whom he named 'Gualtero', and leaving behind two of his party, Francis Sparrey and Hugh Goodwin, a boy, who was still in Guiana when Raleigh returned twenty-two years later. They reached Trinidad and their ships and were back in England by September, eager to convince their backers of the rich promise the future held for them by the Orinoco.

When Raleigh was chided for sacking no towns for plunder, he defended himself that such short-sighted methods would have ruined 'the future hope of so many millions and the great, good and rich trade which England may be possessed thereby'. The excellent relations he had established with the Indians must, he said, ensure success. His specimen rocks, including marcasite, were laughed at, for men remembered Frobisher's black ore. Yet Raleigh was absolutely certain he was on the right track and yet 'this dolt and that gull must be satisfied, or else all is nothing'. Some even refused to believe Raleigh had been in Guiana. When the Queen was not going to commission him to lead a full-scale expedition to annex the country for settlement he wrote his *Discoverie of the Large Rich and Bewtiful Empyre of Guiana* as a company prospectus in language of which he was a past master. 'The common soldier shall here fight for gold, and pay himself, instead of pence, with plates of half a foot broad. ... Guiana is a country that hath yet her maidenhead, never sacked, turned nor wrought, the face of the earth hath not been torn ... the graves have not been opened for gold, the mines not broken with sledges, nor their images pulled down out of their temples.' He needed to dazzle readers with this alluring prospect, yet his real goal was to put the entire area under English control before the Spaniards moved in. Burghley and his son were among the few at court who contributed towards Laurence Keymis being sent out in 1596 to sail by the coast from the mouth of the Amazon to the Orinoco and find a passage that would lead to the mountain region where El Dorado was thought to be. They returned six months later without gold but with news that a great lake was to be found which one could reach from the Essequido. By then Raleigh had other employment at Cadiz, yet the mirage of El Dorado never left him and so he was to bargain with James I for his life in 1617 to find the lost city. As the later history of Venezuela has shown there was gold to be mined, but not the priceless Inca treasure that Raleigh had been deluded in believing lay in the mountains. An ageing sea dog, 'fleshed in Spanish blood and ruin', came out of the Tower of London to prepare the *Destiny* for her ill-starred voyage to the Orinoco. Sir Francis Bacon asked him what he would do if the gambler's throw should fail and his gold mine at Manoa be no more than a figment of

A contemporary engraving of the exotic creatures of Guiana; King Topiawari presented an armadillo to Raleigh.

224

A European idea of the Indians of Guiana.

his imagination. Raleigh replied that if such were the case he could still find gold – from the plate fleet on the Main. But, protested Bacon, such would be sheer piracy and against King James's strict instructions. 'Oh,' answered Sir Walter, 'did you ever know of any that were pirates for millions? They only that work for small things are pirates.'

Before Drake's fate was known plans were being laid for a massive combined assault on Cadiz, to sear the flesh rather than singe the beard. Now that Henry IV had established himself in France a new strategy was possible and the way was open for a fresh offensive in the Peninsula, to make the launching of another armada against England impossible. While preparations were going forward, with the utmost secrecy about the destination of the fleet, the Cardinal Archduke Albert of Austria, Philip's governor of the Netherlands, began a surprise attack on Calais and for a few days Elizabeth was uncertain whether she could afford to answer Henry IV's urgent appeal for aid, but the thought of having an English army again in control of Calais was something she could not resist. She had heard the archduke's artillery from Greenwich and knew the need for haste, yet, as always, she had second thoughts about

225

MEDIO ET TEMPORE

Sir Francis Vere
commanded the *Rainbow*
on the Cadiz expedition.

the soundness of the strategy and of the economics. On the Wednesday after
Easter she sent final orders for the troops to embark and in a note to Essex
warned him not to 'peril so fair an army for another prince's town', unless
the position were desperate; 'God cover you under His safest wings, and let
all perils go without your compass'. But next evening as the transports were
ready to leave came news to Dover that Calais had fallen. Calais, in Spanish
hands! A safe harbour for another armada; and so tremors were felt in
London. The Queen debated whether it were wise now to allow her own fleet
to sail for Cadiz, leaving England unguarded, but having decided to press
forward with the expedition she rebuked everyone from the Lord Admiral
downward for unwonted tardiness. Now Essex and Howard were to be

226

replaced as commanders, then they were reinstated; at one time Elizabeth cancelled the whole expedition, and then she was won round by her commanders at Plymouth into allowing them to proceed and penned her own words of Godspeed to Essex, sending a special prayer she had composed. She rehearsed reasons for the enterprise and 'these being the grounds, Thou that diddest inspire the mind, we humbly beseech with bended knees prosper the work, and with the best forewinds guide the journey, speed the victory and make the return the advancement of Thy fame and surety to the realm, with the least loss of English blood.'

Raleigh had recovered sufficiently from the Queen's displeasure to be appointed vice-admiral of the fleet, commanding the *Warsprite*. It was so long since he had been with a major expedition that he cut it fine in filling his complement and in the end went round with a press-gang from one Thames-side alehouse to another finding sailors. This made him late for the rendez-vous in Plymouth, but the grand fleet of 120 sail was still awaiting the Queen's orders to proceed. This was the most formidable English force that had ever been sent to sea, numbering perhaps as many as 16,000 men of whom 6400 were English seamen, about as many soldiers and the rest Dutchmen under Jan Duyvenoord. As they waited there was bickering between Vere and Raleigh, jealousy between Essex and Howard and general criticism of the Dutch. Everyone was eager to shine and delays in Plymouth Sound brought out the worst in men. At last on 1 June they weighed anchor but almost at once the wind dropped. They did not properly get away for another two days, but soon they were racing towards Cadiz. Ahead were the fastest pinnaces, which intercepted every vessel they came across to prevent news of the fleet's despatch reaching the ports of Spain. While the Duke of Medina Sidonia recuperated under his orange trees, young ruffians disturbed his peace by shouting over the hedge *'Viene el Draque'* – not aware that the chief corsair was dead, but then came news brought by a country-man on a mule as fast as he could ride that the horizon was thick with English sails.

At a council of war it was decided to land the troops as soon as possible to storm the city, and they chose the rocky point of San Sebastian for the landing on 19 June. This was disastrous because of heavy seas and a strong north-westerly wind, and Raleigh successfully argued for his original plan to be followed instead – to wreak havoc in the harbour before attempting to sack the town. On the twenty-first they pounded the harbour and were the target for heavy fire from the shore batteries. Raleigh was slightly wounded in the leg but outshone Essex in his persistent gallantry and beaching parties got to grips with the enemy. In his subsequent account, *A Relation of Cadiz Action*, Raleigh graphically described the end of the proud galleons *St Philip* and *St James*:

The spectacle was very lamentable on their side; for many drowned themselves; many half-burnt, leaped into the water; very many hanging by the ropes' ends by the ships' sides, under the water even to the lips; many swimming with grievous wounds, stricken under water and put out of their pain; and witted so huge a fire and such tearing of the ordnance of the great *Philip* and the rest, when the fire came to them, as if any man had desire to see hell itself, it was there most lively figured. Ourselves spared the lives of all after the victory; but the Flemings, who did little or nothing in the fight, used merciless slaughter, till they were by myself and afterward by my Lord Admiral beaten off.

Two other galleons of the 'Apostles' class, the *St Matthew* and *St Andrew*, were captured and brought to England.

The harbour firmly in English hands, the soldiers under Essex made themselves masters of the town. Looting and firing houses went on for three days, so that the proud city seemed returned to ashes. Many prisoners were taken and for their ransom the English commanders demanded 120,000 ducats in cash, though Medina Sidonia argued in vain to pay in bills of exchange. In the Priory of St Francis Howard and Essex held an investiture, dubbing sixty-six knights, which created a bad impression in class-conscious England, for these Cadiz gentlemen were but soldiers of fortune, said a pamphleteer, and:

A yeoman of Kent with his yearly rent
Could buy them out all three.

Both Essex and Raleigh had wanted to garrison the city and hold it as an English base, much as Gibraltar later became, but Howard and the others thought nothing of the plan. One singular lapse was allowing the *flota* anchored in the roadstead at Puerto Royale, due east of Cadiz, to escape up river with cargoes, it was said, worth twelve million ducats. But effectively it had been a famous victory. Leaving Cadiz behind them the commanders could not agree on their next objective, though most of the men were eager to be home to enjoy their share of the plunder. Essex advocated either hovering off the Spanish coast in the region of Cadiz or making for the Azores to intercept the expected plate fleet, but he was overruled for the others thought it more prudent to swoop down on one of the Portuguese harbours for easy loot and this was popular with the crews. They anchored off Cape St Mary on 13 July where the Lord Admiral, feeling Essex had had more than his fair share of the limelight, proposed leading the men ashore to march on the town of Faro, but he found the intense heat intolerable and it was left to Sir Christopher Blount to lead the attack, while Howard covered the landing with his guns. Essex could not keep away, however, and ransacked for himself the most valuable books in the bishop's library, though the pickings in general were negligible and the army in disgust fired Faro. Moving northwards, the wind made sailing for the Azores favourable and Essex again argued that they should race to the Islands to take the treasure ships. The others by now were even more anxious to make for Plymouth and even refused the earl's plea to be allowed to detach a few ships and patrol the approaches to Lisbon. Instead they decided to continue northwards and *en route* see if Corunna invited attack. Alas, Corunna was bare of shipping, so they proceeded home, arriving in the Sound on 6 August. The decision proved wrong, for they missed the Spanish treasure fleet, carrying gold, silver and jewels worth 20,000 ducats, making for the entrance to the Tagus, by fifty hours.

Once Elizabeth heard of the sack of Cadiz, she sent a message in grand style to the commanders: 'Let the army know I care not so much being Queen as that I am sovereign of such subjects.' Essex was, however, coolly received by his sovereign and wrote to a friend, 'I am as much distracted with the glorious greatness of a favourite as I was before with the supposed happiness of a courtier'. But Raleigh seemed in high favour.

As in all such ventures embezzlement was rife. It was discovered that a great diamond that should have passed to the Queen had been broken up and parcelled out amongst London jewellers and her personal agent, Sir Anthony Ashley, who had accompanied the voyage to look after her interests, was sent to the Fleet Prison. She was aghast to be told that her share of the spoils was no more than £78,000. When in September she learnt that the treasure ships had slipped through her commanders' hands at Lisbon, halving the profits of the voyage, she rated Raleigh and Howard for turning down Essex's plan of campaign, yet though he thought he had been vindicated, she continued to blame the earl for 'mishandling the spoils' and said she would confiscate his share of the ransoms of prisoners at Cadiz. Burghley tried to restrain her, but she bawled at him, 'My Lord Treasurer, either from fear or favour you regard my Lord of Essex more than myself. You are a miscreant! You are a coward!' Apart from haggling over profits, there was bitter quarrelling between Raleigh and Essex as to which of them was the real hero of the expedition, which forced courtiers to take sides. The earl who had no doubt about his own claims endeavoured to set a new fashion – a full square beard, that he called the 'Cadiz style'. In revenge for the attack, which showed the world how vulnerable Spain was, Philip II decided to put another armada, collected from ports other than Cadiz, to sea later that year; but the preparations were inadequate and the weather foul, so the survivors of the October gales of the Bay of Biscay limped home.

At Easter 1597 Essex was busy preparing for a fresh expedition to humble the Spanish in which he hoped to have sole command, with operations centred on the Azores which had been so disastrously neglected the previous summer. After much hestitation the Queen signed his commission on 15 June. He was indeed to sail to the Islands (as the Azores were so often called) to await the arrival of the summer plate fleet from the Indies, but with this proviso: he was first to visit the north Spanish port of Ferrol, where it was understood another armada was being fitted out for sailing to Ireland. If that intelligence was correct he was to destroy all shipping in Ferrol and leave the port in ruins, but if the armada had already left Ferrol he was to abandon all thought of going to the Azores and pursue the enemy. As in the initial instructions to Drake and Hawkins in 1595, Elizabeth was torn

The capture of Cadiz,
1596; a Dutch engraving.

between two irreconcilables – hunting for treasure and defending her realm.

Essex brought the Queen's ships from the Thames, meeting the squadron that the Estates General were again providing in the Strait of Dover, and then faced a howling gale so that he was not only late for his rendezvous in Plymouth with Raleigh's fleet, but his ships were in a sorry condition. Apart from the Dutch there were fifty English vessels, arranged in three squadrons commanded respectively by Essex (in the *Dire Repulse*), Lord Thomas Howard (in the *Merhonour*) and Raleigh (in the *Dreadnought*). The last squadron included the two great galleons captured the previous year at Cadiz. As many as six thousand soldiers were aboard. Soon after leaving the Sound on 10 July they encountered an even worse tempest, which scattered the fleet, battering them mercilessly. John Donne, aged twenty-three, was in the expedition and afterwards recalled the effects of that freak wind:

Some sitting on the hatches, would seem there
With hideous gazing to fear away fear.
Then note they the ship's sickness, the mast
Shaked with ague, and the hold and waste
With a salt dropsy clogged, and all our tacklings
Snapping, like too high stretched treble strings. . . .

Only Lord Thomas Howard succeeded in keeping his squadron together and brought it through the gale to Ferrol, where he challenged the *Adelantado* to come out and fight. Most of the ships found a West Country English port and waited for days for the storm to abate. This was not at all what the Queen had envisaged, for provisions were being used up at an alarming rate. Repairs were put in hand and some men were too ill or too shaken by their experiences to be prepared to continue. Essex decided to dismiss all the English soldiers, who never wanted to go on shipboard again in their lives. Raleigh came to Essex's defence when Elizabeth was incredulous that two months after first sailing they were still in Plymouth Sound: 'God having turned the heavens with fury against us, a matter beyond the power or valour or wit of man to resist.' With Essex he strove to adapt the Queen's instructions into a more practicable scheme: let them send fire ships into Ferrol and then proceed to the Islands. Elizabeth agreed, providing none of her own ships were used, and considered the two Spanish 'Apostles' galleons would be ideal for the purpose and also a wry joke on Philip. At last on 17 August they were off, yet again a gale soon faced them, though it quickly blew itself out. Sir George Carew, commanding the *St Matthew*, had lost his mast and only brought her back to Falmouth through superb seamanship; the *Dire Repulse* had sprung a leak; the *Dreadnought*'s main-mast had snapped in two. Off Lisbon Raleigh was told somewhat improbably that the *Adelantado* had put to sea to convey the plate fleet and he sent a bark to pass the news to Essex, nowhere in sight. The earl made for the Islands, but let it be known that he regarded Raleigh's conduct as insolent; he feared his reputation at court above all.

OPPOSITE Lord Thomas Howard sailed with Raleigh and Essex on the unsuccessful Azores expedition.

TOTI° ANG° THESAVRARI° HONORATISS: Dᵒ THOMAS HOWARI Oᵒ SVFFOLCIÆ ET

The rig͢hte Honourable THOMAS: HOWARD Earle of Suffolke. Lorde Walden and Lorde Tresurer of England and one of his Maᵗⁱᵉˢ most honᵇˡᵉ priuie Counsell and knight of the most noble Order of ẙ Garter.

R. Elstracke sculp:

Spanish galleons of the
'Apostle' class.

Now the expedition became a wild goose chase. The two rivals met at
Flores in mid-September and were outwardly friendly, but Essex was being
goaded on by his minions. At a council of war they planned to descend on
different islands for provisions and easy plunder, but Essex unaccountably
disappeared to look for prizes and Raleigh waited for him off Fayol. The
latter decided to land his men, yet the inhabitants had long enough warning
to desert the town and hide their valuables. When the earl reappeared after
four days there was a terrible argument between the commanders, for each
blamed the other for incompetence and lack of judgement. Their differences
were patched up as best could be, but morale in the fleet was low.

Instead of staying at La Gratioza, the most central of the islands where
they could be well placed for surprising the approaching Spaniards, Essex
ordered them to move east, to St Michael's. This was an elementary tactical
error. Almost at once the galleons were seen on the horizon, twenty
miles away, so the English had to turn about. The plate fleet sensing the

234

danger altered course to make for Terceira, a harbour protected by a good fort. All might not have been lost had the English not turned to deal with three vessels from Havana that were not part of the plate fleet. These were captured and found to contain only cochineal. Three hours had been wasted and by then the galleons were safely anchored at Terceira. Withdrawing in dismay, Essex and Raleigh decided to return to St Michael's, desperate for plunder. The earl landed 2000 soldiers at Villa Franca under cover of Raleigh's guns, intending to take the town of St Michael's from the rear, but the men stumbled on a store of wine and would not move on. Essex was persuaded by his cronies to sit tight in Villa Franca, while Raleigh remained unaware of the change of plan. The Islands Voyage ended in ignominy. The rival commanders did their best to concoct an explanation for the Council, largely blaming the weather, but no one remained ignorant of the weakness of a divided command and the glaring sequence of tactical errors. The voyage marked the end of the naval careers of both Raleigh and Essex. Elizabeth never employed either of them again at sea, nor had either of these 'Shepherds of the Ocean' further maritime ambitions. Henceforth a disillusioned Sir Walter never used a wherry to cross the Thames, but went the long way round over London Bridge.

9 ADVENTURERS

DURING ELIZABETH'S REIGN there had been a complete re-orientation of England's trade in which the sea dogs had played so prominent a part. On the eve of her accession Calais had been lost. That port had been not only the last remnant of England's once formidable dominion on the continent, but the headquarters of the Merchants of the Staple, who held the monopoly of the export of wool, from early medieval times the backbone of the island's overseas trade, though of late overshadowed by the export of cloths woven and finished in England.

More significant in 1558 was the position of Antwerp, the pride of the old Burgundian duchy, which had passed to the Habsburgs. Antwerp had by the end of the fifteenth century become the emporium for all Europe and here the English Merchants Adventurers had their headquarters. Regular fleets arrived from the London docks with English cloths of many varieties, which were sold for a great range of wares – oriental sugar and spices, Baltic pitch and timber, Venetian glass and lutes, Florentine silks and a host of metal ware and other manufactured goods from Germany. From the early 1560s, however, the religious and political upheavals in Philip II's Low Countries threatened the special relationship between London and Antwerp. Until then William Cecil had reckoned that 'one hoy will bring as much in one year as ten merchant ships were wont to bring from the other places in two years', yet the traffic between the Thames and the Scheldt had been conducted not in single hoys, but in regular convoys. In 1564 the Merchants Adventurers, temporarily denied entry to Antwerp, chose the German port of Emden as their staple town and then the embargo on trade with Spanish dominions between 1568 and 1573 turned them first to Hamburg and then to Stade, as alternative gateways to continental markets. As the struggle between Philip of Spain and his Northern Provinces developed it became clear that the international importance of Antwerp was over. There had already been a series of violent outbreaks of iconoclasm which affected the mercantile community and then in 1576 the Spanish army in Flanders mutinied for lack of pay, for with the Channel in the hands of English sea dogs and the Dutch 'Beggars of the Sea' commanding the Narrow Seas, the governor of the Netherlands was completely cut off from supplies of bullion from Spain. In their fury the soldiers sacked Antwerp. Seven years later the French Duke of Anjou, intending to carve for himself a principality in the Southern Netherlands, attacked the city and in August 1585 came the *coup de grâce* under Parma. Antwerp's days as a key trading centre for the western world were past and its bourse ceased to be the hub of the international money market.

Long before the fall of Antwerp English merchants had been seeking fresh markets, spurred on by the slump in the cloth trade, and their efforts redrew the pattern of overseas trade. Instead of concentrating the bulk of their interests in the Scheldt Estuary they were adventuring to the Baltic, the Mediterranean and beyond. English ships were now bringing home from Danzig, Hamburg, Leghorn, the Barbary Coast and the Levant goods formerly obtained at the Antwerp mart. Merchants had been forging new commercial links with distant lands in their endeavours to free themselves from dependence on the Netherlands and though the long naval war with Spain strained their efforts, not least because so many ships and seamen were requisitioned for naval defence, the links were not broken. The design was that London should in the future come to occupy the extraordinary position held for so long by Antwerp as the centre of international trade.

The beginning of this enterprise had been laid as long ago as 1553 with the foundation of the Muscovy Company, but in the next half-century a series of other trading companies was formed under royal charter to exploit markets in such areas as the Baltic, the Levant and the East Indies. In each of them the Queen had a stake – thanks to her proceeds from privateering – there was close co-operation with the Royal Navy and officials of these companies served in distant parts as diplomatic representatives. Accorded privileges in particular regions, the companies jealously defended their monopolies against interlopers. All of them were dominated by London merchants and there was constant complaint from provincial ports such as Bristol, Southampton, King's Lynn and Hull, that they were being denied an entry to profitable markets. If they were to be ineligible for membership to

Antwerp market *c.* 1540; artist unknown.

the club then they would operate independently as 'interlopers'. Drake and the sea dogs had shown the weakness of the Spanish claims to commercial monopoly in the New World, and the interlopers on the chartered companies fought fiercely for a share of the trade in Narva, Hamburg, Venice, Aleppo and elsewhere. Sometimes there were unseemly incidents when shots were exchanged between English merchants in foreign ports and there was a good deal of illicit trading by Englishmen who 'coloured' goods – passing their consignments off as goods belonging to a member of the company – and they even used flags of convenience.

In 1558 the Russians had captured Narva from the Swedes and this port attracted so considerable a number of interlopers that the Muscovy Company sought and obtained a new charter from the Queen and fresh privileges from the Tsar. As a result trading factories were established at Moscow, Novgorod and Archangel. Furs and skins from Siberia, pitch, tar, wax,

240

Elsinore Castle on the
Baltic Sound; a
sixteenth-century
engraving.

timber and cordage from the great forests and even grain were shipped to
England in annual fleets of fourteen stout vessels. Where the English had
pioneered, the Dutch followed and before 1590 had contrived to secure a
foothold in the Muscovy trade.

Merchants trading to the Baltic were formed into the Eastland Company
in 1579. They maintained stations at Elbing and Danzig, but their activities
covered a very wide area – the whole of Scandinavia, Poland and Eastern
Pomerania. English cloth was the staple export and the ships brought back
masts from Norway, deals and clapboard from Sweden, pitch and tar from
the Baltic ports and increasingly large quantities of rye. When the English
harvest was poor, it was estimated that half the urban population fed on
loaves made from 'Danske rye'. Hundreds of English vessels each year
passed through the Sound, guarded by Elsinore Castle, where tolls were
levied by the King of Denmark. The Eastland merchants strove hard to oust
the Hansards from their share of the Baltic trade with England, which had a
long history, and they were largely successful, yet by the turn of the century
they faced intense competition from the Dutch, who seemed ubiquitous. It
was Dutch vessels, exploiting the carrying trade with Danzig and beyond
that helped lay the foundation of the prosperity of Amsterdam long before
peace was signed with Spain. The Dutch republic was founded upon the seas,
with the efforts of the 'Beggars of the Sea' from Brill early in the struggle for
independence, but they moved on from privateering to develop sound commercial links both in the north east and in the Far East.

English trade with Morocco was centred on Safi, the port of Marrakech, and
Agadir, which handled exports of sugar from the Sus district. When the
Portuguese had been driven out of Agadir in 1541, they blamed their rout on
the quantities of arms which English and French merchants had been selling
to the Moors, and this arms traffic continued so that it was said in Lisbon
that the infidel was becoming better equipped than the Christian. In return
for sugar, vessels brought to Moroccan ports ammunition and artillery,
coats of mail, pikes, lances and naval stores, though there was also a good
market here for fine cloths, such as Suffolk kerseys. Spain and Portugal,
however, brought strong diplomatic pressure on Elizabeth in 1574 to forbid
her subjects from trading in that area and to end the arms traffic. For a while
the commerce had to be conducted in a hole-and-corner way using Hanseatic
ships. The chief culprit was Edmund Hogan, a London merchant, who in
March 1577 when he was being cross-examined by the Privy Council defended himself by putting forward a proposal that would cement ties with
Morocco to the mutual advantage of the two countries. He reported that
saltpetre was now being produced in North Africa in growing quantities and
this was a commodity which England badly needed for manufacturing gun-
powder. Saltpetre had become scarce and costly in the Baltic ports, because
of the wars in the Netherlands and France, so a new, independent source of
supply seemed a godsend.

As a result of several secret discussions in Council, Hogan sent out his agent John Williams, who reported that the saltpetre mined in the southern part of Morocco was an excellent product, though the output was reserved exclusively for the Shereef Mulai Mohammed. Williams went to the Shereef who said he would be prepared to sell saltpetre to the Queen of England if she in return would manufacture cannon-balls to his specification. A specimen thirty tons of saltpetre was despatched to London and found satisfactory and subsequently samples of English-made cannon-balls were shipped to Morocco. These arrived too late to be approved by Mulai Mohammed, since he was by now overthrown by Abd el-Malek, though the new Shereef told Williams that if he could guarantee to send him a regular supply of armaments he would then give the Queen's agents an exclusive licence to buy his saltpetre, copper or anything else, provided it was not allowed to fall into Spanish or Portuguese hands. Elizabeth now sent out Hogan as her ambassador to clinch a secret deal. He was received in Marrakech in great honour 'such as hath not ordinarily been showed to other ambassadors of the Christians'. Abd el-Malek at once liked the man and 'took from his girdle a short dagger set with 200 stones' as a present. All was concluded within the year 1577, showing the urgency with which the matter was treated by the English Council. Elizabeth was alarmed when the Shereef talked about sending her a Moroccan envoy because she feared the terms of the secret treaty would be discovered by Mendoza, the Spanish ambassador. The Spaniard, as it happened, already had an inkling of what was afoot, reporting to Philip II about a Morisco named Julio, of princely birth, who was closeted for hours with the Queen and her ministers. He added that a vessel was ready to sail from London for Barbary with many dogs, well-trained horses and rich clothes for the King of Fez: 'the assertion is made that they are going to bring back saltpetre.' The King of Spain did not follow up this clue, or he would have reproved the 'heretic Queen' from allying herself with the infidel. But for this Barbary trade, England might well have been desperately short of gun-powder during the Armada campaign. The traffic soon became extended to dates and carpets, but even in 1600 voyages to Safi were reckoned very risky enterprises, quite apart from the prevalence of corsairs, for 'if the Spaniards take you trading with them [the Moors], you die for it'.

With the overwhelming defeat of the Turkish navy at the battle of Lepanto in 1571 the Levant was again safe for trade and there was added incentive for English merchants to return to those waters, after some thirty years absence, as a result of the decline of Venice. The shipping of the Venetian Republic had taken a terrible buffeting from the Turks, not least in its endeavours to prevent Cyprus from falling to the Turks, which proved impossible. In 1573 English ships were once more seen at Leghorn and before long cloth, tin and great quantities of Yarmouth herrings were finding ready markets there, in return for currants, wine and oil.

The English looked further east, hoping to penetrate Turkey and reach

The eastern Mediterranean in 1571, the year of the battle of Lepanto. The defeat of the Turks opened the Levant trade to English merchants once again.

Sultan Murad III.

the overland trade route to India. Through the initiative of Sir Edward Osborne, a sheriff of London, and Richard Staper negotiations were opened with the Sultan Murad III for granting trading concessions. William Harborne, a Norfolk man, was despatched to Aleppo and journeyed by land to Constantinople to secure a commercial treaty in the face of strong opposition from France, which already had diplomatic representation in Turkey and Venice. To control the new traffic the Levant Company was formed by royal Charter in 1581 for 'trading with the dominions of the Grand Signior'. Osborne was the first governor and the Queen invested £40,000 in their first ventures. A condition of the charter was that the company's resident agents in Aleppo and Constantinople should serve as ambassadors. Harborne held this post in Constantinople for eight years, fostering England's new relations with the world of Islam and overseeing the foundation of an important trade. Because of the resurgence of piracy from Ragusa and the Barbary corsairs, the Levant Company ships were built for speed and usually went in

The illustration bears the inscription: VIVAT ELIZABETH REGINA SEMREADEM

'The great Temple called Sancta Sophia at Constantinople where the great Turke called Sultan Muradd doth inhabitt', drawn by Thomas Morgan, an English mariner held captive on the Turkish galleys for fifteen years.

convoy; if the winds were favourable and the sailing masters skilful they could take as little as fifty days on the trip from Falmouth to the Syrian coast. Harborne was concerned to keep this valuable monopoly firmly in the hands of the members of the company, since interlopers gave the Turk the wrong impression about the ways an Englishman conducted trade and, because they were disorganized and in a weak position for bargaining, they could easily be outwitted by 'the malicious Turk and crafty Moor and faithless Greek'.

John Sanderson had been sent out to Constantinople in 1585 by his master, Martin Calthorpe, to act as an assistant to William Harborne. The ambassador used him for a trading mission to Alexandria and Cairo, which proved disappointing in its results, but he had some success in Tripoli and came home to England in the *Hercules* with a cargo worth over £70,000 just before the Armada sailed. Sanderson's future seemed uncertain, for his master died and the original charter for the Levant Company was expiring, so he joined John Davys's ill-favoured expedition of 1590 in the *Samaritan* to round the Cape of Good Hope. By the time he returned, blaming everything on Davys, all London was talking about the epoch-making journey which Ralph Fitch

244

had made from Aleppo to India and back (see below p. 249), and this stimu-
lated interest in a new charter for the Levant merchants, whose area of
operations was to include Venice and the East Indies, as well as the Ottoman
Empire. Wines from Candia were soon no longer a novelty in southern
England, currants were plentiful and there was optimism that keen factors in
Aleppo could lay their hands on gold dust brought by camels from the
Orient. Sanderson returned to Constantinople full of hope.

He left Tilbury in the *Toby*, which landed him at Patras in the Morea as
she had to go to Zante for her lading, which itself suggests a well-organized
system. Sanderson was able to see something of Corinth, Thebes and Athens
before making for Gallipoli and the capital of the Sultan's dominions, where
he was to remain for seven exciting years. He found the ambassador's household dissolute, compared with the strict standards Harborne had maintained, but Edward Barton, the acting ambassador, discovered Sanderson
to be a quick-tempered fellow, always seeking a fight and determined to make

Aleppo, the centre of the
Levant Company's spice
trade.

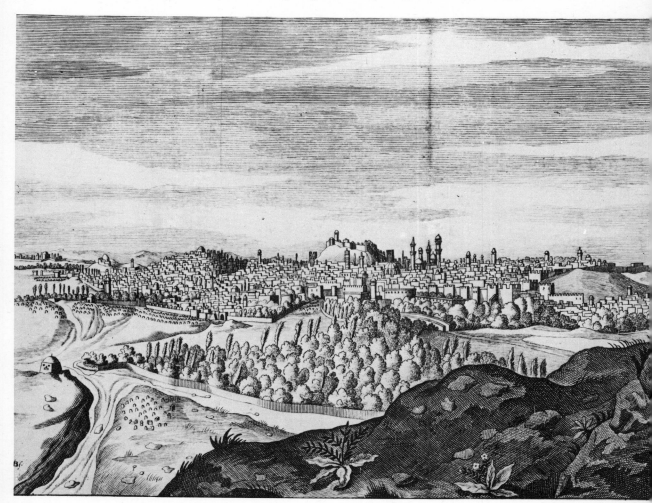

ABOVE A reconstruction of the organ built by Thomas Dallam and presented to the Sultan in 1599.
RIGHT The arms of the Levant Company.

OPPOSITE ABOVE The Indian Ocean charted by Joan Martines of Messina in 1578 showing Portuguese trading posts.
OPPOSITE BELOW East Indiamen attacking Portuguese vessels near Surat.

trouble in the little English colony. When Barton agreed to accompany the new Sultan on his campaign in Hungary he felt he had no option but to leave Sanderson in charge of the English merchants. In time he returned to London, but within the year was persuaded by the Levant Company to take up the new post of treasurer and consul in Constantinople and he took with him an unusual gift from the Queen to the Sultan. This was an organ built by Thomas Dallam that besides being played as a conventional keyboard instrument boasted many mechanical devices, for it struck the hour, sounded chimes, made artificial birds sing and flap their wings and could even reproduce music in five parts. It was not surprising that the Sultan was overjoyed by the demonstrations Dallam gave and Sanderson was able to extract from him wider concessions for English merchants throughout his dominions.

From the time of the Cabots schemes had been proposed and vessels despatched to find a route to the fabled Orient, as we have seen. The English quest for Cathay was reckoned the most promising market for English cloth as yet unexploited and those manufactures would be exchanged for cargoes of spices that would yield a great profit. In 1566 the Queen was told that in the east 'English cloth shall be more esteemed than their gold and silver' and that the traffic would be bound to exceed what the King of Spain obtained from his western dominions or the King of Portugal from his Indies. The

The court of the Mogul
Emperor Akbar at Agra.

English had directed their efforts to the discovery of a shorter and less dangerous route than the long haul round Africa pioneered by the Portuguese and regarded as exclusively theirs. The Levant Company in 1583 decided to send out an expedition from Aleppo to travel overland to the dominions of the Great Mogul and beyond. No one had much idea about distances involved, the natural barriers that would have to be negotiated, the nature of the climate or the time such a preliminary survey might take. The intrepid travellers who undertook this adventurous commission were John Newbery and Ralph Fitch, who left Falmouth in the *Tiger* and landed in Syria without a single stop *en route*; if the first leg of their journey could be accomplished so expeditiously they were hopeful of their travels in the interior. Characteristically Richard Hakluyt had given Newbery a private commission – to ask Arab scholars of the whereabouts of a copy of *Cosmography of Abilfada Ismael*; he had no success in Syria, but promised to try in Persia, Babylon and in Basra.

Crossing the Syrian desert by camel they passed down the Euphrates, noting the ruins of the tower of Babel. At Hormuz, the island in the narrows where the Persian Gulf and the Gulf of Oman meet, there was a Portuguese trading settlement. Here Newbery and Fitch were arrested because they were countrymen of Drake and were told that the English corsair had fired on a Portuguese galleon in the Moluccas – as if the rest of his exploits were irrelevant! Fortunately Newbery had been in Hormuz before, as factor on a Portuguese ship sailing from Lisbon, and he was able to bribe the captain of the fort where they were imprisoned to allow them to take passage by sea to Goa. There they were again put under close arrest and several letters passed between Goa and the Escorial about what was to be the fate of the English interlopers. They feared they would be enslaved, perhaps being condemned to serve in the galleys, yet they succeeded in making their escape to strike north west for the Mogul Kingdom, which meant a long trek across the Deccan. They found Agra and Fatehpur 'two very great cities, either of them much greater than London'. John Newbery was by now anxious to return overland and report on the promising possibilities of trade, so he left Fitch whom he promised to meet with a ship in Bengal in two years' time. Another companion, Master Leeds who was a jeweller by trade, found a *niche* in Akbar's palace at Fatehpur where his skill in setting precious stones earned him a horse, five slaves and a daily allowance of six shillings.

Ralph Fitch had the true traveller's wanderlust and went down the Ganges as far as Hooghly in Bengal, walked in the foothills of the Himalayas and passed by ship to Pegu in Burma (near Rangoon), which was at that time the capital of a thriving kingdom. He crossed into Thailand, then a satellite of Pegu, and came by the Malay coast to Malacca. This was the furthest point of his extensive travels and he had seen and heard quite enough to convince him there was a great role for English Merchants Adventurers to play in India and the East Indies. Fitch returned by the Malabar Coast, the Euphrates Valley and Aleppo to reach London in 1591. Away for eight years he had long ago been given up for dead, but he now heard of London merchants sending a sea expedition round the Cape. The success of such voyages was to lead to the foundation of the East India Company of which Fitch became a founder member.

Philip II's conquest of Portugal in 1580 had closed the Lisbon market to English merchants and the fall of Antwerp five years later denied them the mart for spices in the Low Countries which had come to rival Lisbon. Such was the incentive to seek direct trade with the sources of the spice trade and now that Portugal had joined the ranks of England's enemies all hesitation about offending Portuguese susceptibilities by sailing round the Cape into the Indian Ocean ceased. Drake's voyage round the world had shown that comparatively small craft were capable, if properly handled, of sailing in any seas; he had begun what he hoped would be a regular trade with the Spice Islands and his capture of the *San Felipe* in 1587 had opened doubters' eyes to the riches of the east. In October 1589 a group of London merchants petitioned the Queen for her support in a proposal to penetrate the East Indies *via* the Cape route, now that they had been cut off from normal European markets. They planned to open commercial relations with such countries as India, China and the Philippines and though they hoped their fleet might take certain Portuguese prizes, privateering was not to be the prime object of the expedition. After much discussion three tall ships left Plymouth in April 1591, the *Penelope* in which George Raymond the leader of the expedition hoisted his flag, the *Merchant Royal* commanded by Samuel Foxcroft, who died on the voyage, and the *Edward Bonaventure* under James Lancaster.

Lancaster, born in Hampshire about 1555, had been sent out to Portugal to learn the language and master the special features of the spice trade, probably in Lisbon. As he put it many years later: 'I have been brought up among this people, I have lived among them as a gentleman, served with them as a soldier and lived among them as a merchant.' Perhaps in 1580 he had fought for Don Antonio and then, when his cause was lost, returned at last to England. His experiences had given him an abiding hatred of the Portuguese, who were, he said, 'a people without faith or truth'. He became a freeman of the Skinners' Company and, like so many others, saw service afloat in 1588.

The fleet reached the Cape of Good Hope early in August, but was prevented by contrary winds from rounding it, despite many attempts, so they took shelter in Table Bay where it was hoped the sick men might recuperate. After a month in the roadstead there were still too many of the crews unfit for duty so the *Merchant Royal* returned to England. The other two vessels passed the Cape without mishap, but off Cape Correntes the *Penelope* foundered in a gale and a few days later Lancaster's ship lost her main mast through a flash of lightning. Passing through the Mozambique Channel they came to the Cormoro Islands to water, but nearly a third of the crew, including the sailing master, were massacred by natives. Zanzibar proved less hazardous and here the *Edward Bonaventure* stayed for ten weeks in a sheltered harbour for careening and making good the damage from heavy weather. After they had been badly beaten off course by contrary winds Lancaster managed to reach the island of Gomes, near Acheen in Sumatra, early in June, intending to use this as a base for preying on shipping, but before long they moved on to Penang off the west coast of the Malay Peninsula. They had some minor successes with prizes, but the crew was severely depleted through illness. Lancaster then moved to the Straits of Malacca where he plundered various vessels and then sailed first to Jurkseyla and on to the Nicobar Islands, which he reached in November 1592, desperate for provisions. His crew were anxious that they should begin the homeward

A contemporary woodcut of trade in the Orient.

voyage before there was further illness aboard, so Lancaster made for Point de Galle on the south-west coast of Ceylon, which he had chosen as an ideal base from which to conduct raids on Portuguese shipping. Here, however, the captain was confined to his cabin, being 'very sick, more like to die than to live' and when he was sufficiently recovered his short-handed crew made plain that they had enough of roving.

On 8 December the *Edward Bonaventure* passed the Cape of Good Hope and in April arrived at St Helena for welcome refreshment, which put everyone in better shape. Lancaster now proposed to sail for Brazil, intending to raid Pernambuco, but his crew forced him to alter course for England. Becalmed for days on end, they were running out of water and food, so it was agreed they should make for Trinidad, though on arrival they found that the Spaniards had taken all available supplies, so they pressed on to reach Mona, the small island between Puerto Rico and San Domingo. Here a French vessel spared them essential rations and Lancaster decided to sail for the Newfoundland banks. Off the Bermudas they encountered a terrible north-easterly gale, which forced them back to Mona. While Lancaster led a

251

small party ashore, the mutinous seamen cut the ship's cable to take the *Edward Bonaventure* to San Domingo, where they surrendered to the Spanish. For a month the marooned men just managed to keep alive until they were rescued by French privateers and by devious means Lancaster found a passage to Dieppe and on 24 May 1594 was back in England after an absence of three years. Others were less fortunate, including the purser, Henry May, who had been taken aboard a Frenchman the previous August only to be wrecked in the Bermudas. May was the first Englishman to land in Bermuda and here he made a small craft that he succeeded in sailing to Newfoundland where he found an English fisherman who was prepared to take him home at the end of the season. Lancaster's first voyage had been a financial disaster, with the loss of all three ships, the prizes he had taken in the East Indies and many lives, for of the 195 adventurers who had set out only twenty-five returned. Yet Hakluyt, thinking in wider terms than financial gain, called this a 'memorable' voyage, for Lancaster had sailed the Indian Ocean and reached the Malay Peninsula without opposition from the Portuguese.

Lancaster's next voyage (October 1594–July 1595) was not for trade in the east but to take plunder at Pernambuco, Brazil. It was an audacious attempt in the spirit of Drake, for though the expedition would take any prizes that came its way, the principal objective was to be the coastal town of Recife, where the warehouses were reputed to be packed with spices and other valuable goods that had been rescued from a great carrack cast away at Pernambuco, together with local produce such as brazil-wood for dyeing and sugar that awaited shipment to Lisbon. Aided by John Venner, who joined him in the Cape Verde Islands, Lancaster was able to surprise the place and

Lancaster's ships surround and attack a Portuguese carrack; a seventeenth-century Dutch engraving.

as the booty taken was found to be far more than the English vessels could carry away, a number of Dutch transports were hired. Before they had been able to sail the Portuguese made an unexpected come-back, beginning to build a new redoubt, close to the harbour, and in attempting to destroy these works the English suffered heavy casualties. The booty they brought back to England, though much exaggerated in value, helped to further interest in direct sailing to the Far East and to launch Wood's voyage in 1596, which was financed largely by Sir Robert Dudley. The Dudley emblem of the bear accounted for the names of two of the ships in Captain Wood's expedition – the *Bear* and the *Bear's Whelp*. It was, however, a disastrous voyage for all three vessels perished and not a single Englishman survived, though one of the crew, a Frenchman, succeeded in reaching Mauritius where he was found long afterwards living as a veritable 'Robinson Crusoe'.

Meanwhile Dutch adventurers had been far more successful in the East Indies and in 1598 a fleet of twenty ships sailed from Flushing. John Davys forsook his quest for the north-west passage to accompany that expedition and find out all he could about routes, winds and the nature of the countries the Dutch had visited, for he was jealous of the lead they had acquired over English adventurers. Davys commanded the *Lion* and with her was a sister ship, the *Lioness*, also from England. After troubled days in Madagascar and the Maldives they anchored at Acheen in June 1599, where the King appeared friendly enough at first, but then turned against the visitors. The *Lioness* was captured and many of her crew killed, but Davys cut his cable and opened fire from the *Lion* to the surprise of the natives who 'swam away by hundreds'. The King of Acheen, incensed that his plans had been upset, put to death all the Dutch seamen who were ashore at the time, except eight who were kept as slaves. Next the expedition faced opposition from a fleet of Portuguese galleys and extricating themselves without serious loss they made for Pulo-Botum on the coast of Quedah to water. The voyage had been intended as a trading venture and here at last they succeeded in acquiring a goodly quantity of pepper, even if some of it became 'utterly ruinated' by salt water. Davys himself returned to Middelburg in July 1600 and though he had not succeeded in making his fortune he at least had discovered much first-hand information about India and the Indies which he would soon be putting at the disposal of his compatriots.

English merchants had been alarmed at the extent to which the Dutch had been cornering pepper supplies and as the century closed the price of pepper had risen from 3s to 8s per lb. This crisis provoked the Lord Mayor of London into calling a meeting in September 1599 to consider the best ways of pioneering English interests in the East Indies. The sum of £30,000 was subscribed from those present and a petition to the Privy Council was drawn up which referred pointedly to what the Dutch Provinces had achieved; they had 'made several voyages to some parts of the East Indies and have had returns from thence with their ships richly laden with pepper [and] spices'. The petitioners asked for freedom from customs duties on their exports for

A pepper plant; an illustration from a seventeenth-century herbal.

253

A trading station of the East India Company in Surat, early seventeenth century.

the first six years of their operations and also a licence to export bullion. All this was granted and so it came about that on 31 December 1600 the East India Company was chartered, with a monopoly that would enable it to lay the foundations of a great empire. Among the 218 founder members were several members of the Levant Company, including Sir Thomas Smythe, its governor, who became governor of the new company. One striking feature of the arrangements was that 'for the better advancement of his salary' each seaman sailing in an East Indiaman was credited with a share in the enterprise amounting to two months' wages. This was not to be a variant of the 'truck system' with all its disadvantages to the employee, but a bonus to give every servant of the company a direct interest in its profitability akin to the profit-sharing schemes of certain concerns in the present day.

A company fleet was at once prepared under James Lancaster, who had been nominated a director in the charter. The largest vessel was the *Red Dragon*, purchased from the Earl of Cumberland and renamed from the *Malice Scourge* she had borne at the Queen's suggestion as a privateer and the new name was certainly a prophetic choice for a vessel that was hoping to anchor in the ports of China. The other four vessels had seen service in

254

the Levant. It cost the company £40,000 to acquire and fit out this fleet, they spent £6,860 on purchasing English wares for sale or barter in the east and in addition £21,700 was provided for acquiring goods in the Indies. This sum was changed into Spanish rials of eight in London and those coins can only have come into England as a result of the sea dogs' activities. Rials were thought to be the most acceptable currency in those parts, but as not enough of them could be assembled the Queen was asked whether her mint in the Tower could produce £6000 worth of imitation Spanish rials of eight. Her Majesty thought it absolutely wrong for her to counterfeit coins of a foreign prince, even though an enemy of England, and so instead she ordered the mint to strike coins of similar weight and fineness, bearing her own arms and, on the reverse, the Tudor portcullis. Alas, these English coins were strongly resisted as currency in the east, though they have become collector's pieces.

Lancaster's fleet left Woolwich on 13 February 1601, returning after two-and-a-half years to find the Queen dead. Whereas most of the voyages to the West Indies and North America had begun at Plymouth, the East Indiamen would invariably sail from the Thames. On this first company venture, however, the ships were stayed 'for want of wind' in the Downs for some days and did not in fact leave Torbay until 20 April. They reached Table Bay five months later after a slow crossing of the Doldrums. The other vessels had lost over a third of their crews from scurvy; not so the *Red Dragon*, for Lancaster had brought with him bottled lemon juice and gave each man a dose of three spoonfuls every morning. Later they found oranges and lemons in Madagascar. On Christmas Day they came to anchor at Antongil Bay, Madagascar, where they were to stay almost until Easter, trading with the

The crest of the East India Company.

natives and building a pinnace. After a tricky passage through the Chagos
Archipelago they reached the Nicobar Islands and at last on 5 June anchored
at Acheen on the north of Sumatra. The King welcomed them and, despite
Davys's warnings of his perfidious treatment of the Dutch two years earlier,
was genuinely delighted to co-operate. It was a joy to Lancaster to learn
that his own Queen 'was very famous in those parts by reason of the wars and
great victories which she had gotten against Spain'. But the King jibbed at
entering a permanent commercial treaty, since it was not the practice for
eastern sovereigns to bind their successors, he said, but for the present they
could trade under his protection. In fact they found it was not a very advantageous place for trading, as pepper was dear in Acheen and there was a
negligible demand for English goods. As the King was no friend to the

Bantam, the centre of the pepper trade.

Portuguese, he made it possible for Lancaster to seize the *Santo Antonio* of 1200 tons in the Strait of Malacca; this vessel had left India with a great supply of calicoes suitable for eastern markets which proved most useful to the captors. The *Ascension* was laden for England with local produce, while the *Susan* was sent to load pepper at Priaman on the east coast of Sumatra.

Lancaster himself took the *Red Dragon* to Bantam on the northerly tip of Java, which he had been told was the principal port for the pepper-producing districts. Here he found a large Chinese community. The titular ruler of Bantam was a ten-year-old boy and power rested with his uncle. Lancaster presented the Protector with plate and a letter from the Queen, to secure very favourable terms for trade. English goods reached good prices and there was no shortage of pepper and cloves. Although it was an unhealthy climate

257

The *Tiger*; the ship was boarded by Japanese pirates near Singapore and some of her crew, including her pilot, John Davys, were murdered.

for westerners Lancaster felt he could not do better than establish at Bantam an English factory, so he left behind a group of merchants under William Starkie with a stock of unsold goods, including many of the captured Portuguese calicoes, rather than flood the market with them. From the proceeds Starkie was to buy up pepper in readiness for the next voyage and to trade by pinnace for cloves, nutmegs and other spices in the Moluccas.

Homeward bound, the *Red Dragon* lost her rudder in a storm near the Cape of Good Hope and began to leak badly. The crew feared she would founder and demanded to be put aboard the *Hector*, but Lancaster would have none of it – 'We will yet abide God's leisure, to see what mercy He will show us', he said firmly, though inwardly he was at his wits-end and told the master of the *Hector* to proceed independently, leaving the *Red Dragon* to her fate. He even wrote a letter of farewell to the company. But the master of the *Hector* refused to abandon his companion and hovered near at hand. When the weather improved they were able to fit a new rudder; they made for St Helena and after a spell ashore left for the Downs. All four ships had safely returned and for the first time ever there was a glut of pepper in London. Lancaster was knighted by James I a month after his return and did not again put to sea, though for the rest of his life he guided the affairs of the

258

young East India Company and it was through his personal encouragement that William Baffin took up the challenge of exploring the north west.

John Davys, who had served with Lancaster in the *Red Dragon*, was in no mood to settle down ashore and in 1604 acted as pilot in Sir Edward Michelbourne's *Tiger* which sailed for Bantam and then further east. Anchored at Bintary near Singapore as 1605 was closing they found a Japanese junk that had been roving on the coast of Borneo. After apparently friendly exchanges the Japanese boarded the *Tiger* and Davys was one of the first casualties. The *Tiger* was saved by the master gunner who with great presence of mind trained his demi-culverins on to the pirates, blowing them to pieces. Sir Edward Michelbourne was so shattered by this experience and the loss of John Davys that he at once ordered their return to England. Such was the fickleness of fortune's wheel and it is as well to underline that for every successful voyage in those distant waters, there was a disastrous disappointment.

10 EPILOGUE: THE FRUITS OF ENDEAVOUR

THE SEA DOGS HAD RAISED ENGLISH PRESTIGE to an unprecedented level, for it was through their endeavours that the mighty power of Spain had been curtailed and the advance of the Counter Reformation in Europe halted. Weighing the achievements of Francis Drake, reckoned as the embodiment of England's determination to survive in a hostile world, compatriots thought it 'no less honourable to have enlarged the bounds of the English glory than those of her Empire'.

This glory had a golden tinge, for it was the Queen's return from her private investments in the voyages of the sea dogs that saved her from serious financial trouble and lightened the burden of taxation on her subjects. At first these had been welcome windfalls that reduced the claims on her purse of the inflationary costs of administration and defence, but then she came to rely on such bonuses. Drake's voyage round the world brought Elizabeth £160,000, or a return of 4700 per cent on the sum she had laid out, and this was much more than a normal parliamentary grant. It was because she expected sums of this magnitude from later ventures that made her so angry about the pilfering of the *Madre de Dios* and the fear of being cheated during Essex's raid on Cadiz. Without what she euphemistically called her 'chested treasure' it would have been impossible for her to have subsidized the Dutch patriots to the tune of £1,420,000 from 1585 to the end of her reign or to have sunk even more in reducing Tyrone's rebellion in Ireland. As she told her last Parliament: 'I have diminished my own revenue that I might add to your security and have been content to be a taper of virgin wax to waste myself and spend my life that I might give light and comfort to those that live under me.' She left no national debt behind her. Drake 'her pirate' was her particular hero because he had brought her so much. Apart from her dividends in his expeditions he freely lavished gifts on his sovereign which courtiers could never hope to equal, such as the diamond cross worth 5000 crowns that was his New Year's present in 1581. But there was more to it than that. The economist John Maynard Keynes regarded the Queen's share of the booty brought home in the *Golden Hind* as the 'origins of British foreign investment'. From those proceeds Elizabeth made a notable investment in the Levant Company and from that company's profits in its trade with

OPPOSITE A loadstone, used for magnetizing the needle of a ship's compass. This one encased in an elaborate silver frame belonged to Sir George Sommers who founded a settlement in Bermuda in 1609.

Aleppo and Venice 'there was financed the East India Company, the profits of which during the seventeenth and eighteenth centuries were the main foundation of England's foreign connections; and so on'.

As with the Queen, so with the more prudent of her subjects, whether they were sea dogs themselves, city financiers or county land-owners. Some compulsive gamblers such as Cumberland allowed their rich earnings to slip through their fingers, others like the Hawkins dynasty of Plymouth became affluent, using this wealth to finance maritime ventures of all kinds. Much of the capital for the chartered trading companies derived ultimately from successful privateering. Spanish gold and East Indian spices provided funds for land purchases, building enterprises and the forerunners of public banks. In a materialistic age the mealy-mouthed affected to despise fortunes made from commerce of a somewhat questionable type, just as they disdained the rise of families founded on the spoils of the monasteries under Henry VIII, and we may suspect that in many cases jealousy was the seed of such criticism. William Camden, the annalist, though proud of the sea dogs' martial exploits, was scornful of their pillaging that earned them widespread envy and admiration from 'the vulgar sort of people'.

Sea power had become the fundamental arm of an island kingdom, which stretched out its trade routes to the far corners of the world. England accordingly withdrew from Europe and, once the Dutch Republic had successfully become established as an independent state, reduced her commitments on the continent to a minimum. Her future lay in distant waters. Sir John Hawkins had in 1592 enunciated what was to become the classic principle of English policy in succeeding centuries, that 'we have as little to do in foreign countries as may be, for that breedeth great charge and no profit at all'. A permanent fleet of war-ships, however reduced in fighting strength in times of retrenchment, was essential not merely as 'the wooden walls of England' but for guarding the links between the mother country and her distant outposts, whereas the idea of a standing army smacked of authoritarian rule. The influence of sea power in shaping English policy was all pervasive. It secured the triumph over Spain in the West Indies in the seventeenth century, made possible the wresting of Canada and India from the French in the eighteenth and provoked the opening up of the African continent in the nineteenth. Rooke's capture of Gibraltar in 1704 was to set the seal on the defeat of Philip's Armada and would be followed by the acquisition of Singapore, Aden and Cape Town.

There was, too, the legacy of colonial enterprise. The Roanoke colonies had been badly planned, under-manned, under-capitalized and ill sited, while time and again men and money had been diverted to privateering which destroyed real chance of success. With the coming of the peace with Spain in 1604 fresh attempts were to be made and the lessons so painfully learnt under Grenville and Lane were not forgotten. The men in charge of colonial enterprise in the next twenty years had all served their apprenticeships with the Elizabethan sea dogs. In consequence the great burgeoning of colonial endeavour during the early-seventeenth century was a national sequel to the premature efforts of the Elizabethans, for 'Western Planting' was now to be put into practice on the lines Hakluyt had advocated. In December 1606 the London Virginia Company sent three ships across the Atlantic under Captain Christopher Newport who made a permanent settlement at Jamestown. In September 1620 the Pilgrim Fathers sailed in *The Mayflower* for Massachusetts, and the development of the New England colonies continued with the foundation of New Hampshire in 1623 and Connecticut in 1635. Before then Sir George Somers of Catherine Leweston, where Dorset meets Devon, had colonized the Bermudas and in swift succession came the English settlements in St Kitts and in the Leeward Islands. Stemming from the East India Company's early voyages came the establishment of the first factory on the east coast of India at Masulipatam in Madras in 1611, the settlement of Bengal in 1633 and four years later the opening of a factory at Canton. The flag had followed trade, yet the foundation of the first British Empire would never have succeeded without the exploits of the sea dogs. These contacts enriched the life of the island community so that cheaper sugar, pepper and cloves were followed by a rapid rise in the consumption of tobacco. Later in the century the Englishman's diet would be improved by the introduction of tea, coffee and chocolate as well as citrus fruits.

With the ending of the long naval war with Spain piracy entered a new phase. Many fondly hoped that peace would end the lawlessness that had been threatening trade from time out of mind, and the new Venetian ambassador to the Court of St James's in 1603, who had been robbed by pirates on his journey, looked to the peace treaty as a landmark in international relations. Yet conditions at sea, far from improving, sadly deteriorated. Under James I the policy of a small navy inevitably led to the rise of formidable flotillas of freebooters which sailed the Narrow Seas with impunity. The ships which had saved England from the might of Philip of Spain were laid up and many of the discharged seamen who had manned them drifted into piracy as the only profession for which they were fitted. Thousands of sailors, as one of their leaders remarked, were 'forced for lack of convenient employment to enter such unlawful courses'. Their numbers were swollen by the crews of former privateers, acting under letter of marque, who chose to disobey the proclamation of June 1603 calling on them to cease operations. In ten years the numbers of the outlaws increased tenfold. Adventurous spirits like Sir Francis Verney, Sir Henry Mainwaring and John Ward of Faversham, denied the opportunity of a naval command, settled at Mamora on the Barbary Coast and 'turned Turk'. From Algiers and from bases in Ireland confederations of pirates threatened the trade-routes of the western world, so that in twenty years of uneasy peace under James I London merchants lost many more ships at the hands of the rovers than in the whole of the long naval war with Spain. The privateers proper were succeeded by the pirates in the English Channel, the Western Approaches, the Mediterranean

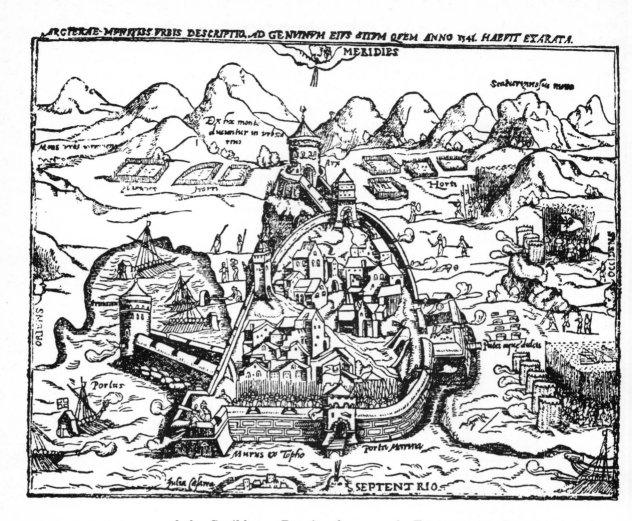

Algiers in the sixteenth century, the centre of piracy on the Barbary coast.

and the Caribbean. Despite the peace in Europe operations continued unabated in the West Indies where hatred of the Spaniard became equated with 'the sacred hunger for gold' and because of his wealth and his religion he was to be hated down to the War of Jenkins's Ear in 1739. Not for many years did it dawn on the Privy Council in Whitehall that those 'which are here called privateers are in reality freebooters, who ought to be wholly supressed'. Such were the dragon's teeth sown by the Elizabethan sea dogs.

Apart from their influence on ship construction and in the preparation of improved charts and sailing directions, the sea dogs contributed to the growing store of scientific knowledge about tides and winds, the practical use of astronomy, the very real problem of magnetism and compass variation and the development of nautical instruments. John Dee's paradoxical compass was impracticable for everyday use at sea, but John Davys's back-staff or quadrant became a standard piece of equipment for a century. Navigation was becoming more complicated and less uncertain. 'The old, ancient rules' of hunches and guesswork were roundly mocked by a new generation of men with a grounding in mathematics. They pointed out that the courses set were essentially 'hit or miss', whereas if they put into practice the teaching of Stephen Burough, 'with a compass and certain lines drawn upon a parchment a man can direct his course to places that he cannot see'. Such was a revelation. Men such as Leonard Digges were insistent that the mysteries of mathematics must be turned to the use of the professional seaman and the instrument-maker, and there was concern in England that the essential rules of this expanding body of knowledge should be popularized and brought to the attention of the ordinary sea-farer. A notable vade-mecum was William Bourne's *A Regiment for the Sea*, first issued in 1574, and it was reckoned so authoritative that it soon earned the compliment of a Dutch translation. The Dutch had, indeed, the reputation of being the most

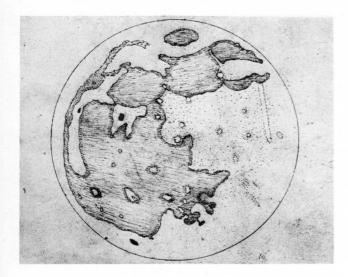

Thomas Hariot's map of the moon.

scientific of navigators and it was through Sir Christopher Hatton's initiative that Lucas Waghenaer's treatise *Spieghel de Zeevaerdt* was brought out in an English edition in the year of the Armada. Not all the innovators were armchair scientists like John Dee. Thomas Digges went on a number of voyages to learn seamen's ways and attitudes, which made him appalled at the 'gross usuage and homely instruments' they employed, so he compiled a useful manual that corrected 'Errors of Navigation'. Raleigh employed the brilliant mathematician Thomas Hariot of Oxford to accompany Grenville to Virginia and the Earl of Cumberland enticed Edward Wright, Fellow of Caius College, Cambridge, to go to sea that he might give pilots the benefits of his learning. The sea dogs had in their way brought about a minor scientific revolution.

Richard Hakluyt had set out 'to bring the Antiquities, smothered and buried in dark silence, to light, and to preserve certain memorable exploits of late years by our English nation achieved, from the greedy and devouring

THE PRINCIPALL NAVIGATIONS, VOIAGES AND DISCOVERIES OF THE

Englifh nation, made by Sea or ouer Land,

to the moft remote and fartheft diftant Quarters of
the earth at any time within the compaffe
of thefe 1500. yeeres: Deuided into three
feuerall parts, according to the po-
fitions of the Regions wherun-
to they were directed.

The firft, conteining the perfonall trauels of the Englifh vnto *Iudæa, Syria, Arabia*, the riuer *Euphrates, Babylon, Balfara*, the *Perfian* Gulfe, *Ormuz, Chaul, Goa, India*, and many Iflands adioyning to the South parts of *Afia*: together with the like vnto *Egypt*, the chiefeft ports and places of *Africa* within and without the Streight of *Gibraltar*, and about the famous Promontorie of *Buona Efperanʒa*.

The fecond, comprehending the worthy difcoueries of the Englifh towards the North and Northeaft by Sea, as of *Lapland, Scrikfinia, Corelia*, the Baie of *S. Nicholas*, the Ifles of *Colgoieue, Vaigats*, and *Noua Zembla* toward the great riuer *Ob*, with the mightie Empire of *Ruffia*, the *Cafpian* Sea, *Georgia, Armenia, Media, Perfia, Boghar* in *Bactria*, & diuers kingdoms of *Tartaria*.

The third and laft, including the Englifh valiant attempts in fearching almoft all the corners of the vafte and new world of *America*, from 73. degrees of Northerly latitude Southward, to *Meta Incognita, Newfoundland*, the maine of *Virginia*, the point of *Florida*, the Baie of *Mexico*, all the Inland of *Noua Hifpania*, the coaft of *Terra firma, Brafill*, the riuer of *Plate*, to the Streight of *Magellan*: and through it, and from it in the South Sea to *Chili, Peru, Xalifco*, the Gulfe of *California, Noua Albion* vpon the backfide of *Canada*, further then euer any Chriftian hitherto hath pierced.

Whereunto is added the laft moft renowmed Englifh Nauigation,
round about the whole Globe of the Earth.

By *Richard Hakluyt Mafter of Artes*, and *Student fometime*
of Chrift-church in Oxford.

Jmprinted at London by GEORGE BISHOP
and RALPH NEWBERIE, Deputies to
CHRISTOPHER BARKER, Printer to the
Queenes moft excellent Maieftie.

1589.

jaws of oblivion'. All succeeding historians have necessarily followed the chart he mapped so thoroughly, adding details acquired under their own 'lodestars of experience'. The author of the *Principal Navigations* was a contemporary historian of the first rank, yet it should be easier with the passage of the years to see the achievements of the sea dogs in truer perspective and to assess their influence on the subsequent development of England. Yet even on impartial estimates these seamen seem larger than life: we think of Drake, the corsair extraordinary, taking the *Cacafuego*; of Raleigh with his head full of schemes, sure he would find gold at the end of a rainbow; of Cavendish rigging damask sails for his entry to Plymouth after his circumnavigation; or of Cumberland, the Queen's own privateer, convinced that Her Majesty's glove was a lucky mascot that must bring him a successful voyage. Luck, indeed, at times was as essential an ingredient in our tale as professional skill or ingrained courage, and the winds were fickle. Martin Frobisher, still in the prime of life, was killed by Spanish bullets off Brittany; John Davys the intrepid pioneer in both the north west and the Far East, was massacred by Japanese pirates. John Hawkins was never the same after the ordeals of the battle of San Juan de Ulua and Drake's incredible luck ran out in the Portugal expedition and on his final voyage with Hawkins to the Caribbean. There was pathos in Humphrey Gilbert's last hours in the *Squirrel* when he felt himself 'as near to heaven by sea as by land' and heroism untarnished in Richard Grenville's last action in the *Revenge*. Those, and many others, together wrote a glorious chapter in England's history and their heritage has profoundly affected the national tradition.

A nocturnal made by
Humphrey Cole in 1580.

FURTHER READING

CONTEMPORARY MATERIALS

The prime source is Richard Hakluyt, *The Principal Navigations, Voyages, Traffics and Discoveries of the English Nation* (2nd edition, 1598–1600). The best modern edition is that by Sir Walter Raleigh (12 vols, 1903–5). Another edition, with an introduction by John Masefield, is available in Everyman's Library (8 vols, 1907 and subsequent reprints).

Since its foundation in 1847 the Hakluyt Society has published a great many accounts and narratives of expeditions and voyages relating to the sea dogs, usually with full-scale introductions, annotations and indexes. Of these may be particularly noted: 1st Series, Vol. 59, *The voyages and works of John Davis the Navigator* (ed. A. H. Markham, 1880); 2nd Series, Vol. 34, *New Light on Drake: a Collection of Documents relating to his voyages of Circumnavigation, 1577–80* (ed. Zelia Nuttall, 1914); Vol. 62, *Spanish Documents Concerning English Voyages to the Caribbean, 1527–68* (ed. in translation Irene A. Wright, 1929); Vol. 71, *Documents concerning English Voyages to the Spanish Main, 1569–80* (ed. Wright, 1932); Vols. 83, 84, *The Voyages and Colonising Enterprises of Sir Humphrey Gilbert* (ed. D. B. Quinn, 1940); Vol. 85, *The Voyages of Sir James Lancaster to Brazil and the East Indies, 1591–1603* (ed. Sir William Foster); Vol. 99, *Further English Voyages to Spanish America* (ed. Irene A. Wright, 1951); Vols 104, 105, *The Roanoke Voyages, 1584–90* (ed. D. B. Quinn, 1955); Vol. 111, *English Privateering Voyages to the West Indies* (ed. K. R. Andrews, 1959); and Vol. 142, *The Last Voyage of Drake and Hawkins* (ed. Andrews, 1972).

MODERN WORKS

General Accounts: The best introductions are J. H. Parry, *The Age of Reconnaissance, 1450–1650* (1963); A. L. Rowse, *The Expansion of Elizabethan England* (1955, chapters 5–8); and Sir Julian Corbett, *Drake and the Tudor Navy* (2 vols, 1898) which is effectively a maritime history of England in the reign of Elizabeth I.

Among a host of works may be singled out – K. R. Andrews, *Elizabethan Privateering, 1585–1603* (1964); C. R. Boxer, *The Portuguese Seaborne Empire, 1415–1825* (1969); *The Cambridge History of the British Empire*, Vol. 1 (1929); G. Connell-Smith, *Forerunners of Drake* (1954); Sir William Foster, *England's Quest of Eastern Treasure* (1936); Garrett Mattingly, *The Defeat of the Spanish Armada* (1959); S. E. Morison, *The European Discovery of America: the Southern Voyages, 1492–1616* (1974); A. P. Newton, *European Nations in the West Indies, 1493–1688* (1933); J. H. Parry, *The Spanish Seaborne Empire* (1966); D. B. Quinn, *England and the Discovery of*

America, 1481–1670 (1974); G. D. Ramsay, *English Overseas Trade in the Centuries of Emergence* (1957); J. A. Williamson, *Maritime Enterprise, 1485–1558* (1913).

Lives: John Barrow, *Memoirs of the Naval Worthies of Queen Elizabeth's Reign* (1845), is still worth reading for minor characters. J. A. Froude, *English Seamen of the Sixteenth Century* (1895) is the text of a lively course of lectures. Among modern works see in particular – Robert Lacey, *Robert, Earl of Essex* (1971); Michael Lewis, *The Hawkins Dynasty* (1969); George Malcolm Thomson, *Sir Francis Drake* (1972); D. B. Quinn, *Raleigh and the British Empire* (1963); A. L. Rowse, *Sir Richard Grenville of the Revenge* (1937); Rayner Unwin, *The Defeat of Sir John Hawkins* (1960); William M. Wallace, *Sir Walter Raleigh* (1959); Neville Williams, *Francis Drake* (1973); G. G. Williamson, *George, Third Earl of Cumberland* (1920); and James A. Williamson, *Hawkins of Plymouth* (1949).

Discovery and Seamanship: E. G. R. Taylor, *Late Tudor–Early Stuart Geography* (1934) and *The Haven-Finding Art* (1956); and D. W. Waters, *The Art of Navigation in Elizabethan and Early Stuart Times* (1958). *The Mariner's Mirror*, the journal of the Society for Nautical Research, contains a great many articles on a wide range of relevant topics.

ACKNOWLEDGMENTS

Photographs and illustrations are supplied by or reproduced by kind permission of the following:

Archivo General de Indias, Seville: 58–9

Ashmolean Museum, Oxford: 72

The Bancroft Library, University of California, reproduced by permission of the Director: 135

Berkeley Castle, Gloucestershire: 122

Biblioteca Ambrosiana, Milan: 50

Bibliothèque du Ministère des Armées, Paris: 85, 95

Bibliothèque Nationale, Paris: 8

Bodleian Library, Oxford: 66, 73 (left), 147

British Museum, London: *endpapers*, 18, 28–9, 33, *38–9*, 42 above), 69, 70, 73 (right), 74, 75, *77*, *78 (below)*, 98 (left and right), 100, 101, 102, *108*, 125, 136, 139, *142–3*, 181 (right), 189, *193*, 206 (left and right), 208, 214, 220–1, 224, 225, 244, 247 (above), 256–7, 267

Cambridge University Library: 13

By courtesy of Christie's, London: 204

Cincinnatti Art Museum, Ohio: 55

City Art Gallery, Bristol: 15

City Art Gallery, Plymouth: *37* (photograph by Tom Molland), 89, 112 (photograph by Robert Chapman)

Department of the Environment, by permission of the Controller of HM Stationery Office, Crown copyright: 154, 158–9, 159

Edinburgh University Library: 163

By courtesy of Lord Egremont: 265

Free Library of Philadelphia: 80

John Freeman: 67, 86, 123, 167, 181 (left), 247 (below)

By courtesy of Commander Walter Raleigh Gilbert: 81

Photographie Giraudon: 85, 95

Hawkley Studio Associates: 198

The Hispanic Society of America: 90–1

Illustrated London News: 246

John Judkyn Memorial, Bath: *141 (above and below)*

By courtesy of the Master and Fellows, Magdalene College, Cambridge: 20, 47, 60

Mansell Collection: 31, 44, 117, 120, 188, 254

Photo Mas: 169 (right)

Musées Royaux des Beaux-Arts, Brussels: 239

Acknowledgments

Museo Navale, Madrid: 169 (left), 174 (left)

National Library of Wales, Aberystwyth: 160

National Maritime Museum, Greenwich: 11, 17, 21, 22–3, 24, 32–3, *40*, 108–9, 109, 121, 127, 128, 129, 134, 137, 138, 148, 174 (right), 176, 178, 179, 184, 199, 202, 211, 217, 222, 230–1, 243 (above), 258

National Portrait Gallery, London: 36, 64, *103*, 107 (left), *196*

Nationaal Scheepvaartmuseum, Antwerp: 236–7

New York Public Library, Rare Books Division, Astor, Lennox and Tilden Foundations: *78 (above)*

Northampton Art Gallery: 118 (photograph by A. C. Cooper)

Orbis Publishing Company: *141 (above and below)* (photograph by Derek Balmer)

By courtesy of His Grace the Duke of Portland: 191

Public Record Office, by permission of the Controller of HM Stationery Office, Crown copyright: 92, 146, 150, 170, 175

Radio Times Hulton Picture Library: 10, 16, 19, 26, 27, 34, 42 (below), 62, 71, 106, 151, 156, 180, 187, 226, 233, 234, 243 (below), 246 (right), 251, 252, 253, 255, 260, 264, 266

The Royal Library, Copenhagen: 240–1

St Faith's Church, Gaywood, King's Lynn: 167

Science Museum, London: *frontispiece*

The Tower of London, Crown copyright: 23

By courtesy of the President and Fellows of Trinity College, Oxford: 99

Ulster Museum, Belfast: *144 (above and below)*

Victoria and Albert Museum, London: 107 (right), 168, 248

Woodmansterne Limited: 66

The Worshipful Company of Apothecaries of London: *194–5*

Numerals in italics indicate colour illustrations

Picture research by Judith Aspinall

Maps drawn by Admakers

INDEX